SCOTTISH WOMEN WRITERS

FROM 1800 TO THE GREAT WAR

Eileen Dunlop

National Museums Scotland

Published in Great Britain in 2022 by
NMS Enterprises Limited – Publishing
a division of NMS Enterprises Limited
National Museums Scotland
Chambers Street
Edinburgh EH1 1JF

**British Library Cataloguing in
Publication Data**
A catalogue record of this book is
available from the British Library.

ISBN: 978 1 910682 47 0

Cover design by Mark Blackadder.
Cover image: *Self Portrait* by Mary Somerville is
    reproduced by kind permission of Somerville
    College, University of Oxford.

Internal text design by
    NMS Enterprises Ltd – Publishing.
Printed and bound in Great Britain by Short Run
    Press.

This product is made of material from well-
managed forests and other controlled sources.

For a full listing of related NMS titles please visit:
www.nms.ac.uk/books

CONTENTS

ACKNOWLEDGEMENTS

I AM HAPPY to acknowledge the help, advice and encouragement of many people in the writing of this book. They have answered my questions, sent me articles, lent and gifted books and generously shared expertise far exceeding my own. I am particularly indebted to Professor Ian Campbell and Dr Andrew Tod for giving me the benefit of their vast knowledge of the life and work of, respectively, Jane Welsh Carlyle and Elizabeth Grant of Rothiemurchus; I thank them, and also the following: John Briggs, Carol Brodie, Hamish Dunlop, Jennifer Dunlop, Dairmid Gunn, Habib Hashmi, Alison Kinghorn, Julie Lawson (Scottish National Portrait Gallery), Ian and Mary Love, Margaret Miller, Vincent Pritchard, John and Mary Robertson, John Summerscales (Summerscales Technology Services, Alloa), the Staff of the National Library of Scotland and of Stirling University Library, Kate Blackadder and Maggie Wilson at NMS Enterprises Ltd – Publishing. Special thanks to Dr Bob Cowan, who advised me on the maladies and medical treatments of the nineteenth century, to my tireless 'book-finder' Ali Dunlop, to my editor Lynne Reilly, and to my publisher Lesley Taylor for many years of encouragement, friendship and support, both to me and to my late husband, Antony Kamm.

In memory of my mother-in-law
Josephine Kamm
1905–1989
novelist, biographer of women, good friend

INTRODUCTION

ALTHOUGH MANY PEOPLE die in the century into which they were born, at least as many are born in one century and live on into the next. It was possible for children born in the later years of the eighteenth century to live far into the reign of Queen Victoria, and for those born in the 1880s to see on television in 1953 the Coronation of Queen Elizabeth II. The lifespan of a number of writers featured in this book belong in this category. Anne Grant of Laggan, born in 1755, published in 1808 a luminous account of her childhood, while Violet Jacob, born in 1863, published her novels in the early 1900s and was still writing poetry in the years immediately preceding her death in 1946. I have taken as a general rule that to be regarded as a nineteenth-century writer, one's work must first have been published after 1800, regardless of the overlap of centuries in terms of dates of birth and death.

It is striking how intensely the memory of childhood coloured the work of Scottish women writers in all genres during this period and although inevitably, due to the unfair imbalance in educational opportunity, most came from the upper and middle classes, how empathetic and unjudgmental they were. Home-educated children and boarding-school girls who became novelists, letter-writers, poets, journalists, scientists, war reporters and travellers in far-flung lands, all were proud of their heritage and keen to impart the importance of 'a Scottish childhood' in making them the adults they became. It is heartening too how, despite all obstacles, the voices of working-class women kept breaking through, strong, proud and determined to tell their stories for themselves.

Considering the restraints placed on them by the expectations of a male-dominated society, it is also astonishing how many Scotswomen made time to write, and to publish work of excellence and variety. Inevitably, in a book of this length, those featured are personal choices, but I have tried to present them as representative of the different genres explored by women as the nineteenth century unfolded. The fact that they all wrote in English is by no means a dismissal of Gaelic literature, only an acknowledgement that the author is not competent to write about it. There is much to explore beyond the confines of this work.

1
BEFORE
FICTION

I have an aversion, a pity, a contempt for all female scribblers. The needle, not the pen, is the instrument they should handle, and the only one they ever use dextrously.

Matthew Gregory Lewis (1775–1818)
Letter to Lady Charlotte Campbell *c*.1817

THIS DERISORY YET deeply offensive remark, first quoted by the recipient of the letter in a book titled *Diary Illustrative of the Times of George the Fourth* (1838), was occasioned by the rumour that Susan Ferrier (1782–1854), the clever daughter of an Edinburgh lawyer, was at work on a novel. Since Matthew Lewis had himself been inspired by Ann Radcliffe's Gothic shocker *The Mysteries of Udolpho* (1794) to publish, in the following year, his gruesomely sensational novel *Ambrosio, or, the Monk*, it is also hypocritical, though fairly typical of much male opinion at the time. If his words came to Susan Ferrier's ears, they may well have strengthened her determination to publish although, like her near contemporaries Fanny Burney (1752–1840) and Jane Austen (1775–1817), she would choose to do so anonymously. Her avowed reason was that she 'could not bear the fuss of authorism', a sentiment shared by her mentor Sir Walter Scott (1771–1832), although it is likely that she also feared the indignation of Edinburgh neighbours whom she had lampooned.

There was, too, a deeper reason why Ferrier and other women concealed their authorship. There was a wide acceptance, in the patriarchal, Bible-influenced society of Europe in the eighteenth and nineteenth centuries, that women were preordained by God to perform a secondary role. Married or single, their obligations were domestic; housekeeping, cleaning, marketing, cooking, child-rearing, the care of elderly parents and providing comfort for their wage-earning fathers and husbands were the only justifications for their existence. Even the reading of fiction was frowned upon by men; books might – heaven forbid – distract women from their proper duties, and worse, give them ideas. Women had no right to vote (although, to be fair, neither did the majority of men) nor, even if they belonged to wealthy families, had they any legal rights. Their income and property became their husbands' when they married, and if a woman had reason to make a contract, a male relative had to sign on her behalf. And even if in snatched moments a woman managed to complete a manuscript, the constant belittling of female capabilities meant that the chance of any book bearing her name, rather than the coy attribution 'By a Lady', being accepted by a publisher was practically nil.

Yet the notion that all women were angry about the injustices which afflicted their lives is a modern one. They too read the Bible, and most accepted that patriarchy was God's will and the way of the world. What alarmed men was the possibility that a small number of ambitious women, who wanted to pick up the pen and be accepted on equal terms, would try to opt out of their 'womanly' duties, thus inconveniencing their male relatives. Realistically, no such opt-out was available. However strong the urge to write, women could not escape from the tasks which the needle represented. This was not a matter of class, although inevitably, before modern times, the vast majority of aspiring women writers were, for reasons of superior literary skills, access to books and social networks, born into the aristocratic and professional middle classes. This group had been adept at juggling responsibilities long before the nineteenth century, which is the main focus of this book. Mary, Queen of Scots (1542–84) had written poetry in the midst of a turbulent and action-packed career, while her lady-in-waiting Mary Beaton (*c.*1543–*c.*1597) presumably wrote hers in moments not occupied by her duties to the Queen. Elizabeth Melville (*c.*1582–1640), mother of six children, had a long religious poem, *Ane Godlie Dream*, printed in 1603.

A supreme example of the ability of female writers to multitask was Lady Grisell Baillie (1665–1746), a woman of diverse literary gifts, who had an unusually adventurous early life. As a twelve-year-old she carried food in secret to her father Sir Patrick Hume, a Jacobite hiding in the vault of Polwarth Church, and married the son of Robert Baillie of Jerviswood, a Covenanter who had been executed for involvement in a plot to assassinate King Charles II. Despite teenage years spent on the run with her parents in Holland, where she cooked, cleaned and mended for the impoverished household as well as discovering her talent for composing Scots ballads about rustic characters, in more peaceful and prosperous times Grisell settled down as a model wife and mother. Thereafter she had less time, and perhaps inclination, to write verse. The writing of her mature years is mostly contained in her *Household Book*, a vast compendium in which she wrote memoranda and instructions, and kept her accounts with the scrupulous detail and zealous economy of one who had endured harder times.

Published in 1911 on behalf of the Scottish History Society, the *Household Book* reveals a compulsive writer with enviable stamina, who was intimately involved in every aspect of the management of Mellerstain, her Borders home. Lady Grisell organised and accounted for everything, from the tuning of spinets and the laying of 'plainstanes' (paving stones) to clothing her family and servants, arranging the transport of '90 frute trees', giving her husband 'poket money', buying a 'putter [earthenware] teepot' and paying 'the scaffinger at Christenmas' five shillings for six months' work. She wrote instructions for the education of her children, described family holidays, jotted down what she paid for chamber pots, a wig and a parrot. She copied and annotated, using the idiosyncratic spelling of her time, 'Memorandums and Derections to Servants and ruels layd down by my Mother both fer their diet and work … made by her Decr. 1743'. One senses in Lady Grisell a fond but strict mother, and a watchful, autocratic mistress constantly at the servants' backs:

> Let not the dirty cheney go into the kitchen till the cook be ready to clean it and empty the meat into pewter dishes … . Whoever breaks cheney, glasses or bottles let me know that day, otherways they will be laid to your charge … . When diner and super is over, cary what leaves of small beer and bread into the Pantry, and the cheese, that nothing may go to waste.

When, between 1731 and 1733, Lady Grisell's husband George Baillie and his friend the Earl of Haddington travelled through Europe, every penny spent was accounted for, and instructions written by the indefatigable Lady Grisell for their accommodation and conduct. From such unlikely material, a masterpiece was made.

The *Household Book*, never republished in full, unfortunately remains little known, and Lady Grisell Baillie is now primarily remembered as a Scottish poet, despite the fact that little of her verse has survived. Two stanzas of 'The ewe-buchtin [sheep folding]'s bonnie', were extended to eight by Thomas Pringle (1789–1834), to form a once-popular song. A poem titled 'Werena my Heart Licht I wad dee' was published in the *Tea Table Miscellany* of Allan Ramsay (1686–1758), and set to music by William Thomson (fl.1695–1759) in *Orpheus Caledonius, or a Collection of the Best Scotch Songs* (1725). A pastoral ballad of love and betrayal between the high-born and the lowly, it was anthologised well into the twentieth century.

It is notable that the writing of upper-class women in the eighteenth and early nineteenth centuries was, apart from private writing such as letters and diaries, almost exclusively verse. Among the most prolific, and best-remembered, is Carolina Oliphant, later Baroness Nairne (1766–1845), a collector and songwriter who, like Robert Burns (1759–96), composed new lyrics to accompany traditional tunes. Many of these, such as 'Charlie is my Darling', 'The Hundred Pipers' and 'Bonnie Charlie's noo Awa'' reflect the strong Jacobite sympathies of her father. Married in 1806 to a husband less politically passionate, so extreme was her fear of his disapproval that she kept her songwriting secret. When her lyrics were printed in *The Scottish Minstrel* (1821–24), she signed them 'BB', or 'Mrs Bogan of

Bogan'. Only after her death were her songs collected as *Lays from Strathearn*, and published under her own name.

Among Lady Nairne's contemporaries, many are now remembered for one or two lyrics which remain popular: Lady Anne Barnard (1750–1825) for 'Auld Robin Gray'; Jane Elliot (1727–1805) and Alison Cockburn (1712–94) for their slightly different versions of 'The Flowers o' the Forest'; Alicia Spottiswoode, Lady John Scott (1810–1900) for her rendering of the traditional 'Annie Laurie'. No doubt the brevity of the form suited the snatched moments these women could spare for writing, and the lyric voice came easily to those musically educated, as they generally were. Nor was their use of Scots an affectation. Before English became the tongue of the educated upper classes towards the end of the eighteenth century, everyone Scottish spoke Scots.

The burden laid on middle-class women, wives and daughters of mostly city-dwelling doctors, lawyers, university professors and merchants, but also of country ministers and doctors, was even more time-consuming than that of the great chatelaines. They were responsible for running smaller households, but usually with only one or two servants and large numbers of children; many were almost continuously pregnant for more than twenty years. Infectious disease was rife and child mortality high, so that women had to be nurses as well as housekeepers and attendants on parents and parents-in-law in old age. Nor was having servants always a boon, for they had to be fed, dressed and supervised like children. Sometimes, in the strict moral climate of the time, they had to be dismissed for misdemeanours, or were quarrelsome and gave notice or 'warning' in the huff, leaving their unhappy employers to cook their own dinners and do the washing until replacements could be found. Contemporary letters and diaries frequently bewail the inadequacies of servants. Susan Ferrier, keeping house for her father in Edinburgh in the 1800s wrote to her friend Charlotte Clavering:

> *I have got a cook, a very bad one, but better than none, and I've invested her with all the regalia of the kitchen … Bessie Mure and Lord John* [Campbell] *dined here on Monday, but they got such a beastly repast, and were so scurvily treated that I've been sick ever since with pure shame and vexation of the stomach.*

Sixty years later, Haddington-born Jane Welsh Carlyle (1801–66) wrote from London to her cousin in Dumfriesshire on the perils of acquiring a second maid:

> [So] *now I am mistress of two servants – and ready to hang myself! … A maid-of-all-work, even in London, will tolerate your directing her, but a "cook" and "housemaid" will stand no interference; you mustn't set foot in your own kitchen, unless you are prepared for their giving warning!*

It is hard to feel fully sympathetic towards these women. Both were unburdened by motherhood and financial responsibility, and they did, after all, find time to read, and to write. Their lives seem privileged in comparison with many of their own class, and much more so with those of working-class women who, with very few exceptions, had no opportunity to express themselves in writing. Some were taught to read, in order to understand the Bible, but they rarely learned to write, and any creative potential was stifled by the exigencies of extreme poverty. At an early age they were worn out by bearing and losing children, and the grind of manual labour on the land and, increasingly, in factories and coal mines. This is not, however, to say that they played no part in Scotland's cultural life. Their memories were the repositories of folk tales and ballads, recited or sung in Gaelic and Scots, handed down orally through the generations, and the working songs that enlivened tasks such as milking cows and 'waulking' or felting woollen cloth woven in the Highlands and the Hebrides. Sir Walter Scott recalled, from his own childhood in a Borders farmhouse in the 1770s, the kitchen where family and farm workers gathered in the evening to hear his grandparents' renditions of ballads such as 'Kinmont Willie', 'Tam Lin' and 'Thomas the Rhymer'.

That some, at least, of these tellers of tales knew the worth of their contribution to their country's tradition is clear from the story of a redoubtable and literate old woman named Margaret Hogg, who lived in a cottage in remote Ettrickdale. She was the mother of James Hogg (c.1770–1835), the 'Ettrick Shepherd' who, around 1802, introduced her to the same Walter Scott, now collecting ballads for his *Minstrelsy of the Scottish Border* (1802–03). Egged on by her son, who was keen to cultivate Scott's acquaintance, she obliged him with a rendering of a little-known (and possibly spurious) ballad, 'Auld Maitland'. When she saw the printed version, however, she was not impressed, telling Scott bluntly:

> There war nane o' my sangs prentit till you prentit them yoursel', and ye hae spoilt them awthegither. They were made for singing and no' for reading, but ye hae broken the charm now, an' they'll never be sung mair. An' the worst thing of a', they're nouther right spell'd nor right setten doun.

Of course she had a point, and during the following two centuries Scott's method, which included 'improvement' of 'orally corrupted' versions and interpolation of his own verses, drew much scholarly criticism. But it is also true that as the nineteenth century dawned and shifts in population threatened the fatal weakening of the close communities where oral transmission flourished, Scott was right to say that on balance their recording in print saved many ballads from oblivion.

Among Scottish collectors, Scott is best known, but there were others, notably Anna Brown née Gordon, 'Mrs Brown of Falkland' (1747–1810). The daughter of a professor of Classics at the University of Aberdeen, she was brought up in the north-east, before marrying the Church of Scotland minister at Falkland in Fife. She made a collection of fifty ballads, modestly explaining her sources in a letter to the jurist Alexander Fraser Tytler:

> *I do not pretend to say that these ballads are correct in any way, as they are written down entirely from recollection, for I never saw one of them in print or in manuscript; but I heard them all sung by my aunt* [Mrs Farquarson], *by my own mother, and an old maid-servant who had been long in the family.*

Generously, Anna Brown supplied her versions of well-known ballads such as 'True Thomas' and 'Burd Ellen' to male collectors, including Scott who, in a classic instance of pot and kettle, repaid her by damning her repertoire as 'inauthentic'. Fortunately, there have been kinder voices. She was admired by the great American collector Francis James Child (1825–96), who published her versions in *The English and Scottish Popular Ballads* (1882–98). In our own time, the critic William Donaldson, in an entry for *The Oxford Dictionary of National Biography* (2004) writes perceptively of her great strengths. Her ballads, he points out, see life from a female perspective, their courtly and magical settings masking everyday brutality. Their heroines are catapulted (in a way oddly familiar in certain modern cultures) from the protection of their mothers to the dangerous world of men and jealous mothers-in-law. As Donaldson writes:

> *The ballads speak of murderous sexual rivalry between siblings and hint at infanticide as a form of revenge upon treacherous males. Adventures in the magical greenwood, a metaphor for transgressive sexuality, have a strong appeal but usually alarming consequences ... the dangers of sex are stressed on every side, along with the sheer physical hazard of being female.*

Whether Anna Brown's versions were or were not 'authentic', her ballads, written down between 1783 and 1801, reflect feminist perceptions which we tend to believe are more modern. And it is worth noting that at the point when the ballads were in transition from the oral to the written, the proud peasant performer Margaret Hogg and the more sophisticated middle-class collector Anna Brown were complicit. One provided the fruits of the long folk memory, the other kept that memory safe in a time when social structures were changing and new literary forms explored. Anna Brown's generosity to other collectors was acknowledged but poorly rewarded by her contemporaries. Her own collection was not published in its entirety until 2011.

2
CALVIN'S
SHADOW

Let your women keep silence in the churches: for it is not permitted unto them to speak; but they are commanded to be under obedience, as also saith the law. And if they will learn any thing, let them ask their husbands at home.

St Paul the Apostle
First Epistle to the Corinthians c.AD 53–54

FICTION IN SCOTLAND, by both men and women, made a slow start in the face of ingrained hostility. Since the Reformation in the 1540s, works of imagination had been sternly discouraged by the Presbyterian Church of Scotland, steeped in the biblical doctrine of the Swiss theologian John Calvin (1509–64), on the grounds that only the Bible, the 'word of God', contained the truth. Secular poetry by men was tolerated, and devotional writing, permitted, but the Church's insistence that unbiblical stories were lies, and thus the work of the Devil, effectively muzzled writers and readers afraid of offending God and his ministers. Not until late in the eighteenth century, when a new set of ideas at last challenged the illiberal mindset of the Kirk, did indigenous Scottish fiction begin to emerge from the shadow of Calvinist belief.

The situation in England had been different. After Puritan times, the less baleful stance of the Anglican church had allowed drama and fiction to flourish, and the 1740s had seen the publication of *Pamela* by Samuel Richardson (1689–1761), *Joseph Andrews* and *Tom Jones* by Henry Fielding (1707–54) and *Roderick Random* by expatriate Scot Tobias Smollett (1721–71), all unrestrainedly vigorous, entertaining and essentially amoral works. Thirty years were to pass before the popularity of such novels, encouraged by new circulating libraries in Edinburgh and Glasgow, created a demand for specifically Scottish fiction. What emerged showed in both style and content the gap between Scottish and English sensibilities.

Modern Scots, largely unacquainted with its core doctrine, tend to equate Calvinism with a pessimistic habit of mind. But in the past, when faith was stronger and the Church more powerful, it was the main tenet of Calvinism which justified such pessimism. In her famous novel of 1930s Edinburgh *The Prime of Miss Jean*

Brodie (1961), Muriel Spark has one of her characters describe this as '[the] belief that God had planned for practically everybody before they were born a nasty surprise when they died,' Calvin having 'made it God's pleasure to implant in certain people an erroneous sense of joy and salvation, so that their surprise at the end might be the nastier.' This is a succinct, merry summary by a modern author of Calvin's teaching that an all-powerful, wise but inscrutable God rules the universe, handing out salvation and the prospect of heaven to his 'elect' and damnation and hellfire to everyone else. In this alarming narrative, although God has already decided one's destiny, it is still the duty of every soul to battle the power of the Devil. Good deeds are necessary because the Gospels require them, but it is heretical to believe that a charitable life can earn God's favour.

This may nowadays seem preposterous, but it was not until the Enlightenment, a pan-European intellectual movement in the eighteenth century to which Scottish philosophers and scholars contributed strongly, that the power of reason won a partial victory over superstition. Even then, the claws of Calvinism were slow to loosen their grip on the Scottish imagination. The terrible struggle between good and evil finds expression in such works as James Hogg's *The Private Memoirs of a Justified Sinner* (1824) and Robert Louis Stevenson's *Strange Case of Dr Jekyll and Mr Hyde* (1886), both psychological studies of the divided mind which the pernicious doctrine of 'election' forced upon the devout and impressionable. Nor did the fascination with this theme fade with the nineteenth century: *Witch Wood* by John Buchan (1875–1942) was published in 1927, *The Awakening of George Darroch* by Robin Jenkins (1912–2005) in 1985 and *The Fanatic* and *The Testament of Gideon Mack* by James Robertson (b.1958) in the first decade of the twenty-first century.

Sir Walter Scott, who rejected his father's Calvinism to become an Episcopalian, dominated early nineteenth-century literature with a series of vividly imaginative and wide-ranging novels, yet among his most powerful are two that take as their subject the extreme Calvinism of the 'Covenanting' years of the seventeenth century, *Old Mortality* (1816) and *The Heart of Midlothian* (1818). James Hogg's first novel, *The Brownie of Bodsbeck* (1818) was set in the same period, while *Ringan Gilhaize* (1823) by John Galt (1779–1839) was conceived as a rebuke to Scott, whose mirthful treatment of the Covenanters in *Old Mortality* Galt found disrespectful.

A fascination with national history, as much as personal belief, inspired these male novelists. When a group of women writers began to emerge around the beginning of the nineteenth century, keenly aware of society's attitude to women in general and to their perceived authorial pretension in particular, they tended to keep to the safer ground of local and domestic themes. For all that they were excluded from academic schools and the universities, many of these women had, by serious reading, become highly educated. Yet the strongly Christian piety which permeates the earliest work by women in this genre suggests that, although the Enlightenment had made works of imagination permissible, the misogynistic doctrine of the New Testament apostle Paul, and his stern enforcer John Calvin, still perturbed them. It is as if for them a moral emphasis was essential to validate the fictional form.

The first significant writer in this mode was intellectually confident Elizabeth Hamilton (1756–1816), poet, novelist and educationist. In 1808 she published *The Cottagers of Glenburnie*, a didactic tale bursting with the improving spirit of sound religion. In this seminal novel, the heroine is middle-aged spinster Mrs Mason ('Mrs' was an honorary title awarded to upper servants in aristocratic households, and occasionally self-awarded by respectable single women), a pious and self-confident former maid to high-born English ladies. Armed with quasi-gentility, she sets herself the task of improving the manners and domestic practice of a Highland peasant family, the MacClartys. As did Sir Walter Scott, Hamilton uses Scots and English speech as markers of class difference, although, as already noted, in the period of which she wrote, described by Henry Cockburn (1778–1854) as 'the last purely Scotch age', Scots was still universally spoken.

The narrative, framed as a *de haut en bas* indictment of the MacClartys' slovenly lifestyle, enjoyed great popularity, and allegedly contributed to an improvement in the squalid conditions of the Scottish peasantry in the 1800s. To the modern reader, the book is redeemed by the entertaining scenes in which prim Mrs Mason attempts to reform the unhygienic ménage of her cousin Mrs Mac-Clarty, to whom bedbugs, moths, hairs in the butter and flyblown dunghills at the front door are slight, unavoidable inconveniences. Presiding over her filthy house and disobedient children with good-natured complacency, her catchphrases are, 'We dae weel eneuch', and 'I canna be fash'd'.

Hamilton's sense of humour is strong, but her need to teach a moral lesson is stronger. The disobedient son who defies his father by going to a country fair falls victim to a press-gang, deserts from the Army and narrowly escapes a firing squad. The family is stricken by an infectious disease, exacerbated by their dirty habits. Deciding that the MacClartys are beyond redemption. Mrs Mason moves out and finds another family, the Morisons, to patronise. They prove more compliant and, installed as the schoolmistress, she succeeds in raising not only them but the whole village from squalor to respectability. Only poor widowed Mrs MacClarty, by her refusal to see the light, is shut out from this paradise, ending her days in lonely bitterness and envy.

Away from Glenburnie, a large portion of the narrative is devoted to the drama of a comfortably off family with an errant daughter who yearns to mingle with wealthier and more genteel people, only to discover too late that she has been conned into marrying the son of a shoemaker. Needless to say, the chief agent in her cruel disabusement is the saintly Mrs Mason, who cannot tell even a white lie. Yet *The Cottagers of Glenburnie*, despite its relentless preaching and assumptions of class privilege, was a key text in early women's fiction, even if, as Henry Cockburn remarked in his posthumously published *Memorials of His Time* (1856), 'One wonders why Mrs Hamilton, with her good Scotch eye, did not put more Scotch into her cottagers than dirt, on which almost solely the book lives.'

Twenty years younger than Elizabeth Hamilton, Orkney-born Mary Brunton (1778–1818) was the wife of a Church of Scotland minister, with whom she eloped at the age of twenty. Although her early education had been conventional, her husband encouraged her to read philosophy and she began to write fiction despite, on her own admission, having previously written nothing beyond letters, recipes and adolescent verse. To the dramatist Joanna Baillie (1762–1851) she candidly admitted:

> I was so ignorant of the art on which I was entering that I formed scarcely any plan for my tale. I merely intended to shew [sic] the power of the religious principle in bestowing self-command and to bear testimony against a maxim as immoral as indelicate, that a reformed rake makes the best husband.

The book referred to was *Self-Control* (1811) and its successor was *Discipline* (1814), forbidding titles which bear witness to the fact that Mary Brunton, like Elizabeth Hamilton, justified her storytelling primarily by its usefulness as a preaching tool. Brunton, however, belonged to a generation with different reading habits, open to the Romantic and Gothic influences of late eighteenth-century poetry and prose. Being young herself, she also realised that young readers of fiction identify with youthful protagonists, and gave them as role models not middle-aged prigs like Mrs Mason, but beautiful and resourceful young heroines, determined to avoid the corruption that assails them at every turn. Thus she was able to excite her readers with scenes of passion, prodigality, duelling, depravity and deceit, while firmly indicating the moral superiority of chastity and its ultimate rewards – a pure conscience and marriage to a refined, wealthy and preferably Scottish man.

In *Self-Control*, virtuous Laura Montreville is involved with two men, one the debauched Colonel Hargrave, the other decent and upstanding Montague de Courcy (Brunton had a weakness for highfalutin names). It is hard to summarise the plot without its sounding ridiculous, which on one level it is; in the course of her struggle against the lecherous passion of Colonel Hargrave, Laura is orphaned and after many trials kidnapped by Hargrave and taken across the Atlantic to Canada, where he intends to rape her and force her into marriage. This wicked plan is frustrated in a scene of transcendent absurdity, in which Laura escapes from the cabin where she is detained by Indian [sic] guards. Finding a canoe among the reeds by a tumbling river, and having first taken the precaution of tying herself to it with her cloak, she resourcefully launches herself into its rapids and is rescued further downstream. A chapter later Hargrave has committed suicide and Laura, having married de Courcy is chatelaine of a Highland castle. As Jane Austen, who is said to have been influenced by Brunton, coolly remarked: '[*Self-Control*] is an excellently meant, elegantly written work without anything of nature or probability in it.' It is vastly entertaining, nonetheless.

Mary Brunton's second novel, *Discipline*, tells in the first person the story of Ellen Percy, an over-indulged and self-centred middle-class rich girl, as she makes a journey, through many trials, towards spiritual and moral enlightenment. Loved by Henry Maitland, 15 years her senior and a friend of her father's, she is nevertheless rejected by him on the grounds that he could not live with such a flawed partner: 'The wife of a Christian,' he tells her sternly, 'must be more than a toy of his leisure; – she must be his fellow-labourer, his fellow-worshipper.' Ellen's reaction to this rebuff is to fall for the advances of the libertine Lord Frederick de Burgh, and narrowly miss being abducted to Gretna Green. Only when her father commits suicide and she is left almost destitute does her life begin to change; she admits her faults and, obliged to earn her living, becomes a governess in Edinburgh to the children of cruel Mrs Boswell, who abuses her to the point of mental collapse. After detention in an 'insane asylum', Ellen is finally rescued by a new friend, Charlotte Graham, and taken to Castle Eredine in the Highlands, the seat of Charlotte's brother, the Chief of the Graham clan. Here, in another of Brunton's highly improbable but satisfying plot resolutions, Ellen meets the Chief, only to find that he is her old friend Henry Maitland, aka Graham, who now finds in her the person, purged of sin through Christian fortitude, conforming to his ideal of the woman he wants to marry.

Of Mary Brunton's two completed novels (she died in childbirth, aged forty, in 1818), *Discipline* is arguably the better book. Although the author never allows the complexity of human nature to subvert her own uncompromising Christian-didactic intention, in Ellen we have a character thoughtfully developed, through whom Brunton confronts the shocking reality of female vulnerability in a male-empowered society. This was a step further than Elizabeth Hamilton had dared to take away from the Calvinist view of women's place in God's plan for humankind. Another was Brunton's willingness to describe passion; *The Cottagers of Glenburnie* was not concerned with sex. As Fay Weldon, writing introductions to new editions of *Self-Control* and *Discipline* in the 1980s, cheerfully summed up: 'Improving the Brunton novels may be, but what fun they are to read, rich in invention, ripe with incident, shrewd in comment and erotic in intention and fact.' The shadow of Calvin was fading, but it had not vanished yet.

3

THE AUTHOR
OF *MARRIAGE*

In the first place I really have not much time that I can absolutely command, for in a town, however privately or retired one may live, they're still liable to be a thousand interruptions; in the next place, I have enough to do with my time in writing to my sisters three, sewing my seam, improving my mind, making tea, playing whist, with numberless other duties too tedious to mention.

Susan Ferrier (1782–1854)
Letter to Charlotte Clavering 1810

SUSAN FERRIER, HELD by many to be the first significant Scottish woman writer of the nineteenth century, was born in an apartment in Lady Stair's Close in the Old Town of Edinburgh on 7 September 1782, during a period of great social change. The medieval city, strung out along a volcanic ridge running from the Castle in the west to the Abbey and Palace of Holyroodhouse in the east, had long been dangerously overcrowded. Rich and poor lived crammed together in ramshackle, vertiginously high tenements; infectious disease was rife, and the capital of Scotland was infamous throughout Europe for its filthy streets, primitive sanitation and noxious smell, compounded of chimney reek and human and animal ordure.

Twenty years had passed since the Town Council had been forced to ease the situation, enabling the building first of a development of new housing on reclaimed marshland to the south of the old city, and then a more ambitious one to the north, with streets and squares of spacious, pale grey sandstone terraced houses – available, inevitably, only to the comparatively wealthy. By the time Susan Ferrier was born, the youngest child of a solicitor who held the elevated rank of Writer to the Signet and a farmer's daughter from Montrose, the first phase of this 'New Town' was nearing completion and the flight from the tenements of the aristocratic and middle classes accelerating. Among them were the Ferriers and their ten children, who ranged in age from 16 to two.

For James Ferrier (1744–1829), the move to 25 George Street was an indicator of professional success. Not only had he established a good practice in Edinburgh, but had also acquired a prestigious position as legal adviser to John Campbell, 5th Duke of Argyll (1723–1806). But it was also a flitting of necessity. Although their apartment in Lady Stair's Close was of the better sort, with wainscotted rooms and decent furnishings, the stress of accommodating so large a family in such a constricted a space must have been considerable. Like the family of Sir Walter Scott, who had moved to George Square on the Southside in 1774, the children would have slept cheek by jowl in box beds that were little more than cupboards, while their father, according to a memoir of him written years later by his daughter, transacted his business in a closet with no fireplace, and entertained his more important clients, including the Duke of Argyll, in his bedroom. Susan herself had no memory of life in Lady Stair's Close, mentioning only in passing that since the middle-class exodus to the New Town, 'the situation is now one of the most beggarly description'.

It would, of course, be a mistake to suppose that physical proximity in the Old Town had meant a blurring of class distinction. While doubtless the presence of so many well-off and well-educated citizens, including historians, scientists and philosophers of the Enlightenment, was a cause of civic pride, inevitably the aristocratic and professional residents led a social life which largely ignored their poorer neighbours. They dined in each other's apartments, attended performances at Carrubber's Close Theatre and the Canongate Concert Hall (despite the intermittently successful attempts of the Kirk to close them), and danced in the Assembly Rooms which opened in the West Bow in 1710. When, as an already homogeneous group, these residents migrated to the New Town, they simply transferred their socialising to other premises. Private dinners became grander and domestic entertainment probably more competitive, while new Assembly Rooms opened in George Street in 1787, and the Theatre Royal, in Shakespeare Square at the east end of Princes Street in 1769. This was the city where Susan Ferrier grew up, the 'other Edinburgh' of the wynds and closes glimpsed only through the windows of a coach on the road south, and contact with its inhabitants limited to formal exchanges with those who worked as servants and suppliers to their wealthier New Town neighbours.

Little is known for certain about the education of Susan Ferrier; she left few clues, believing that personal life should be private. James Ferrier had six sons to educate and launch into the world (the three eldest would become Writers to the Signet like their father, the others would all join the British Army and die tragically young, one in the West Indies in 1801, two in India in 1804). Like other men of his time, Ferrier would have been less concerned about the schooling of presumably marriageable daughters. Susan may initially have attended a small private school, but thereafter she seems to have been taught by her elder sisters. She would also have acquired the 'accomplishments' expected of a young lady, deportment, music, drawing and French, along with activities which nowadays would be regarded as hobbies. For these, as an adult, she could not hide her contempt:

> *I am busied in the Arts and Sciences at present, japanning old boxes, varnishing new ones, daubing velvet, and, in short, as the old wives say, 'my hands are never out of an ill turn'. Then, by way of pastime, I play whist every night to the very death with all the fusty dowagers and musty mousers of the purlieus – and yet I'm alive!*

Certainly the fact that the adult Susan was well-read and able to write long, entertaining letters, pieces of reminiscence and ultimately novels, owed more to her own intelligence and sharp eye for the quirks of human behaviour than from any serious desire of her parents to educate her. The best that can be said is that she grew up with access to the conversation of one of the most sparkling and erudite societies in late eighteenth-century Europe and, when she was not varnishing boxes and playing whist, she was left free to educate herself. She read the Scottish novels of Henry Mackenzie (1745–1831) and John Galt, and also the work of her female contemporaries, Elizabeth Hamilton, Mary Brunton, Jane Austen and the Irish novelist Maria Edgeworth (1767–1849), expressing often severe judgements in letters to her family and friends. She met her father's colleague Sir Walter Scott socially, and knew the influential critics Francis Jeffrey (1773–1850) and Henry Brougham (1778–1868), both founders of the influential *Edinburgh Review*. She showed no respect, however, for the group of Edinburgh women known as the 'bluestockings', much sneered at for daring to discuss political and scientific subjects normally the province of men. She was not a feminist in the modern sense, as is shown in her savage depiction of Mrs Bluemits's literary circle in *Marriage*, where the women are all stupid, technically capable of reading Dryden, Scott and Byron but interested only in their descriptions of dogs.

Mrs Ferrier, of whom Susan later wrote rather dismissively that 'her sole endowments were virtue, beauty and sweetness of disposition', died in 1797, when Susan was 14. This was at a time when her elder brothers were leaving home for careers in law and the Army, and two of her three sisters to be married. For a while, Susan was cared for by her eldest sister Jane, but in 1804 she too married, leaving Susan in the unenviable position of housekeeper to her kindly but demanding father – a responsibility she would bear until his death in 1829, by which time she was 47. Her sense of duty was no doubt reinforced by a strong Christian belief, which helped her to cope at a young age with the deaths of her mother and three brothers, but in her earlier years religion failed to curb her satirical turn of mind. A sharp eye for the ridiculous in the appearance and conversation of her neighbours was evident in her letters long before she turned her attention to fiction. The elderly ladies of Edinburgh were remorselessly described as 'old tabbies', 'toads' and 'fusty dowagers', and no fat, red-faced or dowdy person was safe from her mockery. In 1808 she wrote to her friend Charlotte Clavering:

> *We had Camillia dining with us one day lately in very tolerable preservation.*
> *She went next day to take, as she thought, another family dinner at General Max-*
> *well's instead of which she found herself and her rusty fusty worsted robes*
> *in the midst of a brilliant assembly of powdered beaux and perfumed belles.*

Witty, but catty at the same time. It is, however, improbable that observation of the oddities of her Edinburgh neighbours alone would have given Susan Ferrier the breadth of experience she needed to write the kind of fiction she did. Fortunately, during her formative years, she had the opportunity to witness other ways of living. A sickly child who throughout her life would suffer from persistent colds and coughs, she made several winter visits to her sister Helen, now settled in the south of England, where the climate was generally milder than in cold, windy Edinburgh. These gave her insight into an urbane English society in many ways different from its more downright Scottish equivalent, and impressions that she filed away for future use. But a far greater influence on her writing was gifted to her much closer to home.

As the Duke of Argyll's legal adviser and land agent, James Ferrier was often obliged to visit his distinguished client at Inverary Castle, on the shore of Loch Fyne in the far west. Frequently he took Susan as a companion, and so she was introduced to a landscape of tumbling mountain streams and swathes of sparsely inhabited moorland under tumultuous Atlantic skies, which affected her deeply. Fascinating too was the society at the Castle, where several generations of Campbells resided, their aristocratic eccentricities noted with glee by the legal adviser's daughter. Refined but idle young women pining for romance; flirtatious young gentlemen hoping for wealthy brides; crusty old lairds whose only interest was blood sports; bored, animal-loving ladies who kept dogs, parrots and even an ill-tempered monkey, would reappear, renamed but recognisable, in novels to come. With the ease of a tolerant Scots society, the middle-class Ferriers were made welcome among these grand folk; with one of them in particular, the Duke's youngest granddaughter Charlotte Clavering (1794–1869) Susan became intimate, despite a seven-year difference in their ages.

Much in each other's company at Inverary, and writing long letters (published in 1898 in *Memoir and Correspondence Of Susan Ferrier, 1782–1854: Based On Her Private Correspondence* and edited by John A. Doyle) when Susan was at home in Edinburgh, the two young women discussed their reading and decided that they too could write a novel. What began as a collaboration, however, did not work out, since Charlotte's plot suggestions of Gothic intrigue, murder and suicide were smartly knocked on the head by Susan. 'I will groan for you till the very blood shall curdle in my veins … but I will not enter into any of your raw head and bloody bones schemes,' she wrote. So Charlotte moved aside and when, after nine years of writing in moments snatched from paying visits, shopping for her married sisters, making tea, playing whist and performing the relentless duties of an unmarried daughter, *Marriage* was published in 1818, of its 72 chapters only one very dull one was the work of Charlotte Clavering. Yet it remains likely that without the spur of Charlotte's youthful enthusiasm, admiration and a degree of critical acumen, Susan Ferrier would never have written a novel at all.

In the event, between 1818 and 1831, she wrote three, *Marriage*, *The Inheritance* and *Destiny*, which reveal her as both an innovator and a traditionalist. What was new in women's fiction was her irrepressible tendency to caricature and satire; what was not new was her insistence on an edifying message. 'The only good purpose of a book,' she wrote sternly, 'is to inculcate morality, and convey some lesson of instruction as well as delight.' This habit of mind, so evident in her predecessors Elizabeth Hamilton and Mary Brunton, betrays from the beginning of her writing career a lingering Calvinist sense of unease.

There is a sense in which all of Susan Ferrier's novels might have been titled 'Marriage'. Herself unmarried (there is no convincing evidence of any passionate attachment in her life), she was well aware that for most well-bred young women, in an age when the eldest son automatically inherited the bulk of his father's fortune, future prosperity depended on finding a hopefully kind and loving, but most importantly, wealthy husband. In real life, security easily trumped youthful romance. In *Marriage*, when Lady Juliana, the bored socialite daughter of the English Earl of Courtland, who has heartlessly arranged to marry her off to a squinting, hunchbacked fifty-year-old duke, defies her father and elopes with a Scottish soldier Henry Douglas, she is in the grip of what she imagines is romantic passion. Her disillusionment when she finds herself banged up in the bleak, run-down Highland castle of Glenfern, with her husband's rough-mannered father, three forceful maiden aunts Miss Grizzy, Miss Jackie and Miss Nicky and their clumsy 'blue-faced' nieces, provides much of the comedy in the first part of the book. But its moral, according to Ferrier, is less that tyrannical fathers should be defied for love's sake than that young ladies should be warned against runaway romances. The story, with its version of the age-old tale of faithful love thwarted but ultimately rewarded, is not new, but it is told with infectious verve and is, as the English critic Oliver Elton perceptively remarked in 1912, 'a young book; it is the voice of youth revenging itself on all the bores whom it will tolerate only if it may describe them.'

Marriage abounds in memorable comic figures, the overbearing Lady Maclaughlan and her wimpish husband Sir Sampson, foolish Aunt Grizzy, Mrs

Bluemits, Squire Guffaw, Mrs Downe Wright. Happily Ferrier's impulse to laughter is unrestrained by her need for a virtuous message – one emphasised through the early career of Juliana's humourless but dutiful daughter Mary, who is fostered by an aunt in the Highlands before returning on a visit to her uncaring mother in the south of England. Upper-class English manners are contrasted unfavourably with the simple and sincere ways of the Highlands, Mary's Christian principles and prudence are set against the vacuous vanity of her sister Adelaide and lively cynicism of her cousin Lady Emily. After much angst, however, virtue triumphs. Mary finds a husband to her taste, and the story ends with her restoration to her native land where: 'The hills, the air, the waters, the people, even the peat-stacks, had a charm that touched her heart, and brought tears to her eyes as they pictured home'.

Marriage, for which its author received an advance of £150, was published anonymously by William Blackwood. It gained instant popularity, particularly in Edinburgh where, if readers did not recognise themselves in its pages, their neighbours certainly did. Speculation about its authorship was widespread, and some readers probably guessed correctly, but Susan, laughing inwardly, gave nothing away.

When *The Inheritance*, said to have been largely written at the Ferriers' summer residence at Morningside, was published in 1824, the advance Blackwood offered had risen to £1,000, roughly equivalent to £70,000 today.

Neither *The Inheritance* nor its successor *Destiny* reached quite the degree of popularity achieved by *Marriage*, either at the time of their publication or in the years that followed. *The Inheritance* is the better constructed of the two, but both feature memorably grotesque figures – Lord Rossville and garrulous Miss Pratt in *The Inheritance*, simple Molly Macaulay and the ineffably ghastly Reverend Mr M'Dow in *Destiny*. But the *joie de vivre* of the first book fades as Susan Ferrier grows older, her own health fails and the needs of her aged father encroach on both her writing time and her social life.

In May 1831 Susan Ferrier, her vision blurred by cataracts and still exhausted by the stress of her father's long decline and death, travelled in the Edinburgh–Jedburgh mail coach to Abbotsford to visit Sir Walter Scott. It was not her first visit; she and her father had stayed with the Scotts twenty years before at Ashiestiel, near Selkirk, and she had gone alone at Abbotsford in 1829, the year when her father died. Despite her fondness for Scott, she had not enjoyed that visit, disliking the clutter of his antiquarian collection and bored by his ceaseless flow of anecdotes. Yet she owed him kindnesses; she had received hospitality in his Edinburgh house, and he had paid her a stunning compliment by calling 'the author of *Marriage*' his 'sister-shadow' in the epilogue to *A Legend of Montrose*. More recently, he had persuaded his own publisher, Robert Cadell, to pay £1,700 for the rights to her newly published *Destiny*. Since then, Scott had suffered a number of strokes, and when his daughters, desperate to break his self-punishing work schedule, suggested that Susan's company might divert him, she felt unable to refuse. Many years later, at the insistence of her family, she wrote a memoir titled 'Recollections of Visits to Ashiestiel and Abbotsford', posthumously printed in the *Temple Bar* magazine in 1874.

Although she had watched in Edinburgh his slow physical and mental decline, Susan was still unprepared for the deterioration caused by Scott's most recent stroke. Shown into his library, she was shocked by his swollen, pasty face, dim eyes and slurred speech. His head had been shaved (then a routine and futile treatment for fever) and he was wearing a black silk cap which she described as 'unbecoming'. But he was pleased to see her, and she rallied quickly. Scott's son-in-law, John Gibson Lockhart (1794–1854), would later recall her tact and kindness when Scott's memory failed him in the middle of one of his interminable stories. Not everyone, Lockhart remarked, had shown such patience.

In the past, there had always been many guests of all ages at Abbotsford. Now, apart from Susan, only family were present; Scott's unmarried daughter Anne, Sophia Lockhart with her husband and three children. To add to the gloom and misery engulfing the house, the eldest child, twelve-year-old Johnnie, was terminally ill, probably with osteomyelitis. Susan Ferrier's account of the interaction of this stricken family is unsparing, but filled with a compassion never evident in her better-known work.

Every day, at dinner in the long dining-room, only she, Anne Scott and the Lockharts were present until the dessert was served. Then Scott, whose initial pleasure in Susan's company had quickly faded, was brought in by his servant to join them. Next the children arrived, and Scott's favourite grandson Johnnie, his head swathed in the black bandages commonly used before the twentieth century, was seated at his side. Susan never forgot the expression of 'languor and dejection' on Scott's face as he looked at his once beautiful grandson, 'now tragically transformed into an image of decrepitude and decay'.

> The fair and blooming cheek and finely chiselled features were now shrunk and stiffened into the wan and rigid inflexibility of old age, while the black bandages which swathed the little countenance gave additional gloom and harshness to the profound melancholy which clouded its most intellectual expression. Disease and death were stamped upon the grandsire and the boy as they sat side by side with averted eyes, each as if in the bitterness of his own heart refusing to comfort or be comforted … . [Their] appearance and style of dress, the black cap of one and the black bandages of the other, denoted a sympathy in suffering, if in nothing else.

This bleak eye-witness account of the failure of love and trust under extreme pressure is deeply moving, the more so since it marks a creeping darkness in its writer's mind.

When she left Abbotsford, after a week when beautiful summer weather contrasted cruelly with the shadows and despair within, Susan Ferrier must have known that she had witnessed the end of an era. Johnnie Lockhart, whose bandages concealed a weeping abscess on his neck, died in London in December, his grandfather at Abbotsford nine months later. It was also, whether she knew it or not, the end of her own writing career. She lacked Scott's legendary staying power and, after the publication of *Destiny* in 1831, her creative well ran dry. Beset by bronchial illness and failing eyesight, she became reclusive, spending her remaining 23 years in darkened rooms, lapsing into a Calvinistic religious melancholy where she came to repent ever having written her novels at all. Her letters lost their sparkle, and by 1836 she had admitted defeat: 'I made two attempts to write *something*, but could not please myself, and would not publish *anything*.'

This late Susan Ferrier is hauntingly captured in a marble bust, now in the Scottish National Portrait Gallery in Edinburgh, which was long believed to be by an otherwise unknown sculptor named 'John Gall'. Recent research by Julie Lawson, Chief Curator of the Portrait Gallery, however, strongly suggests a mistaken attribution. It is all but certain that the bust is the work of James Gall (1808–95), a Free Church Minister in Edinburgh and one-time student at the Trustees Academy, forerunner of Edinburgh School of Art. It is known that Susan Ferrier joined the Free Church at the time of the Disruption in 1843, and James Gall may well have been acquainted with his subject in her final years. It is a poignant portrait, but hard to associate this austere, suffering, sightless image with the spritely author of *Marriage*, who made her readers 'screech with laughing', and was defended by later novelist Margaret Oliphant (1828–97) in the never-ending but sterile debate about Ferrier's status *vis-a-vis* Jane Austen, as provoking 'the broader humour and larger laugh of the Scots'.

In 1840, Susan Ferrier sold the copyright of her three novels to a London publisher, Richard Bentley, who published them the following year in an illustrated edition. Her authorship had been an open secret for years, but now for the first time she allowed her name to appear on the title page. She died in her brother's house at 38 Albany Street on 5 November 1854, aged 72.

4

MULTITASKERS

We all know with how womanly and serene a temper literature has been pursued by ... women of admirable genius – how with absolutely no sacrifice or loss of feminine dignity they have cultivated the profession of authorship; and, if we could hear their report, I have no doubt that the little cares of correcting proofs, and the forward-looking solicitudes connected with the mere business arrangements of new publications, would be numbered amongst the minor pleasures of life.

Thomas De Quincey (1785–1859)
*Recollections of the Lakes and the Lake Poets c.*1840

THE WORD 'MULTITASKING' is a modern one, first coined in 1965 to describe a computer function, but used more recently to suggest the necessity in a hectic life of performing a multiplicity of tasks; juggling more than one job while running a household, bringing up children, and, for many people, making financial ends meet. After the end of the Great War in 1918, the ready supply of inexpensive live-in servants had slowed, then dried up, but not until the late twentieth century did the expectation that men would share the responsibility of household chores and bringing up children become widespread. Previously, when the reality of multi-tasking existed without a definition, the burden was laid almost exclusively on women.

As in more recent times, nineteenth-century women writers had different motivations. Some had independent means, so were free to choose their genres and write for their own pleasure; some hoped to supplement a less secure income, while the brave, often driven by necessity, attempted to live by their writing alone. Among the women writers already mentioned, Mary Brunton had the support of her husband and Susan Ferrier of her father. Susan might with justice have seen herself as a multitasker, juggling household obligations to find time to write, but she was not so in a literary sense. Apart from letters she concentrated on fiction, and it is as a novelist that she is known. It was the financially insecure who did not have the luxury of choice. Not for them were proof correcting and business arrangements 'among the minor pleasures of life'. If they found in themselves a talent for writing, exigency forced them to be versatile, moving from journalism to fiction, biography and travel writing to poetry, as opportunity arose. Those women who succeeded in this largely male-dominated industry deserve to be remembered as pioneers.

Elizabeth Hamilton, author of *The Cottagers of Glenburnie* had fewer advantages than Brunton and Ferrier. Unmarried, deprived of her brother's support by his unexpected death in 1792 and unable to find employment due to her own chronic ill health, she had little option but to try her luck as a professional writer. Well-educated for a woman in her time, she had attended school in Stirling, and later public lectures on philosophy in Glasgow and Edinburgh, but most of her formidable knowledge had to be acquired by private reading. Before settling in Edinburgh in 1804, she had already proved her versatility, publishing titles as diverse as *Translations of the Letters of a Hindoo Rajah* (1796), for which she drew on the experience of her brother, who had been in the service of the East India Company, and *Memoirs of Modern Philosophers* (1800), a satirical novel featuring an absurd 'bluestocking', Miss Bridgetina Botherim; such pretentiously intellectual women were fair game for novelists of the period. In 1801 she published *Letters on the Elementary Principles of Education*, the first of many books and articles on educational topics, and in the year of her move to Edinburgh took a subject from Roman history, *Memoirs of the Life of Agrippina, Wife of Germanicus*. This was a brave choice, at a time when classical studies and biography were assumed to be the preserve of university-educated men.

Given the general prejudice against women writers, Hamilton's success was remarkable; apart from an annual pension of £50 from King George III, she supported herself by writing alone until her death in 1816. She was among the first literary multitaskers of the nineteenth century, even if she is now remembered only as the author of *The Cottagers of Glenburnie*.

A literary multitasker of a different kind, whose life overlapped with Hamilton's, was Christian Isobel Johnstone (1781–1857), of whose early years tantalisingly little is known. She has been identified as Christian Todd, born in Edinburgh in 1781, and it seems likely, given her wide knowledge and literary talent, that her parents were of the middle class. But as to who they were, and where and how they lived, nothing has been satisfactorily established. It is believed that at an early age Christian Isobel married a man whose surname was McLeish, and a few years later divorced him. Only after 1812 do facts supersede supposition; in that year she married a Dunfermline schoolmaster, John Johnstone and, when he became owner and editor of the *Inverness Courier*, moved with him to Inverness. The level of Christian Isobel's education and commitment now becomes clear, since she immediately became involved in the business, and is credited with giving the *Courier* a more literary bias than was usual in a provincial newspaper. It was here too that she acquired the deep knowledge of Highland life and culture displayed in her best-known novel *Clan-Albin: A National Tale* (1815).

The Johnstones' decision to move to Edinburgh, then a hub of publishing and journalism which rivalled London, proved their ambition. John Johnstone opened a printing office in James Square and, using funds from the sale of the *Inverness Courier*, bought jointly with the publisher William Blackwood (1776–1834) *The Edinburgh Weekly Chronicle*. This partnership, however, was doomed to failure, since the liberal principles of the Johnstones clashed with those of the arch-Tory Blackwood, leading them to sell their share. Aware of the market for publications which the literate poor could afford, and using their own printing press, the Johnstones then ran a number of periodicals, including *The Schoolmaster* and *Edinburgh Weekly Magazine*, with a cover price of 1½d and written almost entirely by Christian Isobel. This publication was converted in 1832 into *Johnstone's Edinburgh Magazine*, which in turn amalgamated with the better-known *Tait's Edinburgh Magazine*. As well as agreeing to her demand that the price of *Tait's* be cut from 2s 6d (12½p) to 1s (5p), William Tait (1792–1864) showed his confidence by giving Christian Isobel most of the editorial responsibility, along with a salary and half ownership of the magazine.

After that, there was nothing to hold her back. As well as editing the work of contributors, she wrote philosophical articles and literary reviews of her contemporaries, championing in particular the work of other women writers. She attacked the trading of enslaved people and the appalling conditions of the poor, and wrote indignantly in defence of the political agitators tried and executed in the late eighteenth century for their radical beliefs. She had the distinction of being mentioned by name in the condescending essay already quoted by the 'English Opium Eater' Thomas De Quincey – a barefaced attempt at flattery, since the essay first appeared in *Tait's*, and she had commissioned it:

> *Mrs Johnstone, of Edinburgh, has pursued the profession of literature ... as a daily occupation; and, I have every reason to believe, with as much benefit to her own happiness, as to the instruction and amusement of her readers: for the petty cares of authorship are agreeable, and its serious cares are ennobling.*

More gratifying than this havering must have been the opinion of Thomas Carlyle (1795–1881) who admired her moral courage, calling her in a letter of 1838 to William Tait 'the good, brave-hearted lady'. 'Radicalism, I grieve to say,' he added, 'has but few such practical adherents!'

In a market teeming with short-lived literary magazines, some of which did not survive their first few issues, *Tait's*, kept alive almost entirely by the industry of Christian Isobel Johnstone, lasted from 1832 until 1846, when a decline in circulation forced its closure. She was described as 'retiring, amiable and accomplished', appreciative rather than destructive in her criticism, and supportive of new talent. The spikiness of her feminist persona, however, suggests a more combative layer of personality. An article published in *Tait's* in November 1832, titled 'Marriages are Made in Heaven' begins:

> *It may be so, but we have our doubts upon the matter. Heaven, we think, would have made neater jobs than most of them are. Not that we incline with certain Manicheans* [believers in the cosmic opposition of absolute good and evil], *to give the other power the credit of their manufacture. They are a cut above him. That the devil inhabits hell we know; but we also know that he did not make it …*

The substance of the essay is of disillusionment. The beautiful young woman carried away by passion realises too late that she has hitched herself for life to an uncongenial partner, and turns into one whose 'face is like frozen vinegar, and whose life is one perpetual scold', while the short-changed husband turns into a creature '[d]ull, inane, feeble, loveless,' who can 'feel for no one; protect, support or cherish no one; cheer the dull path of life to no one'. The conclusion is bleak:

> *Seeing that 'he who will to Cupar maun to Cupar', the only advice that can be given to aspirants after connubial bliss is not to expect too much. To the man we would moreover hint, that marry whom they may, they ought to eschew silly women … . To the woman we would say, avoid idle men …*

Whether these entertaining but advanced opinions cast light on Mrs Johnstone's first union to 'Mr Mcleish', or on her ongoing marriage to John Johnstone, or simply reflect a journalist's urge to be provocative, is impossible to know. John Johnstone, who provided the money for the couple's acquisitions is, without much evidence, usually supposed a supportive husband, yet he must have been aware that he had been effectively written out of the story of his wife's remarkable career. Whatever the truth, her cool analysis of the married state may well have made uncomfortable reading.

If the literary editor of *Tait's* is still remembered today, however, it is less for her journalism than for two of the many books she also found time to write. One is her most celebrated (and bestselling) work of non-fiction, *The Cook and Housewife's Manual, by Mistress Margaret Dods of the Cleikum Inn, St Ronan's*, both pseudonym and setting lifted without permission from Sir Walter Scott's 1824 novel *St Ronan's Well*. In our own time, such appropriation would probably have led to a court case, but the affable Sir Walter was much amused, entering into the joke by providing a preface. This book, its fame enhanced by Scott's co-operation, provided a supplementary income for the Johnstones for the rest of their lives.

As a novelist – she wrote for both children and adults – Christian Isobel's reputation now rests on *Clan Albin: A National Tale*, first published in 1815 simultaneously in London, Edinburgh and Dublin, and most recently by the Association for Literary Scottish Studies (2003). The narrative tells of the childhood and young manhood of Norman Macalbin, orphaned and forced by poverty to leave his West Highland home and join the British Army. His adventures and misadventures in Ireland, and in Spain during the 1808–09 campaign in the war against Napoleon, provide the main thread of a very long and complex text, which is in part the cry of a Radical writer against the futility of war. Yet a great strength of the book is its presentation of women, whose voices sound more clearly and sympathetically than Norman's – the voices of Lady Augusta, child of a Jacobite family and distantly related to Stuart kings, whose early bewitchment amid the splendour and frivolity of the exiled Jacobite court fades as she encounters temptation, depravity and the wicked intent of villains intent on stealing her child; of the 'wise woman' Moome, the most accomplished storyteller and poet 'in a glen where all were poets', and of Monimia, betrothed to the absent Norman, who is revealed (in the well-used fairytale twist) as the grandson of Lady Augusta, and whose nuptials round off this many-faceted novel, part polemic and part romance.

In her preface to *Clan Albin*, Johnstone disclaims 'heavy-handed moralising and preaching' in favour of 'the plain, direct character and simple-hearted purpose of the old-fashioned novel, to entertain the reader'. Instead, she asserts the power of memory and nostalgia, particularly among Highlanders far from home, 'to meliorate the heart which they so delightfully engage'. Yet though with *Clan Albin* we feel the hold of Calvinism on Scottish women writers loosening, the moral message of the novel is plain enough. Like her contemporaries, Hamilton, Brunton and Ferrier, Johnstone sets her personal vision of the simplicity and sincerity of Highland life as nobler and more satisfying to the spirit than that of the increasingly industrialised and commercial heartland of Lowland Scotland. She is also bitterly aware that with the notorious Highland Clearances, the tragic eviction of people from the land to make way for sheep, the best of Highland culture is also imperiled.

As little is known of Christian Isobel Johnstone's life after the closure of *Tait's Magazine* as of her youth. Her personal papers are lost and, in the absence of diaries and letters, the minutiae of her life, her childless relationship with her husband and their domestic arrangements, are unrecorded. She died in August 1857 and was buried in Edinburgh's Grange Cemetery where, a few months later that shadowy figure, her husband John Johnstone, joined her.

It is sadly true that in the twenty-first century, outside universities, the work of writers like Elizabeth Hamilton and Christian Isobel Johnstone is largely unknown. Neither had the high profile of Sir Walter Scott, who has survived as a 'personality' in Scottish life, though all but a few of his novels are rarely read. It is also true that Elizabeth Hamilton's didacticism is at odds with modern taste. In choosing journalism, Christian Isobel Johnstone committed herself to a form which is by nature, of-the-moment; the political concerns and book reviews of the radical press in the 1800s have as little resonance today as those of *The Economist* and *The New Statesman* will have two centuries from now. The two novels, Hamilton's *Cottagers of Glenburnie* and Johnstone's *Clan Albin: A National Tale* owe their republication to a resurgence of interest in our time in Scottish literature, but neither is likely to have mass appeal. Only the most heroic literary multitasker of the Victorian age, after long neglect, seems to be faring rather better in the modern world.

5

A GENERAL
UTILITY WOMAN

I have written because it gave me pleasure, because it came natural to me, because it was like talking or breathing, beside the big fact that it was necessary for me to work for my children.

Margaret Oliphant (1828–97)
Autobiography 1898

MARGARET WILSON OLIPHANT, the most heroic multitasker among the women writers of her age, was born in the mining village of Wallyford, near Musselburgh in East Lothian. She was the daughter of Francis Wilson, an office clerk, and his wife Margaret Oliphant, who claimed descent from the Oliphants of Kellie, 'an old, chivalrous, impoverished race'. There were two older sons, known as Frank and Willie; three other children, one a girl, had died before Margaret was born, and the bond of love between mother and her youngest child was strong. In a disjointed but deeply moving *Autobiography* written at intervals between 1849 and 1888 and published posthumously in 1899, Oliphant remarks that her father was a dim figure in her early life: 'I had to be very quiet in the evenings when he was at home, not to disturb him; and he took no particular notice of me, or of any of us. My mother was all in all.'

The family moved to Lasswade, a village in Midlothian on the toll road between Edinburgh and Dalkeith, not long after Margaret was born. Her first recollection was of living there, in a little house where '[her] mother kept everything going, and comfortably going, on the small income she had to administer'. The life of a country child in Scotland is poignantly detailed; the great ash trees forming an arch across the road; making toast at the fire on winter mornings; standing in the village forge with her brother Willie, 'wondering at the sparks as they flew up, and the dark figures of the smith and his men'; lying in the grass surrounded by blue speedwells and looking up at the sky. She remembered two kittens, named Lord Brougham and Lord Grey after two enablers of the parliamentary Reform Act (1832), when 'we were all tremendously political and Radical, especially my mother and Frank'.

This rural idyll ended in 1834, when Francis Wilson took up a position in the Royal Bank of Scotland and moved his family across the country to Glasgow. An even greater disjunction occurred four years later, when Margaret was ten; her father was appointed to a post in Customs and Excise, and the Wilsons moved south of the border to Liverpool.

Margaret Oliphant is vague about the circumstances of her education; her parents could have had no money to spare for school fees, or to employ a governess for their daughter. Presumably she was taught to read and write by her mother, the clever, passionate woman who 'had read everything she could lay her hands on all her life, and was fond of quoting Pope'. And having acquired the tools, Margaret used them; in all her spare time she read and wrote stories, and in 1849, at the age of 21, published her first novel, *Passages in the Life of Mrs Margaret Maitland*, with the London firm of Henry Colburn & Co. Only Margaret's mother was more excited than she was. The book is set in the period of the 'Disruption' of 1843 when, after a decade of squabbling over the role of the state in ecclesiastical affairs, almost half of the clergy and their congregations seceded from the Church of Scotland and established the Free Church. It was a live issue at the time, one in which the Wilsons sided with the seceders, and the book did well enough to justify a second novel, *Caleb Field, a Tale of the Puritans* in 1851.

That Margaret Wilson chose to set this book, about a group of English Presbyterians, in England during the Civil War (1642–49) says something important about her attitude to identity. She was a Scot, in that her descent was Scottish, and she was proud of it. Like Thomas Carlyle, she never tried, during the many years she spent in England, to modify her Scottish accent, and some of her best work had Scottish themes and settings. But she lived at a time when nationalism was less of an issue than it has recently become. The Union of the Kingdoms was seen as advantageous to Scots, giving them access to London institutions and English markets; they served willingly in the British armed forces and the colonial civil service, and London-dwellers like Carlyle saw no problem in sending letters to addresses in 'North Britain'. Margaret Oliphant spent to first ten years of her life in Scotland, and the voice and influence of her East Lothian mother never left her. She returned there frequently during the next half-century, but never felt constrained to choose Scottish settings for her work.

The year 1851 was a momentous one for the young author. As well as publishing *Caleb Field*, on a visit to Edinburgh she met William Blackwood, publisher of Walter Scott and Susan Ferrier and founder of *Blackwood's Magazine*, who invited her to become a contributor. She did not know it then, but for the next 47 years her work for *Blackwood's*, familiarly known as 'Maga', would become a mainstay in an increasingly desperate existence. Her articles for the magazine provided a reliable boost to her income, and several of her novels would be serialised in its pages before they were published in book form. She also wrote for many other distinguished publishers of her day, among them Chapman & Hall, Macmillan, Hurst & Blackett, Chatto & Windus, Longmans, W. & R. Chambers and Smith, Elder & Co.

The need for such industry lay in her family life. In 1849, Margaret was sent to London by her parents, to keep an eye on her alcoholic and spendthrift brother Willie, as he pursued his studies to become a minister of religion – a project which inevitably came to grief. By 1852 Willie had been dismissed from his first charge at Etal in Northumberland, fled to Rome, and was supported financially by his sister for the rest of his life. During the three months she spent as Willie's housekeeper, Margaret had become close to her cousin, Frank Wilson Oliphant (1818–59) an artist in stained glass, whom she married just after Willie's fall from grace. Her name was now expanded to Margaret Oliphant Wilson Oliphant (as a writer, in keeping with Victorian convention, she was known simply as 'Mrs Oliphant'). Within seven years after her marriage she had given birth to five children and lost three of them, and nursed her mother through a long terminal illness. At the same time, another tragedy was pending; her talented young husband, who had exhibited at the Royal Academy and collaborated with the architect Augustus Pugin (1812–52) on the windows of the new Houses of Parliament, was stricken with tuberculosis – a diagnosis which, to her lasting resentment, he kept from her. As his condition worsened, the Oliphants, now dependent entirely on Margaret's earnings, travelled with their two children to Italy where, in 1859, Frank Oliphant died and another baby was posthumously born.

Earning now became imperative. Soon Margaret was describing herself as *Blackwood's* 'general utility woman'; every opportunity was grasped, and from the pen that eventually wore a hole in her forefinger flowed novels, short stories, book reviews, travel guides, translations, biographies, art criticism, history, verse. Unfortunately, she had not inherited her mother's frugality; she 'loved the easy swing of life', and, like Sir Walter Scott, had supreme confidence in her own earning power. She became extravagant and ran up debts, her considerable income still insufficient to cover the expense of her fine houses and frequent jaunts to Europe, as well as sending her nephew and two academically gifted but idle and self-serving sons to Eton, so that they might have 'the best education in England'. Her response was to write even more, but there was a price to be paid.

Even in her own lifetime, Oliphant was accused of writing too much, as it became clear that the 'general utility woman' often wrote about subjects for which she had little qualification, cutting corners as she juggled her deadlines. Criticism peaked in the twentieth century when Virginia Woolf (1882–1941) suggested in a lofty polemical essay *Three Guineas* (1938) that Mrs Oliphant had 'sold her brain, her very admirable brain, prostituted her culture and enslaved her intellectual liberty, in order that she might earn her living and educate her children'. Even while admitting that given 'the necessity that is laid upon those who have children to see that they are fed and clothed, nursed and educated, we have to applaud her choice and admire her courage,' Woolf's distaste is clear. Oliphant would no doubt have retorted that she had no alternative; no other career was open to her, and as the years passed she found herself not only supporting her two surviving sons Cyril and Francis (an eleven-year-old daughter died in a cholera epidemic in Rome in 1864), but also Willie and her other brother Frank and his three children, who lived with her from 1868.

Although she claimed always to enjoy writing, she was not devoid of self-awareness. Towards the end of her life, when she was riled by compliments on her industry rather than her literary achievements, she was jealous of George Eliot (1819–80) who was unburdened by motherhood and had a partner to cosset her, and complained that none of her own books had really been a bestseller. The 'general utility woman' admitted ruefully in her *Autobiography*: 'It would have been better if I could have added the grace of thrift, which is said to be the inheritance of the Scot, to the faculty for work,' adding:

> … [that] *a better kind of self-denial should have made a truer artist than myself pursue the higher objects of art instead of the mere necessities of living. I pay the penalty in that I shall not leave behind me anything that will live.*

This frank self-assessment has some truth in it, but is too despondent. A perceptive obituary by the American writer Howard Sturgis (1855–1920), published in the *Temple Bar* magazine in 1899, came closer to the truth:

> *Her best work is of a very high order of merit. The harm that she did to her literary reputation seems rather the surrounding of her best work with so much that she knew to be of inferior quality, that her high peaks of achievement, instead of rising out of the plain, as it were, suffer diminution by the neighbourhood of so many foothills.*

The obituary in *Blackwood's Magazine*, which had published both peaks and foothills, was more effusive. Mrs Oliphant 'belonged to a race of literary giants … [She was] to the England of letters what the Queen has been to society as a whole'. So how to explain her near-eclipse in the years following her death, and is there anything of hers still worth reading?

One suggested reason for her decline in popularity was the transition in publishing, around the time she died, from the three-volume novels, issued in instalments and the norm in the eighteenth and most of the nineteenth centuries, to the one-volume editions we know today. The 'three-decker' required a degree of padding out to make it conform to a required length and format; this necessity could slow the narrative and irritate the reader. Once the transition was made, Victorian novelists fell out of favour with twentieth-century readers appreciative of the pacier, less wordy novels of writers including the Scots Catherine Carswell (1879–1946), Neil Gunn (1891–1973) and Nan Shepherd (1893–1981). It has also been suggested that those Oliphant had disparaged in her book reviews were quick to take revenge, perhaps most memorably Thomas Hardy (1840–1928), who hit back at her scathing review (in July 1897) of his last novel *Jude the Obscure* (1895) by dismissing her criticism as 'the screaming of a poor lady in Blackwood's'. It is likely too that when her *Autobiography* was published after her death, her self-deprecation served only to intensify the criticism of others. But there were more profound reasons.

Like her contemporary Robert Louis Stevenson (1850–94), Margaret Oliphant had the misfortune to die in the 1890s; both suffered from perceived irrelevance to a generation brutally severed from their predecessors by the Great War of 1914–18. The aftermath of this catastrophe was marked throughout Europe and America by the striving for new forms of expression in ideas, art and literature, drawn together under the name 'Modernism'. A new cynicism and disrespect for the past among the young was first given voice by Lytton Strachey (1880–1932) whose *Eminent Victorians* (1918) gleefully trashed the reputations of icons including Florence Nightingale (1820–1910) and Dr Thomas Arnold (1795–1842), the headmaster credited with changing Rugby School from a den of juvenile iniquity into a community of disciplined, Christian young gentlemen. *Eminent Victorians* divided generations, provoking delight and outrage in equal measure, and giggling at the Victorians soon became fashionable among the 'bright young things' of the 1920s. The satirical novels of Evelyn Waugh (1903–1966) and Aldous Huxley (1894–1963) were all the rage and Modernism, exemplified in literature by the experimental 'stream of consciousness' writing of, for example, Gertrude Stein (1874–1946) and Virginia Woolf, separated 'high' from popular taste. Mrs Oliphant's books went out of print, and she disappeared for sixty years.

Margaret Oliphant's rehabilitation began in the 1980s, when Virago Press, dedicated to redressing the gender inequality between male and female writers, published several of her 'Carlingford Chronicles', notably *The Perpetual Curate*, *Salem Chapel* and *Miss Marjoribanks*, all originally published in the 1860s. Although dealing, albeit ironically, with topics which have little resonance with modern readers, centred as they are on the heated mid-nineteenth-century debate within the Church of England between High (Anglo-Catholic) and Low (Evangelical) interpretations of New Testament doctrine, they have other attractions – flawed but believable characters, a deft handling of emotional crises, romantic interest and a seasoning of wit.

The Perpetual Curate tells the story of Frank Wentworth, a popular young clergyman in charge of a chapel in the English country town of Carlingford, who alienates the more Puritan element of his congregation by his fondness for 'floral ornaments and ecclesiastical upholstery'. The new parish Rector, Frank's superior, is equally disapproving and Frank, who wants to marry and is dependent on a future job which is in the gift of his sternly evangelical aunts, is on the horns of several dilemmas. There is much comedy in this situation, and Oliphant shows her gift for creating strong female characters, notably the Rector's unhappy wife and Frank's sparky fiancée Lucy Wentworth.

Salem Chapel deals with a contrary strand of English religious life – one which has echoes of the tensions in the Scottish church, which the author understood well. It features Arthur Vincent, a naïve young non-conformist minister straight from college, who arrives in Carlingford in high hopes of acceptance among the upper ranks of the town's society. His first social engagement, a tea party at the house of his senior deacon, Mr Tozer, abruptly opens his eyes to the truth; his congregation is composed of cheesemongers, greengrocers, butchers, music teachers and dressmakers. His dream of elegant dinner parties and refined conversation vanishes in an instant. As a Scot, Margaret Oliphant was exempt from English class sensitivity, but observed it with a satiric eye; in relating the consequences of the young minister's recoil from the coy advances of Phoebe Tozer, 'pink, plump and full of dimples', and instead falling disastrously in love with aristocratic Lady Western, the author displays sympathy for the young, contempt for bigots and a fine sense of the absurd.

These novels, which have been favourably compared with the more famous books of Anthony Trollope (1815–82), *The Warden* (1855) and *Barchester Towers* (1857), convey deftly the surface tranquillity of English provincial life, while probing its underbelly of snobbery and social division. They were published anonymously, and Oliphant was less than thrilled that many readers supposed them to be by George Eliot. George Eliot was not pleased either.

As the years passed, Margaret Oliphant's work shows a growing concern with the injustices inflicted on women by a male chauvinist society, a preoccupation no doubt fuelled by her own experience. The frustrations endured by independently minded women to achieve career fulfilment are explored in *Hester: A Story of Contemporary Life* (1883), which features the ageing Catherine Vernon, to whom the presidency of a family-owned bank brings power at the cost of personal fulfilment, and *Kirsteen: The Story of a Scotch Family Seventy Years Ago* (1890), in which a young woman escapes the tyranny of her father and emotional blackmail of her peevish mother, rejects marriage and after many trials gains independence as a fashionable London dressmaker. But *Miss Marjoribanks* (1866), was the first to treat women's issues specifically, and shows Oliphant at her satirical best.

Miss Marjoribanks is the story of Lucilla Marjoribanks, daughter of a Scottish doctor, whose wish, on her mother's death and to her father's horror, is to leave her boarding school and come home 'to be a comfort to Papa'. Papa sends her packing, but cannot prevent the inevitable; by the time Lucilla leaves school, her enlarged desire is to be a comfort to the whole of Carlingford – an ambition which Carlingford has little desire to gratify. Bossy, practical Lucilla is stymied at every turn, but her self-belief is unassailable. Even as her dreams fade she ploughs on, redecorating Papa's drawing room as a party venue, meddling in the lives of the drawing master's daughters, setting up a school and pondering marriage to the local MP – though only 'because of her interest in political economy'. In many ways, Lucilla is a monster of snobbery and self-delusion, who confuses duty with the quest for power, and Oliphant tells her story with relish. But she also points out the triviality of Carlingford's enclosed community, and the real problems facing able and intelligent women forced into subservience to inferior men, and the compromises they were forced to make. Lucilla muses that if she had been a man, she might herself have stood for Parliament.

One aspect of Margaret Oliphant's writing that rarely intrudes into her full-length novels is her power to evoke the supernatural. Like many Victorians who had to cope with the death of children, she was intensely interested in the afterlife but, despite her upbringing in a church-going Presbyterian family, there is little evidence in her work to suggest that Calvinist ideas of salvation and damnation dominated her thinking. Perhaps, too, her long domicile in England had rescued her from the moral anxiety of her Scottish literary predecessors over the propriety of women's fiction. Her personal dialogue with God concerned his failure to answer her prayers for the earthly survival of her children, a problem she partially resolved in the hope that after her own death she would be reunited with them on a spiritual plane. In many passages of her *Autobiography* she meditates on the possibility of such a transition from earth to heaven, a preoccupation which fed into some of the most effective ghost stories in the English language.

Many of these tales were published initially in *Blackwood's* in the 1870s and 80s. They are tautly and beautifully written, skilfully using motifs of darkness and light, and often drawing tension from the question of whether they are genuinely occult experiences or the delusions of troubled minds. Influenced by the contemporary taste for Gothic fiction, yet rejecting its crudely sensational devices, they are tales of lost souls in a world where the unseen spirits of the dead are too close for comfort, and where notably the catalysts are frequently children. Disturbing rather than horrifying, they are the product of a speculative Scottish mind, exploring a territory reminiscent of the Border ballads, with their fluid threshold between the worlds of the living and the dead. Much anthologised, masterpieces such as 'Old Lady Mary', 'The Open Door' and 'The Library Window' preserved the name of Mrs Oliphant through the long years when almost everything else she wrote was ignored.

In the last months of her life, Margaret Oliphant was working on *Annals of a Publishing House: William Blackwood and his Sons, their Magazine and Friends*, of which she completed two volumes. While honest about William Blackwood's notorious failures of judgement, such as publishing cruel attacks on the integrity of Samuel Taylor Coleridge (1772–1834) and the 'Cockney School' of poetry represented by John Keats (1795–1821) and Leigh Hunt (1784–1859), the work is affectionate, gossipy and largely good-humoured. Literary giants of the nineteenth century crowd its pages: Sir Walter Scott, Susan Ferrier, James Hogg the 'Ettrick Shepherd', John Gibson Lockhart, James Ballantyne, John Wilson 'Christopher North', John Galt, Thomas De Quincey, Lord Lytton, George Eliot, Elizabeth Barrett Browning (1806–61). It was Margaret Oliphant's tribute to the Blackwood family whose loyalty to her had lasted for more than half a century, and her final published work.

In 1890, Margaret Oliphant's son Cyril died aged 34, followed four years later by his brother Francis, aged 35. Their self indulgence and failure to achieve anything worthwhile in their short lives had caused their mother deep disappointment, but now, after so many other bereavements, despair overwhelmed her. Her strength declined and she suffered increasing attacks of severe pain, but went on working to the end because it was the habit of her life. She died of cancer at Wimbledon on 25 June 1897, aged 69, in the midst of celebrations to mark Queen Victoria's Diamond Jubilee.

6

A CHELSEA INTERIOR

I never sit down at night, beside a good fire, alone, without feeling the need to talk a little, on paper, to somebody that I like well enough, and that likes me well enough, to make it of no moment – whether I talk sense or nonsense, and with or without the rules of grammar.

Jane Welsh Carlyle (1801–66)
Letter to Mary Russell 1843

ON A SUMMER afternoon in 1861, Margaret Oliphant, on a visit to London from her home in Ealing, resolved to call on the author and historian Thomas Carlyle. Her reason was that she was collecting information for a biography of the controversial Scottish preacher Edward Irving (1792–1834) and, knowing of her subject's early friendship with Carlyle, wanted to pick the famous writer's brains. Although she had a letter of introduction from Carlyle's brother, she approached the tall brick house in Great Cheyne Row with trepidation. Its occupant was known not only for his erudition, but also for his workaholic dislike of interruption, and it required courage to mount the steps of No. 5 and apply the brass knocker to the heavy front door. She need not, however, have worried. Carlyle showed no sign of being irked by her intrusion, took her into his library and listened kindly to her questions. He did not, however, choose to provide answers, saying only that '"the wife" could tell [her] a great deal, if she saw her.' As she recalled in her *Autobiography*, Mrs Oliphant took her leave, 'fluttered with the pride of having seen him, and that people might say "Il vous a parlé, grand'mère,"' but also disappointed that a promising line of investigation was seemingly closed.

As things turned out, she was mistaken. Two days later, the doorbell rang at the house where she was staying, and a maid came to announce that there was a carriage at the door, and that Mrs Carlyle begged Mrs Oliphant to go out and speak to her. In the carriage, a 'homely little brougham' she found 'a lady with bright eyes and hollow cheeks' who invited her to drive in Hyde Park and talk about Edward Irving. Later Margaret Oliphant recalled:

She must have been over sixty at this time, but she was one of those women whom one never thinks of calling old; her hair was black without a grey hair in it (mine at half the age was already quite grey), her features and her aspect very keen, perhaps a little alarming. When we set off together she began by asking me if I did not come from East Lothian; she had recognised many things in my books that could only have come from that district. I had to answer ... that my mother had lived for many years in East Lothian, and I had been so constantly with her that I could never tell whether it was I who remembered things or she.

The discovery that they had been born within eleven miles of each other, and both had tales of mothers to tell, was enough to establish a bond between the childless Jane Carlyle and the child-burdened Margaret Oliphant. The recall of her East Lothian youth and her relationship with Edward Irving gave the older woman pleasure, as did the soothing admiration of the younger, and soon visits were arranged, and letters were flying between Ealing and Cheyne Row. Thomas Carlyle liked his wife's new friend, and his approval of *The Life of Edward Irving* (1862) was a source of great delight to its author, as no doubt was his generous tribute to her work in his own essay on Irving, written in 1867 and published in *Reminiscences* (1881).

Posterity has not been kind to Thomas Carlyle. His political views have been misrepresented, and in his domestic affairs he has been censured as a self-obsessed bully who prevented his wife from achieving her own potential as a writer. That the marriage had a difficult spell is beyond dispute, although much speculation about the partners' incompatibility is based on the gossip of London visitors who may have mistaken the nature of their Scottish marital repartee. But that Margaret Oliphant, who called them 'that much maligned, much misunderstood pair', wrote of them with kindly impartiality and posthumously defended them vigorously, is at least a mild corrective to the customary lambasting of Carlyle. They were all Scots, and understood one another.

Jane Baillie Welsh, later to become Mrs Carlyle, was born and brought up in Haddington, a compact, prosperous town 18 miles south-east of Edinburgh. Set down among the fertile agricultural region of East Lothian, it served as a farmers' market and a staging-post for the mail coaches rattling towards England. Since war against France had been declared in 1792, it had also been a barracks town, its society enlivened by the red-coated presence of volunteer and regular troops, primed to repel an invasion on the beaches of Gullane and Aberlady. Here in 1800 Dr John Welsh, a medical practitioner who had recently retired from the Army, brought his bride, Grace (née Welsh, but unrelated) to live in an elegant house in Lodge Street, adjacent to Haddington's High Street. They were a conventionally handsome couple but their only child resembled neither. Born in 1801 and perhaps the inheritor of gypsy blood through her mother's ancestry, Jane Baillie Welsh was small, dark-eyed, black-haired, and loquacious. Skipping around Haddington, an object of affectionate amusement to its townsfolk, little 'Jeannie' was described by her maid as 'a fleein', dancin', lightheartit thing that naethin' wad hae dauntit', and by her husband nearly seventy years later as 'the prettiest little Jenny Spinner dancing on the summer rays in her time'.

Jane was loved and indulged by both her parents, although they disagreed over her education. Her practical mother would have preferred her to acquire ladylike 'accomplishments' leading in due course to a good marriage. It may be that Dr Welsh, had hoped for a son and, when no other child was forthcoming, decided that his daughter should have a boy's education. His will prevailed and, before she was five, Jane had been sent to school locally, quickly learning to read and write and, when she demanded to 'learn Latin, like a boy', it was again her father who agreed. She was bold and precocious, well able to defend herself against masculine teasing, on one occasion at least giving a bigger boy a bloody nose. Her father, gratified by her intelligence, determined to push her further. When Jane was ten, he engaged a tutor, and so Edward Irving came into her life.

Irving, over six feet tall, red-cheeked, black-haired and athletic, had been born in Annandale in Dumfriesshire and studied at the University of Edinburgh. Much later he would have a colourful and ultimately tragic career as a charismatic preacher, but when he came to Haddington in 1810, aged only 18, it was as headmaster of a new mathematics school. Poorly paid, he was no doubt happy to moonlight as a private tutor, and pleased with the introduction the Welshes gave him to Haddington's middle-class society. Latin, advanced mathematics and logic were the staples of the ten-year-old's early morning and late night lessons. Jane and Irving were good companions, but he was strict and under orders to report daily on her progress to Dr Welsh. If she failed a task he told her father, who punished her. Yet she admired them both; she was drawn to strong, authoritative men.

Irving stayed less than two years in Haddington before taking a better-paid post in Kirkcaldy. At this point Mrs Welsh, long sidelined and not unreasonably wondering where all this learning was leading, again asserted the need for her daughter to acquire more conventional skills. She worried that Jane would become unattractively hoydenish if she mixed so much with boys, and this time she won a partial victory. It was decided that Jane would attend a girls' boarding school, recently opened in the town by a Miss Hemmings, to learn sewing and music, drawing and a little French, while continuing to study Latin and mathematics with a new tutor, James Brown. From there in 1818 she was sent to have her ladylike skills polished up at Miss Hall's Finishing School in Edinburgh; in the city she again encountered Edward Irving, and fell in love with him. But their mutual attraction came to nothing; by this time 26-year-old Irving was obliged to tell Jane that he already had a fiancée in Kirkcaldy, and they agreed that he must keep his promise to her. They remained friends, but Jane returned to Haddington in temporary despair. By now an attractive and fashionably dressed young woman, musical, formidably educated but (as her mother had foreseen) frustrated by the unavailability of a challenging career, Jane was not averse to the attentions of other young men. Sadly, none met her exacting standards.

In 1819, Dr Welsh died of typhus, aged only 44. He had been a strict father, but Jane had worshipped him, and he remained her ideal of manhood for the rest of her life. Though in the early days of bereavement mother and daughter clung affectionately to each other, their incompatibility gradually became evident; affable and polite in front of visitors, when alone in their house off Haddington's High Street they became irritable and quarrelsome. Jane, disappointed and prone to depression, became languid and indolent. Deprived even of its Army barracks after the defeat of Napoleon in 1815, provincial Haddington now seemed intolerably dreary: 'Alas! my native place!' she wrote. 'The Goddess of Dullness has strewed it with all her poppies!' But honesty compelled her to add, '[b]ut it is my native place still and after all there is much in it that I love'. She loved her mother. They just could not live long in peace together.

It was on a May evening in 1821 that Edward Irving walked unexpectedly into Mrs Welsh's elegant drawing room, accompanied by a friend, a fellow-teacher in Kirkcaldy with whom he was on a walking tour. Thomas Carlyle had been born in Ecclefechan in Dumfriesshire, the eldest son of a strict Presbyterian stonemason who, with not unusual Scottish parental aspiration, had sent him first to Annan Academy, then to the University of Edinburgh where he intended to study divinity. Accustomed to his parents' clean but sparsely furnished house and to squalid student accommodation, 26-year-old Carlyle was dazzled by the stylishness of the Haddington drawing room and the refinement of its occupants. Forty-five years later, he wrote in *Reminiscences*:

> *The Drawing-room seemed to me the finest room I had ever sat or stood in ... solid and correct as well as pertinently ornamented ... . The summer twilight, I remember, was pouring in; I felt as one walking transiently in the upper spheres.*

Jane's view of him was less ethereal:

> *He scratched the fender dreadfully. I must have a pair of carpet shoes and handcuffs prepared for him the next time. His tongue only should be left at liberty: his other members are fantastically awkward.*

In fact, Carlyle was a handsome man, as his many portraits attest. But Jane was right that his conversation (which was nine-tenths monologue) was wonderful and, so long starved of intellectual company, she enjoyed it. There is little doubt that Carlyle, beguiled by the house and the vivacity of its younger occupant, fell in love that first night, and that Jane did not. But Carlyle was – uncharacteristically – patient. For five years he sent her books, helped her with her German studies, suffered jealousy of a young Haddington physician who was also making advances to her, and waited for her to make up her mind whether to marry him. No doubt there were problems, not least Mrs Welsh's vocal disapproval. She thought that Carlyle was short-tempered, which was true; that he was an atheist which, although he was in the process of disavowing his specifically Christian beliefs, was not true; and that he was Jane's social inferior, which was indisputable. There was also the question of Carlyle's future; he had abandoned the idea of ministry, he hated schoolmastering, the tutorship he was embarking on, in a wealthy family named Buller, must needs be temporary, and his earnings from translations and future literary work were far from assured. But Jane, however much she criticised his manners, and although she may not have been passionately in love with him, liked him and was convinced of his genius. Perhaps now accepting that as a woman her education was in danger of being wasted, and seeing a meaningful role for herself in advancing Carlyle, she put aside her uncertainties.

In the end, Mrs Welsh capitulated, enabling the marriage by renting a small terraced house in Comely Bank, on the western fringe of Edinburgh's New Town and, herself bound for Templand in Dumfriesshire where her family still lived, furnishing it with items from the Haddington house. Jane and Thomas were married at Templand on 17 October 1826. 'I swear,' wrote Carlyle, 'I will love thee with my whole heart, and think my life well spent if it can make thine happy'.

The remark attributed to Samuel Butler (1835–1902): 'It was very good of God to let Carlyle and Mrs Carlyle marry one another, and so make only two people miserable instead of four', belongs to a later period. At the beginning, despite Carlyle's grumbling, self-doubt and chronic indigestion, they were happy. Indeed the affection they felt then would survive for forty childless years, the unsubstantiated rumours of sexual incompatibility mercifully unpublicised until after they were dead. Jane, determined to support and promote her husband, loved their Edinburgh life and the interesting people they met. Carlyle asked her advice, she felt involved in his work, and now there was only one problem; they had no money. Comely Bank proved unaffordable, and by 1828, a vital decision had been taken. They would save money by moving to the isolated farm house at Craigenputtock, in the bleak upland parish of Dunscore in Dumfriesshire, left to Jane in her father's will.

In 1882 the Scottish artist James Paterson (1854–1932), visiting Craigenput-tock on a painting expedition, found the place little changed since the Carlyles had lived there fifty years before. Writing an account of his visit, he described the plain stone house as 'not beautiful ... but not out of keeping with its barren surroundings ... . Flanked by the orange and purple moors and Galloway hills, there is about it a quiet dignity which does not jar with its associations'. Although at the time she drew a cheerful picture of their life in her letters, it certainly jarred with the nerves of Jane Carlyle. Accustomed in Haddington and Comely Bank to busy streets and people visiting, to good conversation interspersed with idle gossip, she had no experience of cooking and housework; in the draughty house, in the silence of 'the little estate of peat bog', broken only by the moaning of the wind and the distant bleating of sheep, she had to learn fast. 'My tea is done,' she wrote to a cousin in Edinburgh, asking her to send supplies, 'my coffee is done and my sugar, white and brown; and without a fresh supply of these, I fear my husband would be done also.' Carlyle might have missed his coffee, but the way of living at Craigenputtock was familiar enough to him. Jane was in more danger of being 'done'.

Breaking point came when, after six years of hardship and frugality, Carlyle's *Sartor Resartus*, the book on which they had both pinned their hopes of a change of fortune, was rejected by London publisher John Murray. In the wake of this ter-rible disappointment, the impossibility of negotiating with publishers at long-distance became clear, and the decision taken to leave Craigenputtock and move to London. After many delays, on 10 June 1834 they moved into 5 Great Cheyne Row, Chelsea, where they would live for the rest of their lives. Thirty-two years later, Carlyle would remember that as they approached the house, Jane's canary, which was with them in the cab, burst into sudden song; they thought it was a good omen, and so it seemed to be. *Sartor Resartus*, described as 'a witty "symbolic myth" in the form of a philosophical treatise on clothing', was published serially in *Fraser's Magazine* (1834–36) and subsequently as a book. It was enthusiastically reviewed, and kick-started Carlyle's career as an important writer and thinker.

The life of the Carlyles in London has been well-documented, largely through the vast collection of the letters Jane wrote to friends, to her cousins in Liverpool and Edinburgh, and to Carlyle when he was away from home. To her mother-in-law: 'I told Mrs Hunt, one day, that I had been very busy *painting*. "What?" she asked, "is it a portrait?" "Oh! no," I told her; "something of more importance – a large wardrobe."' And to Carlyle:

> On that day, I came, saw, and bought – a sofa! It is my own purchase, but you shall share the possession. Indeed, so soon as you set eyes on it and behold its vastness, its simple greatness, you shall see that the thought of you was actively at work in my choice. It was neither dear nor cheap, but a bargain nonetheless ...

She told of nailing down carpets, the horror of bedbugs, troubles with maids, their diet, their sleeping arrangements, their health, what they planted in their back garden. Distinguished visitors streamed through their drawing room – their neighbour Leigh Hunt, Edward Irving, John Stuart Mill (1806–73), Charles Dickens (1812–70), Robert (1812–89) and Elizabeth Barrett Browning, the diarist William Allingham (1824–89), the exiled Italian patriot Guiseppe Mazzini (1805– 72), Alfred Tennyson (1809–92) and Margaret Oliphant – all came to sit on the six-foot-long sofa, to drink tea in the afternoon, to eat porridge in the evening. They came to hear Carlyle talk, and be entertained by Jane's running commentary, her lively wit, sarcastic humour, gifts of mimicry and repartee. But when the visitors had gone, and they were alone together, storm clouds were beginning to gather.

In an 1844 essay published anonymously, but probably by Elizabeth Barrett (then unmarried), it is claimed that Carlyle had 'knocked out his window in the wall of his century' – gratifying praise for a writer who ten years previously had been largely unknown. Life for Jane had its compensations; she was by now one of the most admired literary hostesses in London, and genuinely proud of Carlyle's success. But she was also aware of a changed relationship; the window he was knocking out in the wall of his century was personal, and as his fame grew outside 5 Great Cheyne Row, and inside his bilious attacks, sensitivity to noise and fits of rage intensified, she began to feel sidelined and no longer part of what had once seemed a joint enterprise. Carlyle was never a deliberately unkind man and, as his letters to Jane when they were apart bear witness, he cared for her deeply. But at home he seems to have been oblivious to the effect his constant complaints, gruff manner and self-absorption had on her nerves. As her youth gave way to middle age, Jane's sense of isolation deepened. Her resentment erupted into bitter reproach, she had migraines and slept badly, took too much morphine and suffered a marked decline in bodily health. Photographs of her in her fifties show the hollow-cheeked, saucer-eyed face which Margaret Oliphant noted at their first meeting; she was not the only observer who found Jane Carlyle 'alarming'. In 1851, Carlyle gave himself up entirely to his largest, and in his own estimation greatest work, *The History of Friedrich II of Prussia, Called Frederick the Great*, which would take 14 years to complete. Jane called this period 'living in the shadow of Frederick', a long tribulation made worse by her jealousy of Carlyle's friendship with clever and aristocratic Lady Harriet Ashburton (1805–57), over whom he was lengthily making a fool of himself.

The tone of her letters, always amusing, sharpened. She was obsessed with her own ailments, openly sarcastic about Carlyle's. When he developed lumbago after sitting on wet grass: 'Lumbago, my dear,' she wrote to a friend, 'admits of but one consolation ... viz., perfect liberty to be as ugly and stupid and disagreeable as ever one likes ... and that liberty reserves itself for the domestic hearth!' Of the famous painting 'A Chelsea Interior' by Robert Tait (1816–97), with Carlyle in the fore-ground and herself to the rear, she remarked sourly:

> I suspect that [Tait] aims at more than posthumous fame from this Picture: hopes, perhaps, some admirer of Mr C., with more money than wit to guide it, may give him a thousand pounds for Mr C.'s "Interior", – the Portrait of Mr C. himself, and Mr C.'s Wife, and Mrs C.'s dog included! The dog is the only member of the family who has reason to be pleased with his likeness as yet.

Things got worse: 'It is like living in a madhouse on the days when he gets ill on with his writing … I sometimes feel I should like to run away. But the question always arises: where to?' On hearing of the engagement of her cousin Jeannie Welsh, she revealed openly the depth of her disillusionment:

> Oh, Babbie! How I wish it had not been your idea to pitch your tent in this "Valley of the shadow of marriage" – it is a very relaxing air, I am sure, and peculiarly un-suitable to your constitution. But certainly I am not the best authorised person to tell people how they should manage their lives under the head of Method – having made such a mess of my own life – God help me!

It was only after she was dead that a grief-stricken Carlyle read and was crushed by these devastating remarks.

In recent times, indignant feminist writers have suggested, on the evidence of the brilliant narrative passages in her letters, that Jane Welsh Carlyle might have been a great novelist. If she was not, then surely the wear and tear of life with a self-ish, work-absorbed husband must have been to blame. Yet on the evidence of the body of writing Jane left, the ultra-modern speculation that her talent 'might have been' diverted into the writing of great fiction is hard to sell. After her death, Car-lyle found among her papers part of a journal of the years 1855–56 (the rest she had destroyed), and a brilliant and entertaining piece titled 'Budget of a Femme Incomprise', addressed to Carlyle and setting out the case of his 'unappreciated woman' for more housekeeping money. There were some verses, and also a short story titled 'The Simple Story of my Own First Love', which had an autobiograph-ical element and was probably written at the urging of her friend, the minor novelist Geraldine Jewsbury (1812–80). There were no drafts of novels, opening chapters, character sketches, nothing to indicate that sustained fiction was seriously in her mind.

Rather her life, with its busy domesticity, friendships, crises and dramas, sug-gests that in her compulsive letter-writing, spontaneous and alive with sprightly anecdotes and intimate pen-portraits, she had found the ideal medium for her talent.

Because she wrote in English, and lived so long in London, it is sometimes over-looked that she was a quintessentially Scottish writer; the rhythms of her prose mimic Scottish speech, her vocabulary is rich with Scottish words, and in her observations of English life we hear constantly the sardonically amused voice of the Scot. What she did not have, or understand, was the ruthless work-comes-first attitude of a professional writer like Carlyle. Yet if, while living, she felt that her own light was dimmed by the brilliance of his, it is due to his diligence that so many of her letters were collected, and her posthumous reputation secured. And ironically, by entrusting their joint archive to his far from impartial biographer James Anthony Froude (1818–94), he also ensured that her narrative of their marriage was the one that prevailed.

After the 'shadow of Frederick' faded with the publication of Carlyle's *magnum opus* in January 1865, Jane's health improved slightly. The Carlyles went out to dinner and the theatre together, visitors came to Great Cheyne Row, and the warm, mutually appreciative relationship observed by Margaret Oliphant was again in evidence. This tranquil period was, however, of short duration. At the beginning of April 1866, Carlyle travelled north to be installed as Lord Rector of the University of Edinburgh, an honour which had gratified him and delighted his wife. As the occasion approached, however, his nervousness about speaking in public had intensified, and Jane had fretted about him from the moment he left Cheyne Row. Nothing shows the mutual affection at the heart of their relationship more touchingly than her joy and relief when a telegram arrived from Edinburgh, announcing that the address had been 'A perfect Triumph'.

On his journey back, Carlyle stopped off to visit his family in Dumfriesshire. He was still there when on Saturday 21 April Jane, having organised a celebratory party for the evening, went to lunch with friends in Palace Gate, Kensington. Sitting in her brougham on the way home through Hyde Park, she had a heart attack and died. A week later, Carlyle took her body to Haddington and, as she had wished, buried it in her father's grave. The epitaph he composed for her ended with the words: 'Suddenly snatched away from him, and the light of his life as if gone out.'

7

THE GOOD
WIFE

*I now possess all that renders a husband happy in a wife. I have now been rather
more than eight months married, and am as much in love as ever.*

Hugh Miller (1802–56)
Letter to Sir Thomas Dick Lauder 1837

IN THE EARLY 1830s, while Jane and Thomas Carlyle were escaping from Craigenputtock and beginning their new life in London, away to the north in the small
coastal town of Cromarty another young couple were embarking on a long and difficult engagement. As with the Carlyles, the man was older and destined for fame,
the woman well-educated and determined to promote his genius. Again, there was
class difference, and a mother not slow to voice her objections.

Lydia Falconer Fraser (1811–76), about whose father William little is known
except that he was an unsuccessful shopkeeper in Inverness, was educated on a
pattern similar to that of Jane Welsh, though less dependent on classical learning.
For this benefit she was obliged to her mother, Elizabeth Lydia née McLeod
(?–1865) who had family connections rather more distinguished than her husband's. In 1820, eight-year-old Lydia was enrolled at the Inverness Royal Academy,
a co-educational school where, in the 'Ladies' division, she won awards in French,
Italian, geography and arithmetic. She also had piano lessons, for which her mother
paid from a legacy she had received from her uncle, the interest to be used for the
benefit of her children. This income also enabled her to send her daughter to be
'finished' in Edinburgh, as Jane Welsh had been ten years before.

In 1827, Lydia entered as a boarder 140 Princes Street, the house of George
Thomson (1757–1851), a retired lawyer with a passion for books and music and
who had been a friend of Robert Burns (1759–96). With a few other 'young ladies',
Lydia was to learn painting, music and dancing, and have the benefit of conversation
with some of the literary and artistic figures who crowded Edinburgh in the closing
years of the city's 'Enlightenment Age'. Among these was Mrs Anne Grant of Laggan
(1755–1838), whose *Letters from the Mountains* (1806) and *Memoirs of an American
Lady* (1808) had earned her money and made her famous in her day.

Lydia had been in Edinburgh a year when her father died, and shortly afterwards she had her second experience of life far removed from the quiet Highland town where she was born. A wealthy couple named Dobinson, distantly related by marriage to her mother, invited Lydia to stay with them at Egham Lodge, a mansion house in Surrey, on the edge of Windsor Great Park, perhaps to act unofficially as governess to their four children. The year she spent there was important in that long after, when she wrote her one full-length novel, life at Egham Lodge provided her with her only insight into English upper class life.

It may be that Lydia experienced a culture shock on returning north in 1830 to Cromarty, where her mother had settled after her husband died, but if so, she gave no sign of it. The society of a small, provincial fishing port, clinging to the edge of the turbulent Cromarty Firth, might be culturally undistinguished, but it was also the home of Hugh Miller, a stonemason and self-taught scholar and geologist who, like Thomas Carlyle, was destined to become one the most influential Scots of the nineteenth century. Born in 1802, the elder son of a ship's captain lost at sea in 1807, Hugh Miller had been educated at the local school, where he was disruptive, frequently punished and underachieving, his schooldays ending abruptly in a violent quarrel with a teacher. All was not lost, however; the disaffected youth loved books and nature, and was encouraged to read widely by his two maternal uncles. Aged 17, he became a stonemason, travelling all over Scotland as the work required. But because the trade was seasonal, he was free to use the winter months to study what became abiding passions, the geology of the Cromarty shore, literature, folklore and the history of the Presbyterian Church. Long before he encountered Lydia Fraser, Hugh Miller was known locally for his skilled handiwork and as the author of *Poems written in the Leisure Hours of a Journeyman Mason*, published in 1829.

In a small Scottish community where learning, irrespective of class, was revered, Hugh Miller was a welcome evening visitor to Mrs Fraser's parlour, for he talked well and, once he had washed off the dust of his daytime occupation, good-looking in the way usually described as 'rugged'. No doubt he listened politely to the chatter of Mrs Fraser's newly arrived daughter about the small school she and her mother planned, but he was not as impressed by Lydia as she clearly was by him. Aged 29, he thought she was beautiful but immature, noting that she was 'light-hearted and amiable, but somewhat foolish and affected, and her friends who are much attached to her, love her less as an interesting woman than as an agreeable and promising child'. This would surely have been mortifying to the 'accomplished' Lydia, fresh from the sophisticated ambience of Egham Lodge, but it says much about Hugh Miller. By this time he had left his disaffected schooldays far behind; he was devoutly Presbyterian, impatient with frivolity, and seems not to have had marriage in mind. But Lydia aimed to please, and by degrees convinced the erudite stonemason that she shared his interests, including his austere religious beliefs. Meeting 'accidentally on purpose' on evening walks on the hill above Cromarty, Hugh and Lydia talked of books and philosophy, and decided that they were in love.

The reaction of Mrs Fraser to the growing intimacy between Hugh Miller and her daughter had much in common with Mrs Welsh's reaction to the attachment of Jane and Thomas Carlyle. Mrs Fraser could not have accused Hugh Miller of atheism, but otherwise her objections boiled down to the same things: money and class. It was all very well to invite the personable young stonemason to take tea of an evening, but that did not entitle him to court Lydia, who had been educated as a lady. He had been brought up by a poor widow in a thatched cottage, he had been a bad boy at school, and now he was a low-earning artisan with no prospects. For a while, she forbade them to meet, an interlude which unsurprisingly intensified Lydia's determination to defy her. Only when, in 1834, the stonemason was offered, and accepted, the more genteel post of accountant in the newly opened Cromarty branch of the Commercial Bank, did Mrs Fraser reluctantly agree to a formal engagement. Even so, nearly three more years would pass before, in January 1837, Lydia and Hugh were married, moving into a house adjacent to his childhood home, which his father had built but did not live to inhabit.

Eight months later, Hugh was 'as much in love as ever', but all too soon happiness gave way to sorrow. In November, a first child, known as 'Little Eliza' was born, to her father 'a delight and wonder above all wonders'. Eighteen months later, she was dead. Already there was a second baby, and three more were to come, but the loss of Eliza was a shadow that never lifted. Hugh took what comfort he could in carving a beautiful headstone for his daughter's grave, then grimly turned his attention to a matter obsessing Scotland in his time.

The Church of Scotland, to which the vast majority of Scots belonged, was in the early nineteenth century a considerable power in the land. Organised since the seventeenth century along democratic lines, to the extent that the elders ordained to rule each congregation were, apart from the minister, laymen, one anomaly persisted – the right, known as 'patronage', of a landowner to 'intrude', meaning force on a congregation a minister of his choice, not theirs. This right, supported by Parliament at Westminster, was regarded by many as interference by the State in the internal affairs of the Church, and between 1834 and 1841 trials of strength between the two were enacted in several parishes. Hugh and Lydia Miller supported a proposed ecclesiastical Reform Bill to settle the matter, and in 1839 Hugh published in pamphlet form 'A Letter to Lord Brougham', a powerful plea to Government to end patronage and give congregations the right to choose. This led to his being offered the editorship of a new newspaper *The Witness*, which was being set up in Edinburgh to support the anti-patronage movement. Initially diffident, but strongly encouraged by more ambitious Lydia, he agreed. Five months after Eliza's death, the Millers sold their possessions in Cromarty and moved south to Edinburgh and a new life.

It was now that the pattern of the Millers' marriage veered sharply away from that of the Carlyles. Hugh Miller shared Carlyle's capacity for hard graft; as well as editing a national newspaper from a cramped office in the Royal Mile (although primarily a religious publication, under his editorship the twice-weekly *Witness* contained news, political comment, general interest articles and book reviews), at home in the evenings he pursued his study of fossils, publishing at first serially in *The Witness* his famous book, *The Old Red Sandstone, or New Walks in Old Fields* (1841). But even as he too 'knocked out his own window in the wall of his century', Lydia did not allow herself to experience the sense of exclusion felt by Jane Carlyle. Perhaps the 'Protestant work ethic', unpractised by the religiously sceptical Jane, accounts for this, or perhaps Hugh Miller at this stage regarded a wife as a partner; it seems as likely that he was simply overwhelmed by her determination. Lydia set to work as an assistant on *The Witness*, at first cutting and pasting the copy together, later graduating to writing book reviews. By 1843, when the Church, fatally divided between 'moderates', who could live with the status quo and 'evangelicals' who hankered after a return to the clear-cut, Calvinistic certainties of former times, split asunder in the great schism known as the 'Disruption', *The Witness* was established as an important organ of what was henceforth to be known as the Free Church of Scotland. Hugh Miller was lionised in Edinburgh as a writer and opinion-former, but was also, despite his high-mindedness, keenly attentive to his own image as a Highlander and as a manual labourer. He walked the sober streets in all weathers swathed in a tartan plaid and, rather duplicitously, donned his old overalls for the famous calotypes created by David Octavius Hill (1802–70), a decade after he has ceased to be a stonemason.

Lydia, meanwhile, had embarked on a subsidiary career away from *The Witness*. She had, unusually for her time, continued teaching in Cromarty after her marriage in order to supplement Hugh's meagre income, but the move to Edinburgh and the arrival of three more children made work outside the home impracticable. So in the evenings, while Hugh was slaving at his desk, she settled herself at hers. Between 1845 and 1866, under the pseudonym 'Mrs Harriet Myrtle' she wrote and found publishers for 16 books for children. It was a sensible choice; Lydia was a teacher of young children and skilled in engaging their interest. Stories such as *Little Amy's Birthday* (1846), *Home and its Pleasures* (1852) and *Aunt Maddy's Diamonds* (1864) are simply told, lightsome in content, moral in tone but not overly so. If they are only period-pieces now, it is because the nature of childhood has changed.

Many children's authors, however, hanker after what they presumably see as the weightier reputation awarded to writers for adults, and Lydia Miller seems to have been among these. In the early 1840s she was also at work on a novel forbid-dingly titled *Passages in the Life of an English Heiress; or Recollections of Disruption Times in Scotland*. Although the Disruption had centred on patronage, there were other issues which separated the new adherents of the Free Church from the 'moderates' of the Church of Scotland. The Free Church 'Evangelicals', among whom were the Millers, had much in common doctrinally with the 'Covenanters' of the seventeenth century, taking a literal view of biblical truth and favouring the uncompromising Calvinist doctrines of earlier times. Lydia's ambition, according to her biographer Elizabeth Sutherland, was 'to spread the message to an English readership by encapsulating the essence of the Disruption in a novel'. Setting aside the question of the suitability of such a subject for treatment as fiction, one has to admit that it was a brave endeavour. The old Calvinist belief that novels were intrinsically evil was still alive among the austere Presbyterians who had seceded from the now more broadminded Church of Scotland, so that Lydia, even although she published anonymously, was courting the severe disapproval of her fellow church members. As for her proposed English readership, it must have seemed unlikely even then that members of the less combative Church of England would be swayed by Lydia's earnest admonitions. But she had a missionary's tem-perament, and she forged ahead.

Like Mary Brunton and Susan Ferrier, Lydia Miller was middle-class, yet chose to set her novel in a more aristocratic milieu. The 'English Heiress' of the title is a young gentlewoman, Jane Hamilton Legh, daughter of an English father and Scottish mother, who travels north to an estate in Ross-shire, and then to Edin-burgh, where the themes of patronage and secession are discussed over dinner tables and prolix tales told of the persecution of dissenting preachers by the shady agents of the state. Jane's subsequent elevation to the rank of Countess of Len-traethen (a dream solution already well-used by Ferrier and Brunton) by marriage to a wealthy retired Scottish General, and return to her English estate, give Lydia an opening to harangue her hoped-for audience on the 'evils' of the Church of Eng-land, such as its universal patronage and what dissenters saw as 'popish practices' in the emerging Anglo-Catholic movement.

The most amazing thing about the book, with its contrived plot and relent-lessly didactic tone, is that it found a reputable publisher. In 1847 it was brought out in London by Richard Bentley, who had published Susan Ferrier. Its only known review, a glowing one in *The Witness*, was probably written by Hugh and, although the book sold reasonably for a year or two, it then sank without trace. The authority of Calvinism might linger in some corners of society but, to the great majority of the reading public, it was no longer a moral force.

Yet despite its many faults, there are good things in *An English Heiress* that may make the reader wish that Lydia had managed to follow it up with a less priggish, preachy novel. Her description of the scenery in her native Ross and Cromarty is luminous, and her characters, when they briefly escape from their role as mouthpieces for authorial opinion, have flashes of charm. But there was no second novel. Perhaps Lydia had done what she wanted to do, or perhaps the burden of mounting problems, both with *The Witness* and at home, made it too hard to concentrate on fiction.

Like the Carlyles, both Hugh and Lydia had chronic health problems. Lydia had from girlhood endured spells of trembling and dizziness, and in early middle age developed an unspecified 'spinal complaint', causing intermittent immobility. Hugh suffered from silicosis, an inflammatory lung disease caused by inhaling dust particles when he was a stonemason, but he too had dizzy spells and severe headaches which were, as it turned out, ominous. A brief *Memoir* written much later by Lydia and unpublished in her life time, makes clear that after the move to Edinburgh, his demeanour changed. Although equable in the family circle, he became easily angered and caustically argumentative, and alarmingly bought a revolver which he carried loaded under his tartan plaid. He claimed that it was to protect himself from footpads but, startled in the street on a dark night, he came within an inch of shooting a friend.

The late 1840s brought yet more stress. In 1847, Hugh became reluctantly involved in a bout of in-fighting in the recently established Free Church, and was rattled by a plot to displace him as editor of *The Witness*. His theories about fossil-formation were also under attack. Adamant in his opposition to the idea of evolution, he published *Footprints of the Creator* in 1849; the book was well received, but its author must have been aware that, with *A Theory of the Earth* by James Hutton (1726–97) and *Principles of Geology* by Sir Charles Lyell (1797–1875) the tide of opinion was turning against him. The last of his works to appear in his lifetime, an account of his youth titled *My Schools and Schoolmasters*, was published in 1854. Happily, in view of the dark clouds gathering around the family, the book bears the hallmarks of his best writing; a flowing narrative drawing its fulness from history, folklore and daily life, and animated by a dry sense of humour not much evident in his or Lydia's other work.

In the year that saw the publication of *My Schools and Schoolmasters*, the Millers moved to Shrub Mount, a rather grand stone villa in Portobello. This must have pleased Lydia, whose religious devotion had never overcome her worldly fondness for 'respectable tables and chairs ... painting and garnishing my house', fashionable clothes and 'dainty fare'. For Hugh the attraction was a large garden, where he planned to build a museum for his huge fossil collection. Within a year, however, family life disintegrated, as Hugh's health, mental and physical, rapidly deteriorated. Always superstitious despite his scientific acumen, he believed in ghosts and in childhood had suffered from lurid nightmares. These now returned in force; at the same time his lung inflammation worsened, he became irritable with his children and complained that his capacity for work was failing. Yet he was still up all night writing his final riposte to modernity, *The Testimony of the Rocks*. On 23 December 1856, half-blinded by headache and convinced that he was facing insanity, he went upstairs, wrote a note containing the terrible words, 'my brain burns', took up his revolver and shot himself through the chest.

Thomas Carlyle, who died in 1881 aged 85, had stated his wish to be buried among his kinsfolk at Ecclefechan. It is unlikely, at the age of 54, that Hugh Miller had left explicit instructions, and it was Lydia's task to buy a burial lair in the Grange Cemetery, probably in expectation of a modest Free Church funeral. In the event, when the shocking news of Hugh's death appeared in the newspapers, the citizens of Edinburgh turned out in force to honour him. Led by civic dignitaries, members of parliament, Free Church ministers and mourners estimated in thousands, the black procession proceeded along Princes Street and over the Bridges to the burial ground in The Grange. At home in her widow's weeds, Lydia was inundated with letters of condolence, including one from Thomas Carlyle.

Lydia had been married to Hugh for 19 years, and faced a widowhood of twenty. Fortified by the unquestioning belief in God that enabled her to write to her mother: 'How kind the Lord has been in these deep, deep waters,' superficially she recovered quite quickly, steadied by her determination to devote the rest of her life to the promotion of Hugh's work. Her children, the youngest only six, were despatched to boarding schools or to stay with relations; she moved from Shrub Mount to Ann Street in the New Town and set to work, finding publishers for Hugh's papers, correcting proofs, writing prefaces for new editions, championing his views on creation, even after the publication of Charles Darwin's *The Origin of Species* (1859) had profoundly unsettled the scientific community and the Church. Although it is hard to suppose that there had been no tensions in the marriage of two such highly strung people, one declining over a period from eccentricity into madness, and the other described by Miller's sceptical nephew as a self-obsessed hypochondriac, it had to be a true partnership. No doubt Lydia hoped to cash in on Hugh's books – she had always liked comfort and had four children to support – but her activity was also an outlet for the pent-up energy of a woman whose narrow religious beliefs had spoiled her attempt at fiction but who, judging by the prefaces she wrote for her husband's work, was well able to understand his thought. However misguided they may now appear, they suggest that her real gift was for explication, not for fiction at all.

Sadly, there was a price to be paid both for such fortitude and industry. Three times between 1863 and 1867 Lydia was admitted to mental hospitals for treatment, twice to the Crichton Royal Institution in Dumfries and once to the Glasgow Royal Asylum. Unable to settle anywhere for long, she haunted health spas, paid visits to her daughters and friends, bought and sold houses, moved around Scotland from Dumfriesshire to Inverness. She died in her daughter's house at Assynt in 1876, aged 63.

*

The complete disappearance of Lydia Miller, for more than a century, might be put down to her having published all her creative work anonymously, or to the weight of Hugh Miller's reputation effacing hers. Even feminist publications failed to notice her. In the twenty-first century, however, Lydia has been modestly resurrected, particularly in her native north-east, where the National Trust for Scotland, in its quest for 'footfall' has refurbished Hugh Miller's Cottage as a tourist attraction, along with the adjacent house where Hugh and Lydia spent their first three years of marriage. Elizabeth Sutherland's biography, *Lydia: The Wife of Hugh Miller of Cromarty* was published in 2002, for the first time (despite its status-confirming title) making Lydia, rather than Hugh, the main focus of the text. Unfortunately there are many gaps in the story, due to the fact that most letters and family papers are in New Zealand and were not made available to the author, who is too much thrown back on speculation in an attempt to fill them. Yet the book is a laudable step towards giving Lydia Miller a narrative of her own.

Despite attempts to rescue her from obscurity, however, Lydia remains enigmatic, a smooth-faced, dark-eyed 23-year-old with fashionable ringlets, in the only image of her known to exist. Perhaps it is partly the strange absence of photographs, in an age obsessed by them, and certainly the scarcity of her personal letters that make her so frustratingly hard to fathom. For it is in letters, above all, that writers provide their biographers with clues to the understanding of how and why they wrote, and whether their first love really survived the trials they endured. Which is why it is that other wife of a famous man, the much-photographed, gossipy, sarcastic, self-dramatising, jealous, sceptical, entertaining Jane Welsh Carlyle, who also once fancied for herself a noble supporting role, the brilliant literary hostess who never wrote a novel and lived to resent her husband's prominence as pious Lydia gave no sign of resenting hers, who comes dancing to meet us out of the nineteenth century, telling us in peerless letters never intended for us what being a mid-Victorian was really like.

8

TWO POETS
OF THE WEST

I have ever held, and now express the opinion, that to give a true and graphic sketch or sketches of Scottish peasant life and character in "days of langsyne," it is necessary that the writer should not draw his information from tradition and hearsay alone, but should from childhood, have lived, moved and shared, for a time at least, … in all the habits and actings both of the inner and outer life "of that bold peasantry, their country's pride" —a class which is fast losing its identity.

Janet Hamilton (1795–1873)
'Sketches of Scottish Peasant Life and Character in Days of Auld Langsyne', 1865

SCOTS HAVE ALWAYS been proud of their historic reputation as one of the best educated and most democratic societies in Europe, with both boys and girls attending the 'school in every parish' envisioned by John Knox, and the opportunity for every ambitious 'lad o' pairts' to proceed from school to university. Only in recent years has this complacency been challenged by scholars who have pointed out the poor quality of much of the teaching, overcrowding in squalid accommodation and the rate of absenteeism in a non-compulsory system. Extreme poverty was widespread, and before there was a statutory leaving age, poor parents were strongly tempted to send their children to work, rather than to school. Research into levels of illiteracy reveals that in 1834 only one in 14 children in Glasgow was being educated, and that half the population in the Highlands could not read.

That this situation existed alongside an explosion of zeal for reading among the literate working class, the foundation of free libraries and circulation of inexpensive but serious newspapers and magazines, makes the plight of the illiterate even more poignant; their deprivation was both social and intellectual. The position was, inevitably, worst among working-class girls, whose parents thought it mattered little if their daughters grew up unable to read. What use was reading, after all, for those whose only future was as wives, mothers and household drudges? Yet there were women who surmounted this defeatist attitude, and many had their mothers to thank.

Janet Hamilton née Thomson was born in Carshill in Lanarkshire in 1795, the daughter of James Thomson, a shoemaker and his wife Mary Brownlee, who worked at home as an embroiderer. Like Margaret Oliphant, Janet had an intelligent, literate mother, and her home schooling started early. In later years, she would remember her mother teaching her to read from the Bible, and of the pleasure of reading Bible stories and children's halfpenny books before she was five years old. When she was seven, her parents deciding that their health was suffering from confinement and that they would benefit from a spell of outdoor work, moved to Langloan, a village south-west of Coatbridge. Mainly dependent during Janet's childhood on agriculture and weaving, during her lifetime the village would be transformed by the building of iron, steel and chemical works, leading to a considerable increase in population. But in the first decade of the century it was still rural, and while her parents worked as agricultural labourers little Janet looked after the house, working at the spinning wheel and snatching any spare moments for books. After two years, her parents returned to their indoor occupations – Mary Thomson to work at the tambour frame, often for 15 hours a day, as an embroiderer of fine cloth for ladies' dresses. Janet, to whom she taught the skill, would later recall the daily grind:

> Bending with straining eyes
>   Over the tambour frame,
> Never a change in her weary routine–
>   Slave in all but name.
> Tambour, ever tambour,
>   Tambour the wreathing lines
> Of 'broidered silk, till beauty's robe
>   In rainbow lustre shines ...

But even in these less than favourable circumstances, her reading expanded to encompass William Shakespeare (1564–1616), John Milton (1608–74) and Allan Ramsay, whose works she found lying by a weaver's loom. Her mother, having taught her to read, now disapproved of this secular fare, but fortunately for peace in a devoutly minded household it was the King James Bible, with its strict morality clothed in exalted prose, that retained central importance in Janet's life and imagination.

In 1808, at what now seems the shockingly young age of 13, Janet Thomson was married to her father's assistant, twenty-year-old John Hamilton, with whom she continued to live in Langloan. Fortunately, the young man was sympathetic to his wife's love of books, bringing her armfuls from public libraries, as well as borrowed copies of *Blackwood's Magazine*. Later she recalled reading these while feeding her infants, and how she had stuffed the papers into a hole in the wall if a visitor who might disapprove happened to come in. Most of her reading, however, now had to be accomplished late at night. Aged 17 and already the mother of two, Janet began to compose religious poems in her head where, but for her husband's acting as her *amanuensis*, they would have had to remain. Perhaps surprisingly, given her precocious reading ability, she had never learned to write, and it was not until much later in life that she taught herself to do so, developing a crabbed but legible style of printing. As far as is known, none of these early verses were published in her lifetime and, burdened by household tasks, ten pregnancies and the care of seven surviving children, she gave up composition until she was over fifty. Then, she made up for lost time.

Janet Hamilton, along with other working-class writers of her period, was dependent for her early publication on a enlightened middle-class English publisher, John Cassell (1817–85), a temperance campaigner and social reformer who devoted much of his energy to producing inexpensive books and periodicals. Most radical of these was the *Working Man's Friend and Family Instructor*, priced at one penny, which hosted an essay competition; subsequently the best essays were published in a volume titled *The Literature of Working Men*. It says much for Cassell as well as for Hamilton that, in an age when sex discrimination was so common as to be unremarked upon, her competition entries were favoured; six essays were published in *The Literature of Working Men*, and her poetry, in Scots and English, was accepted for *The Working Man's Friend* and other of Cassell's periodicals.

Janet Hamilton was a deeply serious writer. There is no evidence that she disapproved of fiction as a genre, but writing it would not have suited her habit of mind. Her sense of vocation stemmed from her Christian faith and observation of the toil and hardship of her neighbours in Langloan. She was against the wide availability of alcohol, having seen the pain inflicted, particularly on children, by its misuse, and against the trade of enslaved people and industrial exploitation. She was – give or take one or two poems celebrating the courage of the British armed services – against warfare. She was for Protestant Christianity, literacy and education, especially for women. Her prose essays, on topics ranging from 'The Uses and Pleasures of Poetry for the Working-Classes' to 'Social Science Essay on Self-Education', are earnest and didactic, while in 'Sketches of Village Life and Character' the picture she presents of the changed and changing scene in rural Scotland, where peasant culture and language were under threat, is unsentimental, hard-hitting and undistorted by nostalgia for 'the good old days'. Her poetry she saw primarily as a concise means of conveying her convictions to her chosen readership; an energetic poem titled 'Oor Location', describes the altered face of Langloan in the 1860s, and laments the consequences of population growth in squalid surroundings. First she lambasts the men, then turns her wrath onto women:

> *Oh, the dool an' desolation,*
> *An' the havoc in the nation*
> *Wrocht by dirty drucken wives! ...*
> *Tae see sae mony unwed mithers*
> *Is sure a shame that taps all ithers,*
> *An' noo I'm fairly set a-gaun,*
> *On baith the whisky shop an' pawn*
> *I'll speak ma mind ...*

It is hard not to wonder how popular she was with her neighbours. But she understood their problems, their powerlessness, poverty and susceptibility to disease; she spoke for them and she could be gentle, especially with children:

> *Be pitiful, be pitiful*
> *To children born in crime;*
> *Spawn of the slums, poor waifs,*
> *Cast on the stream of time.*
> *These little bodies, shrivell'd, vile,*
> *Downtrodden in the mire.*
> *Hold each a priceless gem,*
> *A spark of living fire.*

Janet Hamilton was 66 when the American Civil War broke out in 1861. Although she abhorred the trade of enslaved people and would rejoice in its abolition, as reports of slaughter and disease began to appear in the British press she was horrified. Among several poems she wrote on the subject is 'On the Road to Richmond', referencing the 'Seven Days Battles' fought in 1862 around that town in Virginia, where more than 20,000 lives were lost. Only six years after the end of the Crimean War, in which the British were so heavily involved, and in verses strangely prescient of European wars not so far in the future, she shared her despair at the resort to armed conflict as a means of solving problems of politics and conscience:

> *Horror, fed on carnage, lowers*
> *O'er corruption rankly steaming,*
> *O'er Virginia's Eden bowers,*
> *Thousand vultures hover screaming.*
>
> *In one gory mass they lie–*
> *Husband, father, son and lover–*
> *Festering 'neath the burning sky,*
> *Earth no more her stain can cover ...*

Janet Hamilton did not regard her poetry as a Wordsworthian paean to nature, nor as exclusively 'Scottish' in a nationalistic way; her publisher was English, and she was mindful of her English readership. She wrote verses in English about a mining disaster at Barnsley Colliery in Yorkshire, wars in the Crimea and America, visits by the famous Indian Maharaja, Duleep Singh, (1838–93) to England, and to Scotland by Italian patriot Guiseppe Garibaldi (1807–82). She was a great fan of Queen Victoria, calling her 'Victoria, pattern of all virtues rare'.

Yet to modern readers, the most moving poems are surely those in Scots, lyrical and enlivened by the rich vocabulary of the 'mither tongue'. Of these, none is more appealing than 'A Wheen Aul' Memories', a long, elegiac poem in which she recalls a childhood when 'I skepit aff barefit, the hie road alang / Wi'a hap, stap an' loup, an' the lilt o' a sang', and commemorates the village 'worthies' of a pastoral age when:

> ... *The notes o' the mavis an' blackbird wad ring,*
> *And the gowdspink an' lintie fu' sweetly wad sing*
> *In the green braes o' Kirkwud; sic a walth o' wild flouris,*
> *I never saw onie sic bird-haunted bowris.*

But the sky darkens, as industrial Coatbridge creeps out to engulf Langloan:

> *Noo the bodies are gane, an' their dwallin's awa,*
> *An' the place whaur they stood I scarce ken noo ava.*
> *For there's roarin' o' steam, an' there's reengin' o' wheels,*
> *Men workin', an' sweatin', and swearin' like deils.*
>
> *An' the flame-tappit furnaces staun' in a raw,*
> *A' bleezin, an' blawin', an smeekin' awa;*
> *Their eerie licht brichtenin' the laigh hingin' cluds,*
> *Gleamin' far owre the loch an' the mirk lanely wuds.*

When she was in her sixties, Janet Hamilton gradually lost her sight, probably due to cataracts, and by the age of seventy she was completely blind. From then on, she depended on her daughter Marion to read to her, and her son James to act as her *amanuensis*. She died in 1873, aged 78, never having travelled more than 25 miles from Langloan in her life. Her husband John, to whom she was married for 65 years, survived her. In his introduction to her *Poems, essays and sketches* (1880), the poet, memoirist and Burns enthusiast George Gilfillan (1813–78) paid to Janet Hamilton a tribute that would surely have pleased her:

She displays ... a rugged independence of spirit, and a contempt for all "mealy-mouthedness" and gilded humbug, which make her seem almost an incarnation of the better nature of Burns.

*

When Janet Hamilton was publishing her essays and rediscovering her poetic gift in the 1840s, another poet was spending her childhood far from the west of Scotland, with which she would later become associated. Marion Bernstein (1846–1906), a 'Glasgow poet' all but forgotten until the recent revival of interest in women's writing, was born in London, the daughter of Theodore Bernstein, a German-Jewish emigrant and teacher, and a well-bred Englishwoman named Lydia Pulsford. Marion had an elder sister and a younger brother, and spent her early years in a terrace adjacent to London's Victoria Park. As with Janet Hamilton, much of her early life is written into her poetry, which references the intrusion into a sturdy childhood of the defining sadness of her life; a sudden illness, probably infantile paralysis, also known as poliomyelitis, which weakened her constitution and left her chronically infirm. Her father's hope of finding an academic outlet for his knowledge of several languages was also blighted; by 1851 he was working as a tobacconist and thereafter plunged tragically through the humiliation of insolvency, appearance in a debtors' court, and severe mental illness which ended with his death in Middlesex County Asylum in 1859.

The trauma these terrible events caused for Bernstein's wife and children can only be imagined since, while Marion constantly alluded to her illness in her poetry, she failed ever to mention her father. Nothing is really known about the circumstances of the bereaved family in the following decade, except for census references suggesting that Lydia Bernstein took in lodgers and that both her daughters were trained to teach music. Judging by the literary references in her later poetry, it seems that Marion must also have had the opportunity to read widely. An entry in the *Post Office Directory for 1874–1875* shows that by that date the family had found their way to Glasgow, where the author of 'A Song of Glasgow Town' would spend the rest of her life.

There are few obvious resemblances between Janet Hamilton, the proudly working-class, bilingual poet whose insular life belied her intellect and the range of her reading, and Marion Bernstein, the lifelong city-dweller who spoke only English, taught music and spent more than thirty years of her life at addresses in the middle-class West End of Glasgow – and wanted to be a Glaswegian, although not by birth a Scot. Bernstein was half a century younger than Hamilton, and her poetic style was sharper, cheekier and more ironic. What binds them is their preoccupations; both held strong Christian beliefs, both railed against social inequality, the trade of enslaved people, domestic violence, bad housing, inadequate education for women and the misuse of power. Both were concerned with the pollution of the environment in the west of Scotland, its shrinking green space and the squalor of greed-driven industrialisation. The same indignation informs Hamilton's 'Oor Location' and Bernstein's most famous poem, 'A Song of Glasgow Town':

> I'll sing a song of Glasgow town,
>   Where wealth and want abound;
> Where the high seat of learning sits
>   'Mid ignorance profound.
> Oh, when will Glasgow make a rule
>   To do just what she ought–
> Let starving bairns in every school
>   Be fed as well as taught!
> And when will Glasgow city be
>   Fair Caledonia's pride,
> And boast her clear unclouded skies
>   And crystal-flowing Clyde?

Bernstein published no prose, other than the introduction to her only book of verse, *Mirren's Musings* (1876), a carefully arranged collection of unpublished poems and some previously published in the *Glasgow Weekly Mail* and the *Glasgow Weekly Herald*. Both papers, a mix of advertisements, topical news items and the arts, were aimed at the literate working and professional classes in a burgeoning city. The *Weekly Mail* had a dedicated poetry feature, to which Bernstein sent her work, sometimes responding wittily in verse to editorial diktats, such as a ban on poems on love and death:

> 'How's this?' cried [Love], 'insulting me;
>   The poet's pride and glory?
> Refusing to print poetry
>   On subjects amatory?'
> 'Obituary poems are
>   Rejected too!' [Death] cried,
> This is insulting me as well';
>   'It is,' young Love replied.

'A Song of Glasgow Town' was itself a riposte to a complaint by the editor that too much poetry was being submitted extolling the Scottish countryside, too little reflecting city life.

Two preoccupations divide Hamilton and Bernstein generationally, their attitude to men and their expressed political views. Although Hamilton could give men a hard time, she accepted, as many women did before and after, that the natural lot of women was to marry and bear children. She mercilessly called out abusive men but, perhaps because her own marriage was happy, she was less strident about women's rights and representation than the succeeding generation. Bernstein, who never married, was at best ambivalent and more often cynical about men and, living through the heady days of early feminism and the battle for women's suffrage, enjoyed expressing dissident opinions:

> I dreamt that the nineteenth century
>   Had entirely passed away,
> And had given place to a more advanced
>   And very much brighter day.
> For women's rights were established quite,
>   And man could in fact discern
> That he'd long been teaching his grandmamma
>   What she didn't require to learn.

Forms of poetic expression change, and Bernstein's verses may seem old-fashioned to modern readers accustomed to more allusive, elliptical poetry. But her grasp of prosody is assured and her ideas strikingly modern. Her fearless determination to point out the injustices of nineteenth-century society still resonates, because sadly so many of the issues she raised remain unresolved.

The end of Marion Bernstein's life was tragic. As her infirmity worsened and she could no longer teach, she was reduced to soliciting handouts from charitable institutions and, as death approached, was subsisting on paltry grants from the Indigent Gentlewomen's Fund and the Colquhoun Bequest for Incurables. Probably for years she had been clinging to gentility by the skin of her teeth, and as she declined into breadline poverty she identified with the ever cash-strapped Robert Burns:

> I think of the heart of a poet
>   Always unfit to bear
> Sad poverty's heavy burden
>   Of sordid, ceaseless care.

Marion Bernstein died in Kildonan Terrace, Ibrox on 6 February 1906, aged sixty.

9

THE RAINBOW
IN THE CLOUD

Come then, explore with me each winding glen
  Far from the noisy haunts of busy men;
Let us with stedfast eye attentive trace
  The local habits of the Celtic race;
Renown'd even in those old heroic times,
  That live in Ossian's songs and Runic rhymes;
When ardent Valour call'd his children forth
  And Glory lighten'd through the beaming North.

Anne Grant of Laggan (1755–1838)
'The Highlanders' 1803

THERE ARE AS many versions of 'a Scottish childhood' as there are writers. Published or unpublished, some are lovingly nostalgic and others testify to a need to work through early traumas, but all share a powerful desire to record personal impressions of a time already passed away. It would be hard to imagine a childhood more exotic than that of Anne Macvicar, later known as 'Mrs Grant of Laggan', whose long life straddled two centuries, and who recalled vividly in the early nineteenth century events already forty years old. It was never her ambition to 'be a writer'; she published from necessity, and discovered her real talent only when more that half of her life had passed by.

Anne Grant was born in Glasgow, the daughter of Duncan Macvicar, a 'plain, brave, pious' farmer turned officer in the 78th Highland Regiment of Foot, and his wife Catherine Mackenzie, a descendant of a distinguished and recently Jacobitical family, the Stewarts of Invernahyle. In 1757, Anne's father sailed with his regiment to America, called on to support British colonists in what became known as the French and Indian War. Initially no more than sporadic fighting in a routine trading rights dispute between the British colonists of the eastern seaboard and those of the adjacent area of New France, the affair escalated into full-scale conflict when both French and British troops arrived from Europe, and tribes of Indigenous North Americans joined in on both sides.

Despite a fraught situation, a year later Macvicar sent instructions for his wife and three-year-old child to join him, so Anne's earliest memories included a perilous Atlantic crossing under sail and four years in a war zone. A cheerful child who later remembered herself as 'very much disposed to be happy anywhere', she took in her stride the arduous journeys by river and road from Charleston, South Carolina where she landed, to Albany in New York State, then from Albany to Oswego on Lake Ontario. There she experienced life in palisaded wooden forts, where her mother insisted she learn needlework; she liked better to climb trees, chase squirrels and run wild with the other garrison children. On an expedition with her parents she met the sachem (chief) of the Mohawks and camped on a river bank 'in a land of profound solitude, where wolves, foxes and bears abounded, and were very much inclined to treat us as intruders'. On river journeys in winter, advance parties had to break the ice with paddles to let the boats through.

The one element missing in this extraordinary life experience was books. Like so many Scottish girls she was taught the elements of reading by her mother (and also to write by a friendly soldier in his spare time), but the only reading matter available other than the family Bible was a much-used copy of Blind Harry's *The Wallace*. Later she would recall that this epic poem, extolling the exploits of the famous thirteenth-century Scottish patriot William Wallace (*c.*1274–1305), fuelled her enthusiasm for the homeland she could scarcely remember. The story of how Anne Macvicar acquired a book of her own is a touching one:

> *On the night when we returned to Fort Bruerton* [sic], *I found Captain Campbell delighted with my writing, my reading and my profound admiration of the* [Biblical] *friendship of David and Jonathan … I was much captivated by the copperplate in an edition of* Paradise Lost *which, on that account, he gave me to admire. When I was coming away, he said to me, "Keep that book, my dear child: I believe that the time will come when you will take pleasure in it." Never did a present produce such joy and gratitude. I thought I was dreaming, and looked at it a hundred times before I could believe that it was really mine.*

In 1762, a temporary truce was signed, and the Macvicars returned from Oswego to Albany, a town with a mixed population of Dutch, French and British settlers and, on the fringes of the town, summer camps of the Mohawk nation. Here they became friends of Catalina Schuyler (1701–82), a member of a prominent New England family, known for her wide culture and hospitality. Anne loved 'Madame' Schuyler, in whose house she spent three winters while her father remained in the Army, and whose memory she would honour forty years later in *Memoirs of an American Lady* (1808), the source also of her own childhood story.

By the time she was ten, Anne Macvicar had learned Dutch and enough of the Mohawk language to converse with the children whose wigwams she frequented; this experience greatly influenced her adult view of indigenous societies in danger of corruption by contact with 'civilised' and, by implication, morally inferior people. She read classic English authors with Madame Schuyler, listened to good conversation and wrote later, that 'whatever culture my mind received, I owe to her'.

This charmed life was, however, soon to change. In 1765 Duncan Macvicar retired from the Army, his service having earned him a grant of land in Vermont on which he hoped to capitalise. Unfortunately his plans came unstuck when, in poor health, he brought his family back to Glasgow. While he was mulling over the pros and cons of returning to Vermont, the American War of Independence broke out, and his land was confiscated. It seems that during the next three years, Macvicar was involved in a trading enterprise in Glasgow; for Anne they mattered mostly because she made three close friends, one Henrietta Reid and two sisters surnamed Ewing, all important in her later life. In 1773, however, Duncan Macvicar returned to the British Army. He was appointed Barrack Master at Fort Augustus, and his 18-year-old daughter, who eleven years before had been stirred to patriotic fervour by reading Blind Harry's *Wallace*, left the city for the Highlands.

Initially she found the scenery overwhelming: 'The general aspect of the country,' she recalled in 1809, 'made me think myself in a defile guarded by savage and gloomy giants with their heads in the clouds and their feet washed in cataracts,' but, 'When I grew acquainted with the language and poetry of the country, I found a thousand interesting localities combined with those scenes where the lovely and the brave of other days still had a habitation and a name'. Clearly she had become acquainted with the language of Romantic sublimity, which was all the rage at the time. In 1779 she married James Grant, garrison chaplain at Fort Augustus and minister of the neighbouring parish of Laggan, where Anne gave birth to twelve children, and where they lived for the next 23 years.

As a minister's wife, Anne Grant was a great success. Conscious that 'the sentiment with which [the Highlanders and the Lowlanders] regarded each other was at best a kind of smothered animosity', she played down her Glasgow connections, learned Gaelic, studied Highland folklore and avoided appearing 'to wonder at anything local and peculiar'. This sensitivity, along with a naturally cheerful temperament, made her popular; in a letter to a Glasgow friend at this time, she wrote:

> How happy, in my circumstances, is that versatile sanguine temper which is hoping for a rainbow in every cloud; nay, so prevalent is this disposition, that were a fire to break out in the offices [outhouses] and burn them all down, I dare say the first thing that would occur to me would be to console myself by considering how much ground would be manured by all these fine ashes.

She was to need all her optimism in the years ahead, but for now, busy with charitable work and church duties, frequently pregnant and always bringing up small children, she was what and where she wanted to be. Her husband's ministry was a success – the present church at Laggan was built in his time – and Anne still found time to write long, vividly descriptive letters to her friends, and to compose poems (which she did not herself rate highly).

The Grants' marriage was happy but not without sorrow. Three daughters died in early childhood of tuberculosis and, Anne believed, the loss of their eldest son, aged 15, contributed to the swift decline and death of her husband from the same illness in 1801. Now financial hardship became pressing. The Grants had never been well-off but with a stipend of £70, plus other benefits and income from a farm rented from the Duke of Gordon, they had been reasonably secure. Suddenly Anne found herself with eight children to house and feed, and little provision except the paltry pension due to an Army chaplain's widow. Yet it was typical of a woman supported by strong religious faith and a sanguine nature (a characteristic she shared with another child-burdened widow, Margaret Oliphant), that she was less concerned about her poverty than were her friends. Foremost among these were the prosperous women, Henrietta Reid and the Ewing sisters, who had been her teenage friends in Glasgow and recipients of her letters and verses during her marriage. They now became the prime movers in an attempt to persuade her to publish her poetry. At first she dismissed the idea, protesting that she had never intended such a thing, and was too busy and fearful of criticism. Eventually, however, she was convinced by the enthusiasm of friends including the Duchess of Gordon and, crucially, George Thomson, the Edinburgh music collector for whose song books she later wrote lyrics, and in whose house the young Lydia Fraser would meet her 15 years later. As the century turned, Anne Grant riffled in her desk drawers and pulled out sufficient material for *Poems on Various Subjects*; enough subscriptions (orders paid in advance) were raised, and the book was published by Longman & Rees in 1803. To the author's surprise and gratification, the *Poems* were favourably reviewed; more crucially at the time, they were also a financial success and, at the age of 48, Anne Grant was launched on a literary career.

Meanwhile, although she had no desire to leave Laggan, pressure was growing on her to move closer to her friends in Glasgow; what probably persuaded her finally was that on her father's retirement from the Army, her ageing parents had also returned to the city. In 1803, she moved south to Woodend, a farm on the Carse of Stirling in the lee of the Braes of Touch. She described the farmhouse as 'genteel and commodious' which it needed to be to accommodate not only Anne but her eight children, her niece, four teenagers whom she took in as paying pupils, a couple of servants and, as it transpired, her mother, who moved in with her on the death of Duncan Macvicar in the same year. Here Anne tried again to farm, keeping three cows, growing potatoes and weeding her own turnips, but the money from *Poems on Various Subjects* had mostly been used up in paying off debts, and another financial crisis loomed.

Harassed by debt, an unproductive farm, pupils to teach and a son who needed kitting out for an Army career in India, Anne Grant was far too busy to write a new book from scratch, but once again her resourceful friends devised a plan. Over the years, aware of the literary quality of the letters she had sent them from the Highlands, describing her life and commenting on the habits and customs of an area of Scotland far remote in language and culture from the evermore industrialised society to the south, they had kept them in their desks and drawers. Now the friends suggested returning them, so that she could edit and publish them, which, desperate to make some money, she did. Subscriptions flooded in from those who had enjoyed *Poems on Various Subjects* and, after carrying the manuscript to London herself, Anne Grant arranged within three days for Longman & Rees to publish it. *Letters from the Mountains* appeared in 1806 and, while she was peeved that Francis Jeffrey, whom she called 'the Arch-critic' failed to review the book in the *Edinburgh Review*, and complained of male 'philosophers' 'treat[ing] female genius and female production with unqualified scorn', public approbation must have soothed her. Readers loved the book, which sold out four editions in two years. 'I have reaped considerable benefit from the publication of the letters,' she wrote to a friend. In fact they established her literary reputation, and ensured that she and her family were comfortably provisioned for a considerable time to come.

In 1806, Anne Grant moved from Woodend to Stirling, where she wrotetwo more books. The first was *Memoirs of An American Lady*, a tribute in which Catalina Schuyler was unintentionally sidelined by the memoirs of a small Scottish girl in America. The second was *Essays on the Superstitions of the Scottish Highlanders*, an elegiac work in which she reiterated her view, set out in her long poem 'The Highlanders' and already familiar from *Letters from the Mountains*, of the northern region of Scotland as an indigenous enclave endangered, as the Indigenous North Americans were, by the intrusion of a technologically but not spiritually or morally superior society.

Since her girlhood at Fort Augustus, Anne Grant had been an enthusiast for *Fragments of Translation from the Gaelic or Erse Language*, alleged to be by the blind third-century minstrel Ossian, translated into English by James Macpherson (1736–96) and published in 1760. These tales of Fingal, father of Ossian, ancient hero and warrior of Irish mythology, appeared in 1760 and quickly became a publishing sensation. It was not long however, before a fight broke out among the English *literati* as to the authenticity of the *Fragments* – much to the indignation of Anne Grant who was stubbornly convinced that they were indeed the founding myth of the Gaels. In her *Essays*, the virtues of the Highlanders were those of a race descended from heroes; their manners, family relationships, hospitality, loyalty, sexual probity and idea of honour were of the highest order, and even their super-stitions lent intensity to their religious practice. That Anne Grant's vision of the Highlands as 'Shangri-la' derives from her youthful experiences of reading 'Ossian' and living alongside Mohawks, as well as her happy years at Laggan, does not detract from its charm, but it fails to recognise adequately the evils agitating social observers like Hugh Miller in the same period – the grinding insecurity of subsis-tence farming, atrocious housing, lack of sanitation, cattle disease, poor education, and the heartless exploitation of the populace by its equally indigenous overlords. None of which was enough to temper a potent myth; the heroines of Susan Ferrier, Mary Brunton, Christian Isobel Johnstone and Lydia Miller were not alone in viewing the Highlands as, in the words of Robert Burns, 'the birthplace of valour, the country of worth'.

By the time *Essays on the Superstitions of the Scottish Highlanders* was pub-lished in 1811, Anne Grant had moved to Edinburgh, and it was in a new house in Heriot Row where 'everything was airy and pleasant' that she read the reviews. She had been forewarned that they might not be gushing; her friend George Thomson, who had keenly promoted her previous books, had told her tartly before publication: 'I cannot help regretting extremely that you ever forsook that form of writing so well suited to display your powers, and to hide your defects.' He went on to tell her frankly that she should have stuck to letters, and to opine that long essays require 'a more methodical arrangement and clearer connection than is suited to your poetic genius and irregular habits of writing'.

Francis Jeffrey, in the *Edinburgh Review* was more measured; he pointed out what he saw as her weaknesses, limited subject matter and 'ill-regulated fancy', but praised the force of her 'unmediated vision' of Highland culture. Generally, how-ever, the reviews lacked the enthusiasm which had greeted *Letters from the Mountains*, and there was a sense that the *Essays*, less spontaneously, covered much the same ground. No doubt the author was pleased by Sir Walter Scott's reference, in 'A Postscript' to *Waverley* (1814), to the 'highly creditable ... traditional records of the respectable and ingenious Mrs Grant of Laggan', but the book did not go into a second edition. The accidental writer who had quickly learned professional stan-dards did not attempt another prose work. Apart from a lengthy political poem titled 'Eighteen Hundred and Thirteen' (1814), she published nothing but a few lyrics after she moved to Edinburgh.

Gregarious, well-known and well-liked, Mrs Grant was quickly absorbed into the close literary circle of the New Town. Her first visitors at Heriot Row were Sir Walter Scott and Francis Jeffrey; she became friends with Elizabeth Hamilton and Eliza Fletcher (*see* chapter 12), a radical sympathiser with whom politically she had to agree to differ. She dined out and held supper parties which Henry Cockburn, in *Memorials of his Time* praised for their simple hospitality and good conversation. She took pupils, as she had at Woodend, some of whom became close friends; one Joan Glassel arrived in 1811 and stayed with her for eight years.

For the woman long ago 'disposed to be happy anywhere' these Edinburgh years might have been a enjoyable time, had it not been for constant anxiety about money and a catalogue of bereavements that might have unhinged a less godly woman. Of her remaining eight children, all but one died prematurely; even the survivor, her youngest son John Peter, came close to death in 1825, when a steam ship from Inverness to Glasgow was wrecked with great loss of life, and he was the only cabin passenger to be saved. Not only her own children were taken from her; her niece, her nephew, three of her best-loved pupils and her daughter-in-law died in grim succession. In 1820, Anne Grant had a fall on a flight of steps, sustaining injuries which seriously disabled her for the rest of her life, while by 1825 her income had again dwindled to the point where she had to be grateful for a Civil List pension of £50 a year. She began privately to write a memoir, but left it unfinished when her daughter Charlotte died in 1807; it was completed by her surviving son, who published it with a selection of her later letters in 1844. After the death of his wife, John Peter Grant took his mother to live with him. She died of influenza at his house in Manor Place on 7 November 1838 aged 84, and was buried beside her daughters in St Cuthbert's Churchyard in Edinburgh.

10

THE HIGHLAND LADY

The Memoirs were written for her own children, and the daughter of her sister Mrs Gardiner, with no thought but to interest them in those scenes of her early life which she recalled so vividly and has narrated with such lively simplicity.

Lady Strachey, née Jane Maria Grant (1840–1928)
Preface to *Memoirs of a Highland Lady* (1898)

THERE WAS ANOTHER nineteenth-century author named Grant, even more strongly identified with the Highlands than Anne Grant of Laggan. Their long lives overlapped, but 42 years divided them; they were unrelated and, although the younger knew of the elder by name and sometimes they lived tantalisingly close, they never met. Their social status and paths through life were different, but they had one thing in common: both experienced periods of financial stress in which they relied on their ability to write to make ends meet.

Elizabeth Grant of Rothiemurchus (1797–1885), the eldest child of another John Peter Grant, Laird of Rothiemurchus (1774–1848) and his English wife, Jane Ironside, was born at 5 Charlotte Square in the New Town of Edinburgh. With two brothers and two sisters, she was brought up in affluent circumstances in the south of England, in Edinburgh and at The Doune of Rothiemurchus, the Inverness-shire estate inherited by her father in 1790. When Elizabeth Grant's recollections, written in the 1840s, were published posthumously in 1898 as *Memoirs of a Highland Lady*, many readers may have been surprised to learn that eighty years previously she and her sister Mary had published short stories and articles anonymously in the well-regarded *Frazer's Magazine* and the long-defunct *Inspector*, for much the same reason that Anne Grant had published *Letters from the Mountains* – their circumstances had changed, and they desperately needed money.

John Peter Grant (he was not knighted until 1826), described by Elizabeth as 'a little sallow brisk man without any remarkable feature', but with a charm that many people found 'irresistible', was a clever advocate who was for 14 years Member of Parliament for two English constituencies. Unfortunately he had been less clever with money, frittering his inheritance away in extravagant living and costly improvements to his property at Rothiemurchus. After he lost his Tavistock seat in 1826, it became clear to his horrified family that his debts were beyond control and his creditors in unforgiving mood. The pleasant spells of living in London and Oxford, the winters in Edinburgh, the exchange of visits, dinners and balls to which the grown-up children were accustomed, all ceased abruptly. It was then that a sympathetic neighbour suggested to Elizabeth and Mary Grant, more or less confined to The Doune while their father was on the run from his former friends, that they should write for the magazines which were such an important feature of early nineteenth-century communication. Their success provided a contribution to the family finances much needed at the time.

In 1827, John Peter Grant escaped from his creditors when, through the string-pulling of a more successful politician Charles Grant, Lord Glenelg (1778–1866), he was appointed a judge in Bombay (Mumbai) and whisked his family off to India. There, two years later, Elizabeth Grant married Anglo-Irish Colonel Henry Smith (1780–1862), an officer in the 5th Bombay Cavalry. He was not her first love; that had been an unidentified college friend of her brother William's from whom, due to a quarrel between their fathers, she had been forced to part in 1815. But if she found less passion with Colonel Smith, an asthmatic man 17 years her senior, she found a mature contentment and, when he unexpectedly inherited the property of Baltiboys in Co. Wicklow, moved with him to Ireland. The 'Highland Lady' who had only been a Highland lady intermittently during her first thirty years, now became the chatelaine of an Irish country estate. It was a role that suited her well, since the often ailing Colonel Smith appears to have been happy to leave his property largely to her enthusiastic management.

Mrs Smith's capacity for domestic multitasking was remarkable. She had three children, kept the household accounts, collected rents, visited the poor, read voraciously and pursued her career as a writer, regularly submitting stories, travelogues and opinion pieces on British and Irish affairs to magazines in London and Edinburgh. Her relationship with Edinburgh publisher Robert Chambers (1802–71) proved particularly fruitful, and more than twenty of her extended essays were published by him in *Chambers's Edinburgh Journal*. The money she earned enabled her to contribute generously to poor relief, particularly during the famine years of 1847–52, but also provided 'for a private purse these pinching times I can't do without'.

Elizabeth guarded her anonymity carefully, becoming upset when her mother unguardedly let slip to a visitor that an article in *Chambers's* was hers. She also drew a firm distinction between the work she chose to publish and that intended only for the eyes of her family. She regarded herself as an old mother; she was 41 when her last child was born and, suffering over a long period from gastric problems, colds and coughs, was convinced that she would die before her children were grown up. Her private writings were therefore intended to provide them with both moral guidance and an account of her life and times. In fact, she lived to be nearly ninety, and none of the works which in the twentieth century made her famous – the memoirs of her youth and the journals she kept in Ireland during her marriage – were published in her lifetime. When she was dead, it was another matter.

The dilemma of whether private papers should ever be published has been a subject much discussed; to some it is a betrayal of trust, to others a duty to a wider public interest. But whichever side is taken, the outcome is usually to disregard private scruples and go for publication. Among Elizabeth's eleven great-nephews and -nieces was Jane Maria, Lady Strachey (1840–1928), one of whose 13 children was the more celebrated Lytton. It was she who, when the manuscript of her great-aunt's early reminiscences was first circulated in the Grant family, realised its literary and historical importance and persuaded the copyright holder, Elizabeth's surviving daughter Anne, that a version should be published. Abridged and severely edited by Lady Strachey in line with late Victorian sensibility, a limited edition was brought out in 1897 and a commercial one in 1898. The book was hugely successful, with four reprints in its first year and several more before 1988, when the full version was first made available. It was Lady Strachey who hit on the epithet 'The Highland Lady' by which the author was known long after she had become, in her sister's view at least, an Irish Lady.

It is easy to understand the success of the *Memoirs*. There is always a market for books that give a glimpse of the lives of aristocratic people, and the 'Highland Lady's' story had the additional allure, even for its first readers in the 1890s, of evoking a remote era. Written in Ireland in the 1840s, it reveals a faultless memory of people and places in the pre-Victorian nineteenth century, and its geographical range is wide. The writer recalls an early childhood spent mainly in the south of England, touches on the amusements, fashions, entertainments and literary acquaintances of an Edinburgh still in its Golden Age, and ends with the Grant family's emigration to India and her own marriage. The most vivid passages, however, conjure up the Highlands at a time when, as Anne Grant of Laggan perceived, their distinct culture was under threat, and people were being cleared from the land by the class, ironically, to which the Grants of Rothiemurchus belonged.

Memoirs of a Highland Lady does not deal with such big issues. Rather, the reminiscences capture life in a bubble of privilege, brought back to life through a successful blending of middle-aged perceptiveness and the memory of sharp-eyed adolescence. The author is aware that life was hard for the poor, but can't resist making the point that it was also spartan for upper-class children forced to rise in the dark, 'wash without candle, fire or warm water' and practice on the piano and the harp until 'the strings cut the poor cold fingers and the blisters often bled'. She remembers her mother as bad-tempered and unaffectionate, and feels no remorse over the treatment of governesses, openly defied and despised by the disdainful young ladies whom they were inadequately paid to teach. Only the father was the object of affection, at least until he disgraced himself by shady dealings in his financial affairs. But the disposition of the young Grants was to be happy, and any disadvantages were countered by the pleasures of dancing, theatricals and visiting, particularly to neighbouring Kinrara, the summer retreat of the pleasure-loving Duchess of Gordon – the same who was kind to Anne Grant in her widowhood at Laggan, barely 25 miles from Rothiemurchus.

Elizabeth Grant had a genuine affection for the Highlanders on her father's estate and there are poignant vignettes of Highland life in her book: the fate of the young Highlander forced to go out on a wild night of wind and sleet to open the Loch Ennich sluice gates, found in the morning frozen to death with his mother's half-eaten bannock by his side, and of a shepherd who died in similar circumstances on a snowy night, and whose plaid-wrapped corpse was not discovered on the moors until the spring. The dependants of such unfortunates were taken care of, as part of the unspoken contract between the laird's family and their retainers; the fealty and respect of the 'lower orders' were rewarded by the 'higher' with kindness and help in hard times. Acceptance of this feudal contract lasted longer in the country places of Scotland than in the industrialised parts, and it underpinned Elizabeth's view of proper behaviour throughout her life.

Sad tales in the *Memoirs* are countered by humorous anecdotes. Sir John Peter's dancing at harvest-home is described as 'peculiar – a very quiet body and very busy feet, ending in a turnabout which he imagined was the fling; as English it was as if her had never left Hertfordshire'. At the Presbyterian Sunday service, the unaccompanied psalm-singing was 'serious severe screaming, a wandering search after the tune by many who never caught it', causing dogs to bark and babies to cry. The tale of Sir John Peter's disgrace, his daughters' story-writing to help make ends meet, and their departure from the shelter of The Doune for an unknown future in India is told with a sense of drama and ultimately pathos. Lady Strachey's judgement was right. Whatever Elizabeth's original intention in writing about her early life, her book is a masterpiece and her descendants had a bestseller on their hands.

The success of the book naturally created among readers an appetite for more, which lasted for more than a century. After the *Memoirs*, the words 'The Highland Lady' became a marque, their inclusion in a title guaranteeing a readership. The subsequent books, however, have necessarily been in a different category. The *Memoirs* were a one-off retrospective, an artful record of times remembered not sentimentally, but with love. Subsequent volumes have been edited versions of the voluminous journals kept by Elizabeth throughout her life as the wife and widow of an Irish landowner. Their purpose was to record the day each entry was written, with all its tasks, anxieties and crises, and refer to the past only to make relevant points about it.

Of the three most recent, full and scholarly extracts, *The Highland Lady in Ireland* (1840–43 and 1845–50), *A Highland Lady in France* (1843–45) and *A Highland Lady in Dublin* (1850–56), all immaculately edited by Andrew Tod and Patricia Pelly, the first is most illuminating, both of the personality of the diarist as wife, mother, proxy estate manager and accountant, and of her trenchant opinions on every subject – politics, class, religion, Irish and British affairs, education, women's place in society. Displaying a great diarist's gift for infinite variety, the entries hop between the serious and the trivial; from the funding of schools for the poor to the mending of Colonel Smith's flannels; from the iniquity of sending small boys up chimneys to local gossip, not always benign; from trouble with servants to tart observations about the doings of the young Queen Victoria (1819–1901) and her 'stick of a husband' Prince Albert (1819–61). Like most Victorians, Mrs Smith was obsessed with ailments, her own and her family's, recording faithfully her coughs and chronic dyspepsia, Colonel Smith's asthma, scares about measles and scarlet fever.

She also had a talent for wicked pen-portraits. Her neighbour Mrs Hornidge calls at Baltiboys 'looking most wretched, so very fine too, just like a corpse dressed up for the grave in Italy in all the family splendour!' On a visit to her sister in Edinburgh, she meets an old friend, Mrs Cockburn, who 'shews [*sic*] what beauty comes to; so handsome as she was and now a sort of drunken looking cook or fishwife, red and bleared and bloated, from want of care they say and overeating, porter etc.' (She may have been exaggerating Mrs Cockburn's former beauty; Henry Cockburn had himself remarked laconically in 1811: 'I was cleeket to a decent, well-behaved, thickish woman about a fortnight ago, and as yet have no reason to repent of my choice.' It was a long and harmonious marriage.)

Mrs Smith of Baltiboys boasts in a rather un-Scottish way about the attractiveness of her daughters, and is not averse to self-congratulation either. Every good opinion, every compliment paid to her own publications is complacently recorded, along with any derogatory review of a fellow-writer.

The Smiths were 'improving' landlords, among a small group of people of conscience among an Anglo-Irish landed gentry who generally cared very little about the conditions of the poor. They had found much need of improvement. On a visit to Ireland in 1825, Sir Walter Scott had noted that 'the cottages [of the peasantry] would scarce serve for pig styes, even in Scotland', so they must have been very bad indeed. Egged on by his crusading wife, Colonel Smith re-thatched cabins, put in windows, built chimney stacks, drained peatbogs when funds allowed, fed the hungry and encouraged her establishment of non-sectarian schools 'to improve the intellect and control the temper of the poor'. During the terrible years of the potato famine (1845–52), the Smiths worked tirelessly to obtain grants for drainage and road-building schemes from the London government, so that they could keep their tenants in work for as long as possible. Elizabeth redoubled her efforts to earn money by her writing, and at that time of mass distress gave every penny she earned to the famine relief fund. Her kindness and concern were admirable, as was her self-sacrificial determination to get things done. Yet the journals also reveal some interesting contradictions in the personality of this earnest do-gooder.

Elizabeth prided herself on her liberal opinions. She opposed the monarchy in principle as 'a magnificent remnant of barbarism', which was now a 'worn out institution'. She had no time for the English public schools which had educated her brothers, disapproving of their emphasis on ancient languages and opining darkly that they corrupted youth by 'nursing the vices which are matured at Oxford, Cambridge and Edinburgh'. She was concerned by the 'Condition of England question', a phrase used by Thomas Carlyle to highlight the shocking gap between rich and poor. In theory she was impatient with rituals and pageantry handed down from the past, and applauded the advance of democracy, provided that it was gradual and avoided the horrors of violent revolution.

Unfortunately these laudable principles tended to clash with her Scottish Highland belief in the feudal system of loyalty and deference and, in her battle to improve the lives of the poor at Baltiboys it was usually her aristocratic instincts that won out. However enlightened they believed themselves to be, and however tactfully they thought they acted, the Smiths evicted tenants to enlarge their own farms and, apparently unable to understand the attachment of poor people to their own country, coolly regarded the tragedy of Irish emigration during the famine years as an opportunity for self-improvement for the emigrants, and of better conditions for those who remained. For all her generosity and desire to help, Elizabeth Smith's relations with her poor neighbours were occasionally fraught. Unlike Anne Grant of Laggan, who learned Gaelic and carefully avoided offending the Highlanders' sensibilities, she seems never quite to have understood the difference of temperament between the sober, deferential Highland Scots and the more volatile Irish, describing her peasant neighbours at Baltiboys as idle, slovenly, duplicitous and given to unseemly displays of pique. In true nineteenth-century fashion, she reserved her best efforts for the 'deserving poor' who showed willingness to help themselves.

Nor was the 'Highland Lady' shy about criticising the religious beliefs of her neighbours. An Anglican of Presbyterian descent, she again proved herself more sensitive to their needs than to their feelings by panning Roman Catholicism as ignorant and superstitious, and making enemies of the local priests – although amusingly when introduced at a ball to 'the better rank of Roman Catholicks [sic]', she liked them, and decided that: 'One of the best features of our improving times is the greater sociability of sects and classes'.

Class was important to Elizabeth. For all her Whiggish sentiments and strictures about English public schools, she sent her son Jack to board at an Irish one, which she hoped would 'confirm in him the habits and feelings of a gentleman while making acquaintance with the very best of the society he is to live among'. She wanted her daughters to make socially advantageous marriages. At the same time, believing that one's class, and the obligation it imposed on the privileged to aid the poor, were preordained by God, and that it was the duty of the poor to be grateful, she was puzzled when her rather bossy benevolence was sometimes resented. There were fallings out and petty acts of revenge; servants stole, deliberately broke china and had 'fits of the sullens', while tenants failed to pay their rent on time, and even the loyal steward had a 'fit of temper' when Mrs Smith grabbed a hoe and demonstrated a superior method of weeding turnips. 'Unhappy Ireland!, how much have your wild children yet to learn?' she wailed. 'With such passions, how are they ever to be raised into the pre-eminence their talents and their energy seem to have destined them to occupy?' With some justice, she saw herself as the victim of ingratitude, but it seems not to have occurred to her that lecturing and exhorting might be resented. Yet she knew the worth of what she and Colonel Smith had achieved, and she was not exaggerating when she wrote in 1845:

> When I look back on the condition in which we found our pretty little property, I can hardly believe that fifteen years should or could or would have worked out so improved a state of things. Now we have larger farms, larger fields, some good fences, much finer cattle, a few sheep, even some turnips, five new slated houses, three of them two stories high, good clothing, meal and bread and bacon and a 'bit of beef betimes'. Draining a rage, planting, clearing, good schools, a night school, a lending library, and much approach towards cleanliness. Fifteen years more, and what may we not hope for?

In truth, the next 15 years brought mixed fortunes. The Smiths spent some time in France, during which Elizabeth's sister Mary died. Then came the disaster of the famine years, bringing sacrifice of time and personal earnings, and trying to hold the British government to account. In December 1850 Anne Smith married, and the following year her parents moved with their elder daughter Janey from Baltiboys to Dublin, where they were drawn into a social round of levées and balls at the Castle, concerts, plays and the opera. They met the Lords Lieutenant appointed by the British government, and mingled with Anglo-Irish families like themselves.

Back at Baltiboys, anxieties continued. 'Ribbonists', members of an undercover organisation of poor rural Roman Catholics formed to oppose the Protestant

Orange Order, were briefly active in Co. Wicklow during the 1850s and suspected, in the Smiths' absence, of setting fire to the front door at Baltiboys House. Elizabeth made visits to the estate to collect rents and keep an eye on her schools; she had difficulty in finding competent teachers, and attendance went up and down. In 1851 Elizabeth's aged aunt came to live with the Smiths, necessitating a change of accommodation; the family lived at five Dublin addresses between 1851 and 1856. Colonel Smith's health continued to decline, while their son Jack, after a school career which suggests that St Columba's College was no more a perfect educational Eden than Eton or Harrow, defied his mother's wishes and insisted on an Army career. There were constant worries about cash flow, exacerbated by the behaviour of Anne's spendthrift husband James King and his miserly father, which caused a painful though temporary breach between mother and daughter. Every story went into the journals, interspersed with advice to Jack on how to conduct himself when he inherited Baltiboys, and particularly how to avoid any financial dealings with his profligate brother-in-law. And all the while she was writing her *Memoirs*, churning out essays for the magazines, worrying about money and keeping meticulous accounts.

As 1856 draws to its close, Elizabeth remarks ominously, but as ever valiantly, 'I don't well see what I write. Instinct guides the pen'. A fortnight later she was with Anne at the birth of her son George, a pleasure spoiled when the baby became ill, had convulsions and almost died. His 59-year-old grandmother was up all night every night for two weeks, only to be called home to nurse her 76-year-old husband through an attack of bronchitis. On the last day of the year, she reveals the full extent of her eye problem: '... a vessel which should only contain serum admits a clot of blood ... . Also the lens of both eyes is thickening ... . And so farewell dear journal for a time.'

After a period of almost total blindness, a cataract operation restored partial sight in one eye, and the journal was continued, but never with the regularity and vigour of old. There were other griefs. In 1862, Elizabeth lost her husband, who against the odds had survived until he was 82. In the absence of the new proprietor Jack Graydon Smith on Army duties, the estate was temporarily and badly managed by Elizabeth's thriftless son-in-law James King; it must have been a great relief when this unsatisfactory man was appointed Clerk of the Peace one hundred miles away in Co. Fermanagh, and Elizabeth took back control.

The most desolating event of a long life, however, was yet to come. Elizabeth Smith had never wanted her only son to enter the British Army. She was a loving but clear-sighted parent who recognised his weaknesses and feared that he might be influenced by the moral laxity common among Army officers at that time. Too late, she was proved right. Although he had risen to the rank of captain in the Royal Fusiliers and married a young woman whose parents were family friends, Jack had got into serious debt and, after postings to notoriously insalubrious locations in Europe and North America, was obliged by ill health to resign his commission in the early 1870s. He died in November 1873 of a disease discreetly recorded on his death certificate as 'Congestion of the Lungs following General Paralysis', the nineteenth-century code for tertiary syphilis. Aged only 36, he left a young widow who, the following year, gave birth to a posthumous daughter. Although the real cause of his death may have been kept from her, the restrained words carved on the family gravestone, 'deeply regretted', were surely an inadequate expression of the private distress and sense of futility felt by the mother of this wayward, much loved son.

But the 'Highland Lady', who had endured so much, was not one to turn inward. There was her granddaughter Elizabeth, now the heir of Baltiboys, to instruct, the estate to manage and the poor to be supported. The brilliant, opinionated, self-contradictory, provoking, amusing, larger-than-life 'Highland Lady', born in the eighteenth century and living, despite her early intimations of her own mortality, almost until the end of the nineteenth, soldiered on, never knowing how in the future she would be celebrated among the most-gifted writers and social commentators of her age. She died at Baltiboys in 1885, aged 88, and was buried with her husband and son in St Mary's Churchyard at Blessington.

11

THE IMMORTAL
JOANNA

I had seen nothing of the kind before, but a puppet show in a poor little out-house when I was a mere child. But now I beheld a lighted-up Theatre with fine painted scenes and gay dressed Gentlemen & Ladies acting a story on the stage, like busy agitated people in their own dwellings and my attention was riveted with delight. It very naturally touched upon my old passion for make-believe, and took possession of me entirely.

Joanna Baillie (1762–1851)
*Memoirs written to please my Nephew, William Baillie c.*1848

IF FICTION IN Scotland had a difficult start, the same might be said of drama in the same period, but with one significant difference. The fiction that emerged in Scotland in the later eighteenth and early nineteenth century, powered by Sir Walter Scott, James Hogg and John Galt and encompassing work by Elizabeth Hamilton, Mary Brunton and Susan Ferrier, was essentially a new genre. Theatre, on the contrary, had a recorded history stretching back at least to the twelfth century, when it had first been used by the Church to convey to an illiterate population some knowledge of the Bible. Unfortunately this pious intention had been compromised by early attempts to graft the new religion of Christianity to stubborn old pagan beliefs and, since many pagan rites involved sexual practices and symbolism, the 'plays' acquired a reputation for lewdness that persisted long after paganism had been officially disavowed.

In the later Middle Ages, much street theatre centred on celebrations of the Holy Days of the Church, most commonly with enactments of stories from the Old and New Testaments. These performances were most often staged to coincide with the feast of Corpus Christi in early summer, and were organised by the trade guilds of each burgh; Dundee, Arbroath, Perth, Aberdeen, Lanark, Edinburgh and Glasgow are known to have hosted cycles of such plays. All the actors were men, and surviving scraps of text and descriptions suggest that the productions were fun; the costumes were ingenious, the scenery colourful and there were parts for biblical characters (including a splendid Serpent in the tale of Adam and Eve), for angels and devils and, delightfully if unscripturally, a mermaid. The plays drew large crowds and, inevitably, the excitement of the day occasioned outbreaks of drunkenness and debauchery which offended the Church's desire for propriety. Although, as these 'Passion Plays' declined, a more serious and literary strain of drama was discernible in the Latin plays of George Buchanan (1503–82) and the masterpiece of Scottish poetry and theatre, *Ane Satyre of the Thrie Estatis* by Sir David Lindsay (*c.*1485–1555), the clerical attitude to the drama remained uneasy.

The Union of the Crowns in 1603, which occasioned the hasty removal of the entertainment-loving Royal court from Edinburgh to London, robbed stage performance of powerful patronage. When the eager Reformers who suppressed Roman Catholic observance also swept jugglers, strolling players, musicians, guisers, acrobats and dancing animals from the towns and villages of Scotland, theatre was forced underground; its reputation for lax morals and roguery generally unchallenged. It was, however, too important an expression of the human spirit to wither entirely.

It was not until the eighteenth century, with the coming of the Enlightenment, that a way was gradually cleared for a new flowering of the arts. Allan Ramsay, an Edinburgh wigmaker who was also a poet and founder of Scotland's first lending library, published in 1725 a pastoral play, *The Gentle Shepherd*, which four years later was performed at Taylor's Hall in the Cowgate by the boys of Haddington Grammar School. Undeterred by the growlings of the Kirk, and encouraged by the success of his play on the London stage, Ramsay went on to support a repertory company, the Edinburgh Players, and in 1736 bought a theatre in Carrubber's Close in the High Street. The existence of this building, opened in 1715 and previously used by comedians and strolling players, proved the durability of performance in the face of official disapproval, but Ramsay had a higher purpose. His was to be a proper theatre to match those that had flourished in London, notably in Drury Lane and Covent Garden, since the Restoration of Charles II in 1660 had put an end to Puritan rule. In the event, the venture was short-lived – the theatre was closed a year later by a Government Licensing Act – but theatre was back in Edinburgh and, despite continuing guerrilla war with Kirk and Town Council, thrived in an ever more tolerant society. The New Town expanded and the purpose-built Theatre Royal was opened, attracting famous actors, both male and female, from the London stage. Theatre-going became fashionable – a development which of course failed to dent its raffish reputation among the city's 'unco guid' (those who profess a strict morality).

Meanwhile, across the country in the mercantile and religiously conservative city of Glasgow, theatre was enduring its own troublesome birth. Its first playhouse, a wooden booth erected against the wall of the Bishop's Palace to accommodate a company on tour from London, was burned down in 1754 by a mob whipped to frenzy by the preaching of a fanatical Methodist minister, George Whitefield.

Taking their cue from London's siting of the earlier Globe, the next promoters built outside the city boundary at Alston Street in the village of Grahamston, where Glasgow Central Station now stands. On the opening night in 1764 another arson attack on 'the Devil's house' was prevented, but the interior was trashed by furious sectarians. After repairs, the Alston Street Theatre re-opened and survived until 1780, so it must have been in this theatre that a star-struck teenager, on a group outing from her Glasgow boarding school, had the enthralling experience that would change her life.

Joanna Baillie was born in 1762 in Bothwell, Lanarkshire, the youngest child of the parish minister, the Rev. James Baillie and his wife Dorothea Hunter. Her twin sister had died at birth, and she grew up with her sister Agnes and brother Matthew (1761–1823), who would later follow his maternal uncles, the celebrated physicians and anatomists William (1718–83) and John Hunter (1728–93) into a distinguished medical career. Most of what is known of Joanna Baillie's early years is contained in two *Memoirs* she wrote in old age, one at the instigation of her friend Mary Berry (1763–1852) and the other of her nephew, Matthew Baillie's son William. By her own account, Joanna was a late developer, an idle child who enjoyed running through the manse garden and paddling in the Clyde, and liked listening to stories better than trying to read them. Her parents were provoked by her indifference, but it was not until she was about to go to boarding school and feared loss of face among her companions, that she suddenly learned to read – but not to spell, as proved by her unorthodox orthography in later life.

Unlike many clever girls who found the genteel boarding schools of the period, with their emphasis on deportment, needlework and smatterings of music and French, a waste of time, Joanna Baillie seems to have been happy enough at Miss Macdonald's school, where she made friends for whom she invented bedtime stories, and enjoyed music and drawing. But it seems certain that her visit to the theatre (perhaps a rather progressive choice of treat for young teenagers on Miss Macdonald's part, given the indecorous reputation of the stage) was a highlight of her time there. The part of the programme which most appealed to the girls was *Taste*, a farce by Samuel Foote (1720–77), which had first been produced at Drury Lane in 1753. Satirising a contemporary craze for antiquities and the gullibility of *nouveau riches* collectors, the play features Lady Penwheezle, an alderman's wife from Blowbladder Street with more money than wits, and the attempts of con men Puff and Brush to swindle her. So amused were the young ladies by this burlesque that on their return to school, they asked and received permission to re-enact it. Awarded the starring role of Lady Penwheezle, Joanna Baillie appeared in front of Miss Macdonald's friends 'dressed in a wide hoop and paper lappets and ruffles of my own cutting out', and was greeted with a gratifying roar of laughter. So this normally shy girl was drawn imaginatively into a world of plays and performance, further enhanced by acquaintance with *Bell's British Theatre*, a vast illustrated com-pendium of plays and theatrical illustrations, which she read in the library of a friend. She wrote a tragedy in her spare time, began to read Shakespeare and Mil-ton, and to develop the intellectual interests which had been so conspicuously absent from her childhood.

Not long after Joanna left school, her father was appointed Professor of Divin-ity at the University of Glasgow, and moved with his wife and daughters into a house in the College precincts. Joanna now had the opportunity to make several more visits to the theatre, courtesy of a fellow-enthusiast, her neighbour Professor John Millar; she read widely in English and French drama and began to write, mostly ballads and songs which circulated in her private circle. This pleasant urban life was shattered by the sudden death in 1788 of Professor Baillie. Obliged to leave their College residence, his widow and daughters found shelter at Long Calderwood, a family-owned estate near East Kilbride. They had little money and might have rus-ticated indefinitely, had not Dorothea's brother William Hunter died in 1783, leaving to his nephew Matthew his London house, with a room full of antiquities and medical artefacts; these later provided the nucleus of the collection in the Hun-terian Museum at the University of Glasgow. Since Matthew was unmarried, it was natural that his mother should keep house for him, so Dorothea Baillie and her daughters exchanged the rural seclusion of Long Calderwood for the city clamour of Windmill Street, a stone's throw from London's grimy Tottenham Court Road.

It was not an easy transition and Joanna, contrasting the view of dirty facades across the street with the winter beauty of Long Calderwood, set herself to write a long, nostalgic blank verse poem, 'Winter Day', extolling the countryside left behind. She added rather endearingly in her *Memoirs* that 'I would much rather have written in rhime [*sic*]; only rhimes with me in those days were not easily found and I had not industry enough to toil for them.' Nonetheless, her first pub-lished work was a poetry collection, and *Poems: Wherein it is Attempted to Describe Certain Views of Nature and of Rustic Manners* (1790) shows a deft control of verse forms. Published anonymously, it was not a commercial success, and Joanna turned her attention back to drama, completing a tragedy, *Arnold*, which was never published and has since disappeared.

In 1791, Matthew Baillie married and, his career established, moved to Gros-venor Street in fashionable Mayfair. Dorothea Hunter and her daughters, after a few temporary stops, found a house to suit them in Colchester, fifty miles north of London on the Essex coast. It was here that Joanna, while sitting sewing in the garden with her mother, conceived the idea of writing the *Plays on the Passions* which would make her famous in her own lifetime. These were to 'attempt to delin-eate the stronger passions of the mind – each passion being the subject of a tragedy and a comedy'. The first volume was, with the encouragement of her brother

1. Elizabeth Hamilton, *c.*1812
(1756–1816)
Writer and educationalist
by Henry Raeburn

NATIONAL GALLERIES SCOTLAND, PG 1486

2. Mary Brunton
(1778–1818)
EMMELINE, (1919)

3. Susan Edmonstone Ferrier
(1782–1854)

ROBERT THORBURN, WIKIMEDIA COMMONS

4. Christian Isobel Johnstone
(1781–1857)
Memorial at Grange Cemetery, Edinburgh.
MARK BLACKADDER

5. Margaret Wilson Oliphant
(1828–97)
*THE VICTORIAN AGE OF ENGLISH
LITERATURE* (1899)

6. Jane Welsh Carlyle
(1801–66)

*JANE WELSH CARLYLE LETTERS TO HER FAMILY,
1839–1863,* LEONARD HUXLEY (ED.) (1924)

7. Lydia Miller
(1811–76)
Lydia, Hugh Miller's Wife by William Kay.
© NATIONAL TRUST FOR SCOTLAND

8. Janet Hamilton
(1795–1873)

The Langloan Poetess
by Joseph Wright Esq.

© NORTH LANARKSHIRE
COUNCIL MUSEUMS

9. Marion Bernstein
(1846–1906)

MIRREN'S MUSINGS (1876)

10. Anne Grant
of Laggan
(1755–1838)

WIKIMEDIA COMMONS

11

12

J Baillie

11. Elizabeth Grant
of Rothiemurchus
(1797–1885)

*MEMOIRS OF A
HIGHLAND LADY (1911)*

12. Joanna Baillie
(1762–1851)

*THE DRAMATIC AND
POETICAL WORKS OF
JOANNA BAILLIE (1851)*

13. Eliza Fletcher
(1770–1858)

*AUTOBIOGRAPHY OF
MRS. FLETCHER: WITH
LETTERS AND OTHER
FAMILY MEMORIALS
(1875)*

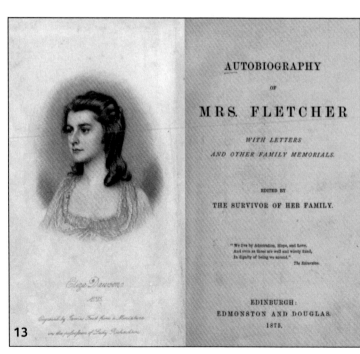

13

14. Mary Somerville
(1780–1872)

SOMERVILLE COLLEGE,
UNIVERSITY OF OXFORD

15. Elizabeth Isabelle
Spence
(1768–1832)

LA BELLE ASSEMBLEE (1824)

Yours very truly
Constance F.ᵏᵃ Gordon Cumming

19. Lady Florence Dixie
(1855–1905)

GLORIANA (1890)

20. Christina Keith
(1889–1963)

At her graduation in 1910.

COURTESY OF FLORA JOHNSTON

21. Violet Jacob
(1863–1946)

HENRY HARRIS BROWN,
WIKIMEDIA COMMONS

THEATRE-ROYAL, EDINBURGH.

For the Benefit of
Mr CALCRAFT.

This present Evening, MONDAY, May 29. 1820,
Will be performed, *for the First Time*, a Tragedy, called,

CONSTANTINE PALÆOLOGU
OR
The Last of the CÆSARS.

With appropriate Scenery, Machinery, Dresses, and Decorations.
Written by Miss JOANNA BAILLIE,
And adapted for Theatrical Representation at the Theatre Royal, Edinburgh.

Constantine Palæologus, Emperor of the Greeks, by Mr COOPER,
Justiniani by Mr J. FARREN—Othus by Mr GRAY—Hugo, for this Night only, by Mr MACKAY,
Rodrigo, a Genoese Naval Commander, by Mr CALCRAFT.
Petronius by Mr ANDERSON—Marthon by Mr BELL—Phocas by Mr M'GREGOR,
Othoric, the Hungarian, for this Night only, by Mr DUFF,
Mahomet II. the Turkish Sultan, by Mr ALEXANDER—Osmir by Mr DUFF,
Greek and Turkish Soldiers by Messrs Armitage, Bramley, Chartres, Drewry, Eames, Fawdington, Goodwin, Hayley, Jac
Field, Aylesford, Brodie, Dunstable, Eckles, Fotheringham, Gesmer, Henry, Irvine, Kerry, Larder, Merry, Norfolk,
Guards by Messrs Zeigler, Yester, Lawrie, Upton, Trimmer, Salford, Riccardson, Quin, Paterson, Ord, Naamyds, Manders
Prescott, Richards, Grimwood, Goddard, Hurst, Hawthorn, Hubbard, Isaacs, Irvine, Jacobs, Johnston, Keeling, Leybu
The Empress Valeria by Mrs H. SIDDONS,
Ella, for this Night only, by Miss ROCK—Lucia by Miss STANFIELD.

A FAVOURITE PAS SEUL BY MISS
After which, a favourite INTERLUDE called,

Where shall I D
Sponge, First Time, by Mr JONES
Grumpy by Mr MACKAY—Dick Discount by Mr GRAY—Squire Flint by Mr ANDERSON
Farewell by Mr J. FARREN—Diggory by Mr ALEXANDER—Bailiffs by Mr HAZLETO
Mrs Grumpy by Mrs NICOL—Dorothea by Miss NICOL—Mrs Discount by Mrs EYRE—De

To conclude with the celebrated Farce of The

Budget of

To-Morrow, th

On Wednesday

On Thursday
On Friday, the
On Saturday,

TALES OF THE PUNJAB
F.A. STEEL
ILLUSTRATED BY J.L. KIPLING
Macmillan & Co.

"CARE OF THE BRITISH ARMY"
by
A Fool in France.
BEHIND THE LINE

"To the nicest of all the pippins
Who sleeps near La Bassee."

Written down at the time - 1918/1919 by CHRISTINA KEITH, autho
The Castle of May. The Russet Coat and The Author of Waverley

"One little hour, how swift it flies
"When poppies flare and lilies smile;
"How soon the fleeting minute dies,
"Leaving us but a little while
"To dream our dream, to sing our song,
"To pick the fruit, to pluck the flower.
"The Gods – they do not give us long.
"One little hour."

THE
LAND BEYOND THE FOREST
FACTS, FIGURES, AND FANCIES
FROM TRANSYLVANIA

BY
E. GERARD

IN TWO VOLUMES-VOL I

WILLIAM BLACKWOOD AND SONS
EDINBURGH AND LONDON
MDCCCLXXXVIII

Korea: Isabella Bird

Matthew and his friend, the eminent scholar and philosopher Archibald Alison (1757–1859) published in 1798 – at the author's own expense. It contained *Basil*, a tragedy on love, and what became the most famous of the plays, *De Monfort*, a tragedy on hatred. It also contained a confident and well-considered preface, in which the author, promising more to come, stated her intention to provide 'a complete exhibition of passion; with its varieties and progress in the breast of man'. Promoted among the London *literati* by Alison, who had a wide circle of acquaintances, the plays at first provoked curiosity as to their authorship, with most readers assuming that they must be written by a man. It is said that only the unusually large number of women's parts aroused the suspicion that they might, however improbably, be a woman's work. Two editions were published anonymously; the third, in 1800, with her name on the title page, led first to correspondence, then to warm friendship with Sir Walter Scott.

One of those who had been intrigued by the question of the author's identity was Mary Berry, a socialite and minor writer who enjoyed a number of literary friendships, most famously with the Gothic novelist Horace Walpole (1717–97). Claiming to have sat up all night in her evening dress reading *Plays on the Passions*, in 1800 she brought the tragedy *De Monfort* to the attention of John Philip Kemble (1757–1823), the distinguished actor-manager of the Theatre Royal, Drury Lane. *De Monford* tells the story of the resentment, originating in a childhood quarrel, between two aristocratic gentlemen, De Monford and Rezenvelt, which is rekindled by a chance meeting in adulthood. When De Monford is joined by his beautiful sister Jane, his simmering dislike of Rezenfelt is inflamed by suspicion that his enemy plans to marry Jane. Maddened by rage, he pursues Rezenfelt into a wood where he murders him and, when arrested, dies of remorse before he can be brought to trial. Reduced to its plot line, it is hard to see what attracted Kemble, other than the poetic intensity of the language which supports it, but he seems to have found enough dramatic potential in De Montford's incremental fury to bring the play to the stage. A lavish production was mounted with Kemble himself in the title role, playing opposite his equally illustrious sister Sarah Siddons (1755–1831).

This surely was the opportunity that any aspiring dramatist might have dreamed of, but theatrically *De Monfort* was not a success, playing to sparse audiences for only 13 performances. Kemble not unnaturally received coldly suggestions of further productions of Baillie's plays, and most of them, though well received by readers, remained unstaged. A notable exception was a production, under the auspices of Sir Walter Scott, at Edinburgh's Theatre Royal in 1810, when in Scotland the popularity of the 'National Drama' was on the rise. This movement, which would gather pace with dramatisations of Scott's 'Waverley Novels', aimed to invigorate the Scottish stage by bringing plays with Scottish themes, and by Scottish authors, to the attention of the theatre-going public. One of Joanna Baillie's plays, *The Family Legend*, fitted this scheme perfectly, and Scott, who loved the theatre, undertook to produce it, boasting: 'The piece [was] entirely of Scotch manufacture.' There were frustrations in the production, especially the delay of the opening night when the leading lady and manager's wife Mrs Harriet Siddons developed a 'cruel inflammation and swelling of the eyes' – but on 29 January 1810 the show did go on. The verse drama, founded on a fifteenth-century Highland legend of a feud between the Lord of Argyle and the Chieftain of Maclean, featured dynastic marriage, threatened infanticide, murder, clan pride, jealousy and revenge; the stage was awash with tartan and the audience, swelled on the first night by the nineteenth-century equivalent of bus parties from Glasgow, was wildly enthusiastic, responding with 'thunder of applause, with cheering and throwing up hats and handkerchiefs'. In a letter to 'Miss Baillie' dated 30 January 1810, a delighted Scott, with his customary genial desire to make his friends happy, reported:

> You have only to imagine all that you could wish to give complete success to a play, and your conception will still fall short of the complete and decided triumph of "The Family Legend". Everything that pretended to distinction, whether from rank or literature, was in the boxes; and in the pit such an aggregate mass of humanity as I have seldom, if ever, witnessed in the same place.

No doubt Miss Baillie was gratified by this account, but one might wonder why she, who was neither very old nor averse to travel, was not in the theatre to witness for herself the triumphant scene. Although her letters reveal her annoyance with critics who dubbed her plays 'closet dramas' (plays suitable for reading), indignation at accusations of lack of stagecraft and the conviction that she was discriminated against because she was a woman – 'John Any-body would have stood higher with the critics than Joanna Baillie', she remarked sourly to Scott – she was keenly ambitious to have her plays performed in the public theatres. What she perhaps did not realise was that her own retiring personality worked against this aspiration. John Kemble has been blamed for failing to explain to her points of stagecraft which might have improved the production of *De Monford* in 1800, but in truth he had little opportunity. Although, according to his biographer and friend James Boaden (1762–1834), he made some trifling alterations, they were not made with the co-operation of the author. She refused to attend rehearsals, turned up reluctantly at first-night performances and, particularly in her early career, could prove intractable when producers, experienced in the practicalities of stagecraft as she was not, suggested changes to the script. Her passion for the theatre was unquestionable and her writing on the subject formidable, but she remained, to her cost, a Scottish minister's daughter. Fastidious and shy of the dissolute ambience of the Regency stage, she was not a theatrical type.

Over the years, however, a few productions of her plays did take place. The reasonable success of *The Family Legend* encouraged the manager of the Edinburgh Theatre Royal, Henry Siddons (1774–1815) to revive *De Monfort*, and the play was also given a second chance at Drury Lane in 1821, with the great Edmund Kean (1789–1833) in the title role. Meanwhile, *Constantine Paleologus*, a drama rejected by Kemble in 1804, had a late flowering. Featuring the last Byzantine Emperor Constantine XI, who died in the Fall of Constantinople to the Turks in 1453, it was adapted as a melodrama, *Constantine and Valeria*, in 1820 at the Surrey Theatre, before going on tour in its original form as a tragedy to Liverpool, Dublin and Edinburgh. There Joanna Baillie, on her last visit to Scotland, overcame her shyness and attended a performance at the Theatre Royal. The evening was a great success, according to an Irish reviewer who wrote: 'The house was crowded, the audience liberal in applause and the authoress delighted.' It is also on record that *De Monfort*, *The Family Legend* and *Constantine Paleologus* were produced at the Park Theatre in New York.

In 1791, Joanna Baillie moved with her mother and sister Agnes from Colchester to the north London suburb of Hampstead. At first they lived at Red Lion Hill and, some time after Dorothea Baillie's death in 1806, the sisters moved to a substantial red-brick terraced house in Windmill Hill, which was to be their home for the rest of their long lives. Whatever the setbacks she suffered in the stage productions of her plays, their publication was enough to make their author a respected figure in 'Romantic' circles, and she was quickly drawn into London's literary society. Sir Walter Scott, William Wordsworth (1770–1850) and Lord Byron (1788–1824) paid visits, the poet Samuel Rogers (1763–1855) and actor Daniel Terry (*c.*1780–1829) were often in her house. The American novelist James Fenimore Cooper (1789–1851), spending a 'poetic morning' in London, called in, and a regular visitor in later years was the 'Arch-critic' Francis Jeffrey, reconciled at last after a long stand-off caused by his savaging of Joanna's early work in the *Edinburgh Review*.

It was, however, her long-lasting, mutually supportive friendships with other women that most clearly underscored the quiet feminism displayed in her work. Mary Berry, Anne Grant of Laggan and Elizabeth Hamilton were devoted to her, as were the Irish novelist Maria Edgeworth and the journalist and critic Harriet Martineau (1802–76). The mathematician Mary Somerville (*see* chapter 13), called her 'Joanna, my dear and valued friend to the end of her life'. The only person who seems, comically, to have demurred from this appreciation was 18-year-old Jane Fletcher who, sent by her mother Grace (*see* p. 92) in 1815 from Edinburgh to London to stay with the poet Anna Laetitia Barbauld (1743–1825), spent a night or two en route at Hampstead with Agnes and Joanna Baillie. Writing from Stoke Newington in July 1815, Jane confessed to her mother that meeting Joanna a second time at Mrs Barbauld's:

The dreadful fear I had of Mrs [sic] *Joanna Baillie, the hopelessness of pleasing her ... gave a feeling of constraint which I hoped I had got over, but which, whenever I saw her composed figure enter the room, returned with painful force.*

There is indeed a steeliness in the serene yet formidable portraits of Scott's 'Immortal Joanna', whom he enthusiastically if daftly compared to Shakespeare, which makes this reaction in a younger woman understandable.

Having told Scott in 1812 that she was 'getting her knitting needles in order', Joanna Baillie changed her mind about retirement and went on writing. She composed new plays and republished old ones, but drama was never the only component of her literary oeuvre. In 1821, inspired by Scott's 'heroic' ballads, she published *Metrical Legends of Exalted Characters*, which included poems on the Scottish patriot Sir William Wallace and Lady Grisell Baillie, from both of whom she claimed descent. In 1823, to help a friend in financial trouble, she edited *A Collection of Poems* by living authors which included work of her own, and in 1836 attempted to reassert her significance as a dramatist with a three-volume edition of *Miscellaneous Plays*. Her last collection of poetry, *Fugitive Verses* (1840) drew together poems that had been published without attribution in magazines and anthologies. Many of these were lyrics in Scots she had written at the behest of George Thomson, and were published by him in *Thomson's Collection of the Songs of Burns, Sir Walter Scott, Bart. and Other Eminent Lyric Poets* (1822–25). Her final volume of poetry, *Ahalya Baee: A Poem* (1849) was based on the career of Ahilya Bai Holkar, female ruler from 1767 to 1794 of Indore in the Indian state of Madhya Pradesh. Printed for private circulation, it was published in 1904.

Joanna Baillie spent most of her long life in the south-east of England, and although she and her sister travelled quite widely in Europe, her visits to her native country were few. But in the comfortably British nineteenth century, when political nationalism was dormant, her place of residence did not define her identity. Although described to this day in England as 'an English poet', the enthusiastic reception of *A Family Legend* in Edinburgh shows that Scots readily accepted her as a Scottish writer. Like those other famous expatriates, Margaret Oliphant, Thomas and Jane Carlyle and Robert Louis Stevenson, she was proud of her Scottish heritage, retained her Scottish accent and quietly believed in the moral superiority of the Scots. It is tempting, however, to wonder whether her ready assumption of Britishness, and her desire to model her dramatic style on Classical and English forms, were not at the expense of a more vigorously Scottish, and arguably more durable reputation. Her shorter poems, and the lyrics she contributed to George Thomson's song collections, show her at ease with the flexible Scots of her childhood. In a farmhouse kitchen on an eighteenth-century wedding day:

It fell on a morning when we were thrang,
  Our kirn was gaun, our cheese was makin' …
Veal florentines in the oon baken
  Weel plenish'd wi' raisins an' fat;
Beef, mutton an' chuckies are taken
  Het reekin' frae spit an' frae pat.

In chillier mood, a shepherd haunts the 'trysting bush', marking its lengthening shadow as he pines for his dead lover:

My sheep-bell tinkles frae the west
  My lambs are bleatin' near;
But still the sound that I lo'e best,
  Alack, I canna hear!
Oh no! Sad and slow!
  The shadow lingers still,
And like a lanely ghaist I stand
  And croon upon the hill.

Whether she wrote in Scots or English, Joanna Baillie's version of pastoral was fashioned by her early years in the Lanarkshire countryside.

There is no disputing the high regard which Joanna Baillie enjoyed in her own lifetime. In a letter of 1846, Elizabeth Barrett Browning, who by then might have claimed the accolade for herself, described her as 'the first female poet of all the senses in England'. Yet despite her stellar reputation, after her death in 1851 Scott's prophecy of her 'immortality' quickly proved unfounded and, half a century later, she had disappeared almost completely from literary discourse. The moral emphasis of her plays seemed heavy-handed in the age of J. M. Barrie (1860–1937) and Oscar Wilde (1854–1900), and even in Scotland her poetry was rarely anthologised. In the twentieth century she received only a cursory mention in Kurt Wittig's magisterial *The Scottish Tradition in Literature* (1958), and she has no entry *The Oxford Companion to the Theatre* (1972).

Only since the 1990s, carried along by the desire to celebrate Scottish women's writing, has there been, in academic circles at least, renewed interest in her work. There have even been a few modest attempts to bring *De Monford* to the stage, though in studio theatres where the limited seating capacity reflects a realistic expectation of attendance. Scholarly enthusiasm, however, has been slow to trickle down to the general reader, with whom *Plays on the Passions*, with their one-dimensional heroes and anglicised blank verse, unsurprisingly fail to resonate. In recent years only *Witchcraft* (1836), a late play with a Scottish setting, has received some belated attention. In 2008, it was staged, and well reviewed, at London's Finsbury Theatre, and in Canada in 2011 was the subject of an extensive study, culminating in performance, at Concordia University in Montreal.

Aside from *The Family Legend*, there is little evidence that Scottish history and culture were major influences on Joanna Baillie's dramatic imagination. Only in *Witchcraft*, written in old age, did her mind revert to the darkest and most traumatic period of her nation's past. It seems that the theme was initially suggested by an incident in Scott's Gothic novel *The Bride of Lammermoor* (1818), and she may also have been influenced by his *Letters on Demonology and Witchcraft* (1830). But the play's main inspiration was certainly a dark and psychologically disturbing incident which took place not far from her childhood home in the west of Scotland. This was the notorious witch trial in Paisley in 1697, when the 'evidence' of a hysterical and possibly vengeful child, along with the ignorance and credulity of her elders, led to the last mass execution for witchcraft in Europe. The action, which loosely follows the same course of events, transcends indifferent stagecraft and the resort to a *deus ex machina* resolution through its other merits; powerful roles for women, a fine indignation at the victimisation of the poor and unattractive, contempt for the superstition which fuelled cruelty in a culture of fear, and the elusive nature of the Devil. Scott, in grouchy mood, told Baillie that she should write the play in verse, but mercifully his advice was ignored. For the reason why *Witchcraft* lives in a way that the *Plays on the Passions* never do is that Baillie chose to write it in prose, fitting theme and setting to the familiar intonations of everyday Scots speech. It is hard not to wish that she had written more often in this vein, or to think that a Scottish performance is long overdue.

Joanna Baillie, still writing, entertaining guests and revered for her charitable generosity, died in 1851, aged 89, in the Hampstead house where she had lived for more than thirty years. She and her sister Agnes, who died eight years later aged one hundred, were buried with their mother in St-John-at-Hampstead Churchyard. On 11 September 2018 Joanna was celebrated with a Google Doodle on what would have been her 256 birthday [google.com/doodles/joanna-baillies-256th-birthday].

12

TELLING
MY STORY

We also met a fine specimen of the noble, intelligent Scotswoman, such as Walter Scott and Burns knew how to prize. Seventy-six years have passed over her head, only to prove the truth of my theory, that we need never grow old. She was "brought up" in the animated and intellectual circle of Edinburgh, in youth an apt disciple, in her prime a bright ornament of that society.

Margaret Fuller Ossoli (1810–50)
Journal entry for 27 August 1846, *At Home and Abroad,* 1856

IN OUR OWN time, in Scotland as elsewhere, the last survivors of the Holocaust and the twentieth-century wars are passing into history. This inevitability has fuelled an increased public awareness of how technological advance has made obsolete the life patterns of even more recent generations, in turn intensifying an eagerness to capture, in their own words, the experiences of the old in a world soon to be beyond memory. This project has been driven less by professional historians than by ordinary people, who have encouraged their parents and grandparents to put on record their recollections of their youth. Some of these have found their way into print, but most have been compiled in the first instance for the interest of their descendants, who thus become guardians of their past. That such narratives, transcending status and class, can exist is of course due to universal literacy and new technology, enabling an inclusive people's history for the first time.

In past centuries, the privilege of recorded reminiscence was, as with every other form of writing, largely the preserve of the educated classes, ensuring that most memoirs were by men. Nonetheless, in Scotland during the years between the second Jacobite Rising in 1745–46 and the end of the nineteenth century – the period during which the majority of the women featured in this book were born, lived and died – a considerable number of women, not all from privileged backgrounds, recorded their recollections, particularly of their childhood. A few were intent on publication, but more wrote at the urging of their children. Few had in mind a readership beyond their intimate circle, and it was usually the next generation who, like Elizabeth Grant's niece Jane Maria Strachey, saw the pecuniary advantage in going public.

Interestingly, women novelists in the nineteenth century seem to have felt less compulsion to write at length about their early years than those who wrote non-fiction; perhaps they found the stories they invented more interesting than their own. Elizabeth Hamilton wrote only a short 'biographical fragment' chiefly concerned with her family's pedigree, which was incorporated into *Memoirs of the late Mrs Hamilton* (1818) by Elizabeth Benger (1775–1827). What we know of Mary Brunton's early life we owe to a posthumous *Memoir* written by her husband. Any information about the youth of Susan Ferrier, a notoriously private woman, has to be gleaned from her letters, a brief memoir she wrote of her father and occasional remarks in the recollections of other people. Margaret Oliphant wrote luminously in her fragmentary *Autobiography* about her first years in Lasswade, but her account of her later childhood and adolescence was sketchier, as if she was anxious to get on to a more interesting part of her life.

Among non-fiction writers, the contexts in which they framed their early experiences varied. Although Anne Grant of Laggan did once attempt a conventional autobiography, she abandoned it in 1807; the better known account of her childhood in America is encased in a memoir ostensibly of someone else. Janet Hamilton wrote, sometimes lyrically, in verse and prose about her upbringing in rural Langloan, but her true adult theme was the contrast between the perceived merits of a clean, God-fearing, agrarian Scotland and what she saw as its pollution and social corruption by the encroachment of heavy industry. Jane Welsh Carlyle wrote into letters her poignant memories of her youth in Haddington, which she came to regard as a sunlit period of her life. Elizabeth Grant's account of her girlhood at Rothiemurchus and elsewhere was a one-off and not, as readers may have hoped, the first volume of a full autobiography. Instead our knowledge of the remainder of her long, active life is derived from the less formal journals she kept during her Irish years.

It seems from the sprightliness of their childhood recollections that all of these women enjoyed writing them, but it seems too that most were too busy in their adult lives, too preoccupied with juggling the writing of novels, plays, travelogues, diaries and letters with the demands of housekeeping and child-rearing, to feel attracted to the idea of a full-scale autobiography. Yet there were a few who, conscious that their experiences had been peculiarly interesting, and with more leisure towards the end of long lives, yielded to family pressure and set themselves a final task of recording them.

The 'noble and intelligent Scotswoman' whom the American feminist writer Margaret Fuller (1820–50) sought out in the Lake District in 1847 was not really a Scotswoman at all, though it is generally agreed that her 37 years' residence in Edinburgh, her charity work in the city and her sympathy with Scotland's struggle in the 1820s and 30s for political reform, qualify her for the status of 'honorary Scot'. By

1847, she had been widowed and living in England for almost twenty years, although her numerous friendships in Edinburgh drew her back, sometimes for months at a time. It seems likely that in 1846 she and her new acquaintance at Ambleside in the Lake District found interests in common; the recently married Margaret Fuller, who tragically did not live to test her theory 'that we need never grow old', was an ardent reformer and champion of women's rights, while the 'intelligent Scotswoman' had also been a fervent young radical in her time.

Eliza Fletcher née Dawson (1770–1858) was born at Oxton, near Tadcaster in Yorkshire, where her father, Miles Dawson, was a land surveyor and owner of a small estate. Her mother died a few days after giving birth, and Eliza was cared for by her father and grandmother, with an assembly of aunts and neighbours happy, by all accounts, to look after an unusually beautiful and good-natured child. Aged eleven, she was sent to the Manor School in York, an establishment of which, like the majority of intelligent boarding-school-educated girls of her time, she had little good to say.

> It was a place where nothing useful could be learned, but it did me some service, because I had something to unlearn. It taught me that all my reading was not to be compared with the graces that other girls had acquired at the dancing school, and my rusticity subjected me to many wholesome mortifications.

These wry observations from her posthumously published *Autobiography* (written, of course, in response to chivvying by her daughters) were only an opening salvo; Eliza went on to describe the headmistress as 'a very well-disposed, conscientious old gentlewoman, but of limited understanding', who seemed blind to the marginally depraved behaviour of some of her pupils. Her husband, who acted as school chaplain, was 'a choleric old man' who 'thumped our fingers so often for bad writing, with his mahogany ferrule, that we listened to his prayers with any feelings other than love and devotion'. Eliza Dawson was throughout life a deeply religious woman but, despite endless catechising and Bible reading, she '[did] not remember to have received a single religious impression at this school'.

The four years she spent there were not, however, entirely futile. Despite the damning observation that 'four volumes of the *Spectator* constituted our whole school library', Eliza and other resourceful girls found ways to smuggle in books and hold 'little reading parties', helping her to develop a taste for literature. And perhaps most importantly, she found in herself the gift for making and keeping friends that would prove her most endearing characteristic in the years ahead.

When Eliza left school in 1785, a friend of her father's gave her a gift of £20, a substantial sum at the time, to 'make addition to [her] slender stock of books'. Among her first purchases were Milton's *Lesser* [*Minor*] *Poems*, and the first edition of the poems of William Cowper (1731–1800), whom she admired all her life. Her father's gift was a six-week tour of the Highlands of Scotland, during which she saw the sea for the first time, was impressed by the situation and history of Edinburgh, and found agreeable 'the frankness and urbanity of Sottish manners'. Her delight in the Highland scenery and observations on the national character and customs were jotted down, and later fashioned into a journal which her proud father kept in his bookcase. Her own view of this production, seen from the perspective of later life, was that its attempt at 'fine writing' was ludicrous, that it 'abounded in the bad taste of the time' and was no more than 'a sort of "sentimental journey"'– a genre concerned with personal taste and emotional response to landscape à la Laurence Sterne (1713–68). Which was doubtless true, but she was only 16 at the time.

For the next two years Eliza lived at home in Oxton with her father, a keen supporter of the progressive Whig party, long in opposition to the ultraconservative Tories. It was a time when, in the aftermath of British humiliation in the American War of Independence and on the threshold of the French Revolution, Radical anger over the rights of working people and the paucity of the franchise was becoming more strident and, although the notion of votes for women was at best a distant dream, Eliza eagerly absorbed her father's Radical sympathies. Though she was unaware of it at the time, this exposure to political ideas was preparing her for the most momentous event of her life.

During her Highland tour the previous year, Eliza had visited a former school friend who had married George Meliss, a Scottish Radical campaigner, and now lived in Perth. In the spring of 1787, Meliss was appointed to travel to London, to plead before Parliament for the reform of the notoriously corrupt and unrepresentative Burgh Councils which passed for local government at the time. Since his journey would take him close to Oxton, his wife decided to pay a return visit to Eliza. Travelling with them, in support of George Meliss, was Edinburgh Advocate Archibald Fletcher (1746–1828) and all three spent a couple of days with the Dawsons before the men rode on to London. It does not appear that 41-year-old Archibald Fletcher made any great impression on 17-year-old Eliza, but she certainly made an impression on him. Comparing her to Sophia Western, the beautiful and virtuous heroine of Henry Fielding's novel *Tom Jones*, he sent her a copy of the 'Ossian' poems and struck up a correspondence, sensibly confining himself for the moment to literary topics. Meanwhile Eliza went on a visit to Ripon where, to her father's satisfaction but not to her own, she acquired another much older admirer, the second Lord Grantley. It is not entirely clear how a literary correspondence turned into a mutual declaration of love, but Archibald Fletcher made further visits to Oxton and, because Eliza scorned deceit, her father became irately aware of her desire to marry him. Perhaps surprisingly, Miles Dawson's objection was not to the 24-years discrepancy in the couple's ages; he had actually hoped Eliza would marry

Lord Grantley, who was nearly fifty. The formerly dutiful daughter, however, proved obstinate, and, on 16 July 1791, married the Radical Scottish advocate at Tadcaster, while her father sulked at home. Half a century later, Eliza recalled in her *Autobiography* the sorrow she felt as she left her former life behind, and, in a few self-revealing lines, the speed with which she got over it:

> *The pang of parting with my father and all my family had almost broken my heart, but I was not of a morbid temperament. Youth and hope, and affectionate confidence in my husband soon reconciled me to the separation. I was received by Mr Fletcher's circle of friends in Edinburgh with a warmth of hospitality and kindness I had never before met with among strangers.*

Her affectionate confidence was not misplaced. The difference in age troubled neither husband nor wife; the Fletchers were harmoniously married for 37 years, and had six children. Initially they suffered financial hardship, due to distaste in Tory-leaning Edinburgh for Whig advocates who supported burgh and parliamentary reform and admired the French Revolution; indeed both husband and wife were regarded by many conservatives as alarming incendiaries. The subsequent 'Reign of Terror' in France, however, induced Fletcher to tone down his views, and though both he and Eliza remained staunch Whigs, legal briefs became more plentiful. Thereafter Eliza was reconciled with her father, who in 1794 bought them a fine house, 20 Queen Street and, dying in 1798, left Eliza the life-rent of his Yorkshire estate. There was money for servants, governesses, travel and hospitality, and as the eighteenth century slipped into the nineteenth, Eliza Fletcher's beauty, intelligence and sociability placed her among the most popular residents of the New Town of Edinburgh. And because she was well-read and eagerly admiring of the authors who frequented that small and distinguished enclave, she acquired the status of a 'literary lady'; educationists sought her opinions, young writers asked her advice, and she became a respected figure among those who wrote more and better than she did herself.

In 1804, when the Fletchers with their six children outgrew 20 Queen Street, another substantial bequest to Eliza from a friend of her mother's enabled them to move to 51 North Castle Street, where they became neighbours of Sir Walter Scott. Eliza became friendly with Scott, despite their opposing political views; by this time she was on visiting terms with Henry Brougham, the poet Allan Cunningham (1784–1842), Henry Mackenzie, Henry Cockburn and Francis Jeffrey. She knew the Poet Laureate Robert Southey (1773–1843) and the East Anglian poet George Crabbe (1754–1832), who turned up in Edinburgh in the middle of George IV's famous visit in 1822. But it was her friendships with women writers which were notable, mutually supportive and kind.

Among those who, in 1791, had welcomed Eliza to Edinburgh with 'a warmth of hospitality and kindness' were novelists Elizabeth Hamilton and Mary Brunton, childless women who enjoyed the affection of the Fletchers' four daughters, Bessy, Grace, Margaret and Mary. In 1811, Eliza extended the same welcome to Anne Grant of Laggan, who wrote of the society she joined in the New Town that 'all the persons most distinguished and admired speak with a degree of respect and kindness of each other – no petty animosities or invidious diminutions, even though differing much on political and other subjects'. And even if the merciless satire of Susan Ferrier somewhat undermines this rosy picture, it is worth remarking that others wrote in the same vein. Eliza Fletcher seems not to have encountered Susan Ferrier until 1832, and the occasion was sorrowful, being shortly after the death of the Fletchers' eldest son, Miles. In the strange web of Scottish connection, Miles was married to Susan Ferrier's one-time friend Charlotte Clavering. Although their early intimacy had lapsed long since, the now middle-aged Susan expressed sympathetic interest in Charlotte's children, who were also Eliza's grandsons.

Setting a pattern for many years to come, the Fletchers frequently crossed the Border, visiting Eliza's family at Oxton and Tadcaster, and on a number of occasions travelling on to London. Here, while her husband lobbied for parliamentary reform, Eliza made new relationships, particularly with the poet Anna Laetitia Barbauld with whom, at different times, she left her daughters Bessy and Grace to experience London society. She also met Joanna Baillie and her sister Agnes, staying with them in Hampstead and through them becoming acquainted with Mary Berry. All of these women wrote lengthily to one another, letters which were lovingly preserved, evidence of a golden age of literary comradeship. Eliza's only reservation concerned the Irish novelist Maria Edgeworth, who visited Edinburgh in 1822, and whose bouncy familiarity mildly offended the more decorous advocate's wife.

It would have been surprising if, surrounded by so many literary women, Eliza Fletcher had not at some point tried her own hand at composition. The family always rented a house out of the city in the summer months, principally at Auchendinny near Penicuik, and for some years in the 1820s owned Hall Park, a farm on the Carse of Stirling near Balfron. It was, however, on a holiday at Callander in 1822 that Eliza found leisure to compose two 'dramatic sketches' in blank verse, titled *Elidure* and *Edward*. Both have 'historic' settings: *Elidure* is a refashioning of a Brittonic legend, in which a bad king, Artegal, is deposed in favour of his virtuous brother Elidure. When, destitute and repentant after long exile, Artegal returns to his native land, he is reunited with his brother, who nobly returns the crown to his father's firstborn. *Edward*, only slightly better grounded historically, hinges on the alleged machinations of a wicked stepmother, Queen Ælfthryth, who contrives the murder of the boy King of the English, Edward 'the Martyr' (978 AD) and the elevation of her own son Ætheldred to the throne. Possibly the inspiration for *Elidure* was

William Wordsworth's poem 'Artegal and Elidure' (1821), but when, in 1825, Eliza Fletcher was persuaded by her family to have her work privately printed and circulated among her friends, it must have been obvious how greatly it was indebted, in content and style, to Joanna Baillie. But kind Joanna wrote loyally in praise, and the letter of Anne Grant of Laggan is typical of many:

> I fear you will scarce consider it a compliment when I tell you that [the dramatic sketches] far exceeded my expectations – not that I expected less, in some respects, than I found. I looked for exalted moral feeling, purity of sentiment and the utmost purity of style, but – truth to say – I did not expect you to be so poetical, or to understand – what one might call the technical part – the management of the drama so well.

In fact, Eliza's real writing talent would emerge much later in a different form, but it is to be hoped that in 1825 her friends' loyal sentiments comforted her, since she was enduring the most stressful period of her life. Her eldest daughter Bessy had made an injudicious marriage, causing much parental anxiety. Her second daughter Grace, a much loved and gifted young woman, had died of typhus in 1817 aged only twenty, and her son Miles, still in his thirties, was ill with the tuberculosis that would kill him in 1831. Between these two tragedies, however, a more natural but deeply distressing event occurred – the death at Auchendinny House in 1828 of Archibald Fletcher, aged 82. Miles was too ill to attend his father's funeral.

Eliza was not yet sixty. She had thirty years of widowhood ahead of her, and when, in her clear-sighted way, she contemplated the future, she realised that with her children grown and only the youngest, Mary, left at home, there was nothing to keep her in Edinburgh. The house in North Castle Street was put on the market, the lease of Auchendinny House terminated, and in January 1929 – only a month after Archibald Fletcher died – Eliza and Mary left Edinburgh for Tadcaster. By early summer they were installed in a cottage at Bilton, near Rugby, their business to settle one of Eliza's grandsons into Rugby School. There Eliza met the famous headmaster, Dr Thomas Arnold and his wife Mary, the first of a new group of friends.

There is no doubt that Eliza Fletcher had loved her husband (in the months after his death she would write a warm-hearted, proud memoir of him for his grandchildren), but, as she had observed in her account of her wedding day, her temperament was not morbid, and she faced the future bravely. Yet it is clear that until very late in life, she could not settle anywhere for long. Year after year she criss-crossed the country, staying with her daughters, renting houses in Dorset, in Kent and the Lake District, visiting Paris and Switzerland, making new friends and corresponding with the old. She made visits to Edinburgh; in Manchester, she met the radical novelist Elizabeth Cleghorn Gaskell (1810–65); in London she sat at a meeting next to a disappointingly uncommunicative Thomas Carlyle. She also befriended Jane Carlyle's protegé, the Italian patriot Guiseppe Mazzini.

But even Eliza's robust constitution could not sustain an itinerant life for ever, and as she moved into her seventies the idea of a more permanent home became appealing. She had always been fond of the Lake District. Her friends the Arnolds had bought a retirement house at Fox How near Rydal, and through them she met William and Mary Wordsworth and their daughter Dora. Her own daughter Margaret and her family had settled nearby, and a house that Eliza liked had become available. In 1839, through the agency of William Wordsworth, Eliza bought Lancrigg House near Grasmere, moving in with Mary in 1840. A new circle of friends surrounded her, and only one more surprise was to come. In 1847, at the age of 45, Mary Fletcher became the third wife of the Dumfries-born naturalist and Arctic explorer Sir John Richardson (1787–1865). A naval surgeon, Sir John was then stationed at Haslar, near Portsmouth in Hampshire, so soon Eliza's carriage was rattling on the road again.

Apart from *Elidure* and *Edward*, private memoirs of her husband and daughter Grace and a few occasional poems, Eliza Fletcher had written nothing but letters until, aged 68, she sat down to write the story of her life. In an elegant, unassuming narrative, proving a gift for lucid prose, she wrote of her Yorkshire upbringing, her life with her husband and children, the causes she had espoused and the people she had known, for she had walked among giants and she knew it. It is unfortunate that when, 17 years after her death, *The Autobiography of Mrs Fletcher* was published, it was so inexpertly edited by her surviving daughter Mary Richardson, who chose to pepper her mother's narrative with personal interpolations and barely relevant letters. These distract from the flow of unclouded recollection which gives the book its unassuming charm. Eliza Fletcher witnessed history; she had seen King George IV riding though a tartan-decked Edinburgh in 1822; she had witnessed at the Cross of Edinburgh the first democratic election of Members of Parliament after the Reform Act of 1832; she had been in Lord Jeffrey's house in Moray Place and shared a 'good greet' with Lord Cockburn, as the elected members, Lord Jeffrey and James Abercromby (1776–1858), later appointed Speaker of the House of Commons, were carried home in triumph in the presence of a delighted crowd. In 1845 she had travelled on the railway from Lancaster to London, and in 1855, aged 85, led a women's group at Grasmere in sending supplies to British troops fighting in the Crimean War. Above all, she had lived to see the return of the Whigs to government, and the beginning of the political reform for which she and her husband had campaigned so valiantly.

There is a persistent but incorrect belief that Eliza Fletcher died in Edinburgh in 1858. In fact, her last visit was in 1851, when she spent some days with friends in Heriot Row. It was a bittersweet occasion, on which she visited her husband's grave in the burial ground at Calton Hill, and attended the marriage of her eldest grandson Henry, son of Miles Fletcher and Charlotte Clavering in St John's Episcopal Church. But many of her old friends were dead, and although she wrote that her 'farewell visit … was not blemished by one dark spot or painful recollection', the account has an elegiac tone. She died seemingly of little more than the debility of great age, at Lancrigg on 5 February 1858, and was buried in Grasmere Churchyard.

*

The *Autobiography* of Eliza Fletcher is the life story of a fortunate, God-fearing woman with a conscience. During her Edinburgh years, in accord with her Christian beliefs, she spent much time in the slums of the Old Town, trying to alleviate poverty and turn hopeless and criminal lives towards a better future. Of course she was not alone in this; indignation at the wrongs of the poor was a hallmark of Radical ardour and, among Eliza's literary contemporaries Christian Isobel Johnstone through her journalism, Elizabeth Grant of Rothiemurchus on her Irish estate, and Joanna Baillie through the donation of half her income to charity, shared her sense of duty to the poor. But driven by human sympathy and spiritual obligation as they were, at the end of the day these women went home to comfortable rooms, good dinners and cultured conversation; they never experienced the horror of extreme economic distress from within.

Much rarer were literate working-class women who could speak from their own experience of hardship; Janet Hamilton, publishing in John Cassell's *Working Man's Friend and Instructor* in the 1860s, was probably the most formidable of these. At the same period, however, a younger woman was emerging from an underprivileged background to whom, no less than to Hamilton, the lifestyle of Eliza Fletcher would have been the stuff of dreams. She was, however, proud of her own class and, when an opportunity arose, not averse to telling her story.

Ellen Johnston (*c.*1835–73) was a poet rescued from obscurity in the late twentieth century by scholars concerned with the history of women's writing and women's rights. Known throughout her short life as 'The Factory Girl' – an acknowledgement of her employment from an early age as a power-loom operator in the textile industry – she grew up unusually well-read and with a facility for verse. In the 1850s she began to send verses to the newspapers and periodicals established to appeal to a literate and politically involved working class, and first had a poem publihed in the *Glasgow Examiner* when she was 19. Ellen Johnston was prolific and versatile, her work exploring a complex range of topics, moods and preoccupations. Inevitably her experience of the long hours, drudgery, bullying, exhaustion, poor wages and danger of factory work is a recurring theme. In 'Lines to Edith' (a correspondent who became a friend) she wrote:

> *It is within the massive walls of factory dust and din*
>   *That I must woo my humble muse, her favour still to win …*
> *It is amidst pestiferous oil that I inhale my breath,*
>   *'Midst pond'rous shafts revolving round the atmosphere of death.*

Yet she could also celebrate moments of kindness and bonhomie; in 'Galbraith's Trip', she recalls the shared pleasure of a works outing down the Clyde from Glasgow to Rothesay:

> *… No matter where we went, we still could trace*
>   *The sweet endearments of enjoyment there:*
> *No gloomy care, with chilling breath did nip*
>   *The hearts of those that were at Gabraith's trip.*

She wrote poems of love, poems marking public events and in praise of natural beauty. Like Janet Hamilton, she published verses celebrating Queen Victoria and the Italian freedom-fighter Guiseppe Garibaldi, and railed against the Crimean War. She was predominantly an urban poet, with a mission to show the dignity of working people ensnared by a culture of greed and exploitation by the wealthy, but her verses drew pathos from a sense of nature defiled.

> *'Tis not within the fragrant vale I gather flowers,*
>   *Nor is it in the garden fair I roam through woodland bowers …*

Her style and expression are over-elaborate and hardly original, but the poet understood her readership; her sentiments chimed with their pride and working-class aspirations, their desire for self-improvement and democracy in an age of change. Relatively few of her poems were in Scots, which is a pity, because those there are show a refreshing vigour and directness:

> *It is the puir man's hard-won toil that fills the rich man's purse;*
>   *I'm sure his gowden coffers they are het wi' mony a curse:*
> *Were it no' for the working men, what wad the rich men be?*
>   *What care some gentry if they're weel, though a' the puir wad dee!*

The scarcity of Scots suggests that the poet had a wider audience in mind; certainly the ornate English she habitually used was far removed from the pithy language of the Glaswegians and Dundonians among whom she lived, and which she must have spoken herself.

Unfortunate in most of her life, Ellen Johnston had one great stroke of luck. Just as Janet Hamilton caught the attention of John Cassell, Ellen at much the same time found an enthusiastic supporter in Alexander Campbell (1796–1870), a keen socialist and advocate of women's rights who edited the Glasgow *Penny Post* between 1860 and his death a decade later. The *Penny Post* during Campbell's tenure had a circulation of around 30,000, due mainly to its Scottish emphasis and his success in making purchasers of the paper feel involved; he gave poetry prominence, and encouraged comment and correspondence between writers and readers. He and Ellen Johnston formed an enduring bond and, when there was a large enough body of her work to justify it, he found a diverse group of subscribers, including the Duke of Buccleuch, the Bishop of Brechin and many respectable middle-class worthies, willing to cover the cost of a book publication. Realising that such a volume required an introduction, Campbell suggested to Ellen that she might write a short autobiography. This presented her with an opportunity but, one supposes, also a degree of anxiety, since the truth, shorn of poetic mystique, contained elements that she had previously felt it prudent to conceal.

As far as can be ascertained, the facts were these. Ellen Johnston was born in Hamilton, Lanarkshire, probably in 1836, the daughter of stonemason James Johnston and Mary Bilsland, an 18-year-old who subsequently became a dressmaker. James Johnston, according to his daughter's account, was a poet with unfulfilled ambitions to become a teacher and to see his work published. When a spell of employment on an extension to Hamilton Palace came to an end, he decided to emigrate to America, taking his wife and seven-month-old child with him but, just as the ship was about to depart the Broomielaw, Ellen's mother, fearful that her child would die on the voyage, refused to accompany him. Living with her mother and grandparents in Bridgeton, then a rural suburb of Glasgow, Ellen had a secure childhood and some schooling, although she claims to have been a self-taught scholar, 'gifted with a considerable amount of natural knowledge for one of my years'. By the age of 13, she had read many of Sir Walter Scott's novels; other references suggest that she also read Samuel Johnson's (1709–84) *Rasselas* and *The Vicar of Wakefield* by Oliver Goldsmith (1728–74).

The years she spent reading and wandering along the banks of the Clyde were terminated by two events; news from America that her father had died there, and her mother's remarriage to a violent factory worker who subjected his stepdaughter to sexual abuse. Within a short time she had absconded more than once, attempted suicide, been beaten by her mother and forced by her brutal stepfather to work alongside him as a power-loom weaver, an occupation which would destroy her health. She got on, perhaps too well, with her male colleagues, drawing dislike and maltreatment, sometimes violent, from other women. She had an illegitimate daughter, wandered round the British Isles in search of work, settled temporarily in Belfast and Dundee and wrote poems, constructing a self-image that attracted sympathy without infringing the conventions of mid-Victorian morality. She was back in Glasgow when a dreadful piece of family news came from America. Her father, long presumed dead, was actually alive and, when informed by letter of his wife's unintended bigamy, committed suicide. Melodramatic as it sounds, there is no reason to disbelieve the outline of this appalling story.

Ellen Johnston was proud of her reputation, hard-won achievement and popularity among her readers. Magazine verse, in its brevity and selectivity, had been for her the ideal form, providing occasions to be philosopher, romantic, nature-lover, social commentator and advocate of human rights, without revealing more of her private life than she chose. Autobiography was an altogether trickier matter. Given the nature of her experience, the charming candour of middle-class Eliza Fletcher was impossible; Ellen Johnston wanted to be honest, but she also had to present a version of the truth that would not unduly disturb the more censorious readership of the *Penny Post*, shock the ultra-respectable patrons of her book, and run the risk of being contradicted in the correspondence columns by someone who remembered her from earlier times. The clue to the form she settled on may be found within the *Autobiography* itself.

Addressing the 'Gentle Reader' of her tale, she recalls: 'Before I was thirteen years of age I had read many of Sir Walter Scott's novels, and fancied I was a heroine in the modern style.' It is as a 'heroine in the modern style' that Ellen Johnston casts her story, using the device of mystery familiar from eighteenth-century 'gothic' novels she had clearly read: 'Mine were not the common trials of everyday life, but like those strange, romantic ordeals attributed to the imaginary heroines of "Inglewood Forest".' The sexual abuse by her stepfather is alluded to as 'a dark shadow, as a pall, enshroud[ing] my soul … a shadow which had haunted me like a vampire', while Victorian censoriousness of single mothers is dismissed, somewhat unconvincingly, as 'the false accusation of those who knew me as a fallen woman while I was as innocent of the charge as an unborn babe'. She had used the rhapsodic literary language of an earlier age to colour her verse; now she used it to disguise as tragic romance the reality of suffering, exploitation, and degradation in Victorian industrial life. It is a curious narrative, self-justifying and self-protective, but moving because we sense that this was the only way she could bear to deal with traumatic experience, and allow strangers into her life.

Autobiography, Poems and Songs, published in 1867, sold a creditable 800 copies, justifying a second edition in 1869. For this the author revised her autobiography, expressing gratitude for gifts of £50 from government funds administered by the Chancellor of the Exchequer and future prime minister Benjamin Disraeli (1804–81), and of £5 from Queen Victoria. She deleted references to her illegitimate child, and toned down her account of the violent spats with her spiteful female fellow-workers – suggesting that the sympathy she had hoped to arouse had not been universally forthcoming. *Autobiography, Poems and Songs* was the pinnacle of Ellen Johnston's achievement, but it was also her swan song. After the death of her mentor Archibald Campbell in 1870, her name disappeared abruptly from the pages of the *Penny Post*. As her health deteriorated and she could no longer work, there is some evidence that she lived for a time with her daughter, but must at some point have been made homeless. All that is really known is that this brave, talented woman, not yet fifty, died in Glasgow's Barony Poorhouse, a vast institution sheltering paupers and lunatics, probably in 1874. She then disappeared for a hundred years.

13

THE MOST
EXTRAORDINARY
WOMAN

Mrs Somerville is little, slightly made, fairish hair, pink colour, small, grey, round, intelligent, smiling eyes ... remarkably soft voice, strong but well-bred Scottish accent; timid, not disqualifyingly timid, but naturally modest, yet with a degree of self-possession through it which prevents her being in the least awkward, and gives her all the advantage of her understanding, at the same time that it adds a prepossessing charm to her manner and takes off all dread of her superior scientific learning.

Maria Edgeworth (1767–1849)
Letter to Sophy Ruxton 1822

AMONG THE WOMEN who, like Eliza Fletcher, frequented dinners and supper parties in early nineteenth-century Edinburgh was one described by her contemporary Sir David Brewster (1781–1868), scientist and pioneer of physical optics, as 'the most extraordinary woman in Europe – a mathematician of the very first rank ... also a great natural philosopher and mineralogist'. This is indeed how Mary Somerville (1780–1872) is best remembered; her contribution to the sciences of mathematics, geology and astronomy was awe-inspiring, the more so for the struggle she had to gain an education in a circle more concerned with female decorum than personal achievement. Even her friend David Brewster, in paying tribute to her brilliance, could not resist the patronising qualification that her genius came 'with all the gentleness of a woman'. That there was gentleness in Mary Somerville's manners is well attested, though the 'prepossessing charm' Maria Edgeworth noted in her may have been calculated to disarm. Her more intimate circle observed a sharper, wittier personality and when, late in life, she wrote her *Personal Recollections from Early Life to Old Age*, she made clear her anger at the impediments she had suffered, the extra burdens placed on a scholarly young woman by a hidebound society, including her parents whose expectations were so limited that they actively tried to undermine her.

Mary Somerville was born Mary Fairfax in the Church of Scotland manse at Jedburgh, home of her maternal aunt Martha (née Charters) and her husband Dr Thomas Somerville, parish minister and author of *My Life and Times, 1741–1814*.

Mary was the second child and only surviving daughter of Margaret Charters and William Fairfax (1739–1813), a naval officer who, until he attained the rank of Vice-Admiral, was never well off. At the family home in Burntisland Mary and her brothers were raised in a state of 'genteel poverty'; the appearance of sufficiency was maintained, but Mary's mother had to supplement her income by growing vegetables and keeping cows for milk, while her daughter, growing up, was expected to help with the household chores. These she frequently neglected, preferring to wander on the beach 'looking at the starfish and sea urchins, or watching the children digging for sand-eels, cockles and spouting razor-fish'. She collected and arranged shells, and marvelled at the leaf-patterns on blocks of limestone by the pier. Her mother taught her to read the Bible and recite the bane of pre-modern Scottish childhood, the *Shorter Catechism of the Church of Scotland*, but attempts to teach her needlework stalled. Mary showed no interest, instead bunking off to read the books in her absent father's library and provoking a visiting aunt to remark to her mother: 'I wonder that you let Mary waste her time in reading, she never shews [sews] more than if she were a man.'

Mary was 'annoyed that [her] turn for reading was so much disapproved of, and thought it was unjust that women should have been given a desire for knowledge if it were wrong to acquire it'. Sent briefly to the village school to improve her sewing skills, she observed sourly that the boys were taught Latin, but 'it was thought sufficient for the girls to be able to read the Bible; very few even learned writing'. When she was ten, in response to her father's arrival home on leave to find her 'no better than a savage', enough money was scraped together to send her for a year to a girls' boarding school in Musselburgh, where she was obliged to wear a steel corset with a rod down the spine to correct her posture; she wept a lot and learned little except rudimentary French and English grammar. Two years later she was in Edinburgh with her mother, envying her elder brother his place at the High School. She attended classes to improve her handwriting and, at the insistence of her impatient father, to learn 'the common rules of Arithmetic'. It must have been a joy to this gifted but misunderstood girl that, frustrated in an attempt to teach herself Latin, she found an ally. While on holiday in Jedburgh she confided in her uncle Thomas, who assured her that in Renaissance times many women has been excellent classical scholars, and taught her to read Virgil.

When the French Revolution kicked off in 1789, Mary Fairfax was only nine, and the long war against Napoleon was the background of her youth. When her father, against whom she seems to have felt little personal rancour despite his extreme views on education, performed courageously at the Battle of Camperdown in 1797, earning a knighthood and promotion to Vice-Admiral, she was proud of his achievement. But this did not prevent her forming political opinions in uncompromising opposition to his. Seventy years later, she wrote in her autobiography:

*Great dissentions were caused by difference of opinion in families; and I heard
people previously much esteemed accused from this cause of all that was evil … .
The unjust abuse of the Liberal party made me a liberal. From my earliest years my
mind revolted against oppression and tyranny, and I resented the injustice of the
world in denying all those privileges of education to my sex which were so
lavishly bestowed on men. My liberal opinions, both in religion and politics have
remained unchanged (or rather have advanced) throughout my life …*

Not only had she rejected the conservative views of her parents; the inflexible
Calvinism of the *Shorter Catechism* had failed to impress her, or the hellfire preaching she had to endure in Burntisland Parish Church.

In the closing years of the eighteenth century, Mary Fairfax spent time in
Edinburgh, experiencing the 'rites of passage' from adolescence to womanhood
usual among the class to which she by birth belonged. In London, conventions of
this 'coming out' were formal, the young women strictly chaperoned, but were in
Edinburgh much more relaxed: 'Girls had perfect liberty … . We walked together
in Princes Street, the fashionable promenade, and were joined by our dancing
partners'. Although shy in conversation, she enjoyed the dinners and evening
parties where she danced reels and played games, indulgently supervised by her
distant relation, the elderly Countess of Buchan. Unlike her friends, however, Mary
had another, private life. She was learning to play the piano and teach herself Greek
and, finding a puzzle in a monthly fashion magazine, was intrigued to discover
that its solution involved elementary algebra. Mathematics had not been a particular interest until this point, but that was about to change. Attending painting classes
held by the artist Alexander Nasmyth (1758–1840), she heard him recommend to
a fellow-student the work of the Greek mathematician Euclid (*c.* 300 BC) as a foundation of perspective and astronomy. Since it would have been regarded as
improper for her to visit a bookshop on her own (perhaps Edinburgh was not so
informal after all) she persuaded her brother's tutor to buy for her the two mathematical staples of her time, Euclid's *Elements* and *Introduction to Algebra* by John
Bonnycastle (1751–1821).

Now parental persecution notched up a gear. Mary rose early on freezing
Scottish mornings to paint, practise the piano and explore algebra. At night she
read Euclid into the small hours, until a clyping servant told her mother that 'it
was no wonder that the stock of candles was soon exhausted, for Miss Mary sat up
reading till a very late hour'. Immediately an order was issued to take away the
candle as soon as Miss Mary was in bed, forcing this determined scholar to lie in
the dark, working out Euclidean problems in her head. Pouncing in one of his disruptive visits home, and somehow finding out what his daughter was up to, the
Vice-Admiral roared at his wife: 'Peg, we must put a stop to this, or we shall have

Mary in a strait-jacket one of these days.' That the study of mathematics strained the female brain to the point of insanity was a common belief at the time, but Mary knew nonsense when she heard it.

In 1804, Mary Fairfax got to know her second cousin Samuel Greig (1778–1807), a naval lieutenant and son of an admiral who had been seconded as a young officer to the Russian court, to help improve the efficiency of the Imperial Navy. Now British Consul in Russia, Greig seemed an impeccable match for a Vice-Admiral's daughter and, although they insisted that Mary should not go to live in Moscow, her parents probably heaved a sigh of relief when she married him. The couple settled in London and had two children in quick succession, but the marriage was an uneasy one. Greig did not forbid his wife to study, but he made clear his disapproval of her learning trigonometry while feeding her baby since 'he possessed in full the prejudice against learned women which was common at that time'. There was little time, however, for disappointment to harden into resentment, since Greig died suddenly in 1807, while Mary was still nursing her younger son.

Aged only 27, Mary Greig came back to Edinburgh a widow, but now financially secure through inheritance and free to cultivate friendships with people who valued her intellect. She met John Playfair (1748–1819), Professor of Mathematics and Natural Philosophy at the University of Edinburgh, who introduced her to his former pupil William Wallace (1768–1843), Professor of Mathematics at the Royal Military College in Buckinghamshire. In correspondence with Wallace, Mary discussed problems set in the College's publication the *Mathematical Repository*, and won a silver medal for solving one of them. It was the first of many honours to come.

Yet for all her erudition, Mary Greig was no 'bluestocking'. Maria Edgeworth was not alone in finding her attractive, and on her own admission she loved to be fashionably dressed. She was not likely to be a widow indefinitely, and in 1812 she married her first cousin William Somerville (1771–1860), making her Jedburgh aunt and uncle also her parents-in-law. The marriage was not without its critics in the family circle; William's sister, no doubt echoing others' opinions, wrote suggesting that Mary should 'give up [her] foolish manner of life and studies, and make a respectable and useful wife to her brother'. Mary was indignant, but over the years she had to become accustomed to this attitude. When she made some jars of currant jam for a sick relative, astonishment was expressed that she could do anything so useful. (Her jam-making skill was not always unappreciated, however. When in 1825 she made a huge quantity of orange marmalade for the crews about to set out on Sir Edward Parry's (1790–1855) third Arctic voyage in search of the Northwest Passage, she was rewarded by having a small island named after her.)

In the event, her second marriage was a happy one, despite the distressing nineteenth-century loss of children – three died before reaching the age of ten. William Somerville, an Army surgeon who in 1813 was appointed Deputy Inspector of Military Hospitals in Scotland, recognised his wife's intellectual superiority and encouraged her; they studied geology together and, at the suggestion of William Wallace, Mary read the work of the French mathematician Pierre-Simon Laplace (1749–1829) which stimulated her interest in astronomy. During the four years they spent in Northumberland Street in Edinburgh, the Somervilles were part of a brilliant circle, scientific, political and literary. Mary formed an important friendship with Henry Brougham, politician and co-founder of the influential *Edinburgh Review,* and around the same time, through her parents-in-law in Jedburgh, she met and formed a warm relationship with Sir Walter Scott and his family. Visiting Abbotsford during Scott's most convivial years, she recalled: 'I shall never forget the charm of this little society … when Scott was in his highest glee, telling amusing tales, ancient legends, ghost and witch stories.' It is poignant to contrast her delight with Susan Ferrier's sombre experience twenty years later, when Scott's light was flickering and the shadows had gathered round the scene of so much joviality.

In 1816, on William Somerville's promotion to Inspector of the Army Medical Board, the family moved to Hanover Square in London, where Mary added botany and physical geography to her studies, as well as bringing up her daughters and supervising the education of her son Woronzow Grieg (1805–65). The Somervilles met William's fellow-physician Dr Matthew Baillie, who introduced them to his sister Joanna, with whom Mary enjoyed a long, supportive friendship. John Stuart Mill (1806–73), a strong advocate of women's rights, the ubiquitous Mary Berry and the Irish novelist Maria Edgeworth, disliked by Eliza Fletcher but loved by Mary Somerville, also joined their circle at this time. But it was Mary's acceptance by a wider scientific community that mattered most; she made the acquaintance of many of the leading mathematicians and astronomers of the time, including Sir William Herschel (1738–1822), his son John (1792–1871) and his sister and collaborator Caroline (1750–1848), the metallurgist William Hyde Wollaston (1776–1828) and George Peacock (1791–1858), mathematician and Dean of Ely. She became the friend and mentor of Lord Byron's daughter Ada Lovelace (1815–52), who collaborated with inventor Charles Babbage (1792–1871) on a prototype mechanical computer, the 'Analytical Engine'. When the French astronomer François Arago (1786–1873) and physicist Jean-Baptiste Biot (1774–1862) came to London, the Somervilles were invited to meet them. But although she presented two papers to the Royal Society in 1826, for most of the 1820s awareness of Mary Somerville's brilliance was mainly confined to other mathematicians.

Her breakthrough to a wider public came through the agency of Henry Brougham, who in 1827 invited her to translate Laplace's *Méchanique Céleste* for publication by the Society for the Diffusion of Useful Knowledge, an association dedicated to publishing affordable books for working-class readers. At first Mary would have none of it, suggesting '[her] self-acquired knowledge was so inferior to that of the men who had been educated in our universities that it would be the height of presumption to write on such a subject'. When Brougham persisted, she pointed out, somewhat self-contradictorily, that such a book could never be popularised, since 'the student must know at least something of the differential and integral calculi, and as a preliminary step I should have to prove various problems in physical mechanics and astronomy'. Only when her husband weighed in eagerly on Brougham's side did she agree to try, provided that 'should [she] fail, the manuscript shall be put into the fire'. It seems tragic that such a formidably learned woman should have so little self-confidence, but heartening that some men at least believed in her.

Mechanism of the Heavens took three years to write. In the end, Henry Brougham was impressed by its substance but baulked at its length, and the work was published in 1831 by John Murray III (1808–92). It was no mere translation of Laplace's words; instead Mary Somerville explained in detail the mathematics used by the French astronomer, which were still largely unfamiliar in Britain, turning algebra into 'plain English' which readers could understand. Some readers, at least. Mary herself recognised that only the introductory chapter would be comprehensible to non-mathematicians, and had it printed separately as *Preliminary Dissertation to The Mechanism of the Heavens*. Although the book was admired by those who could understand it, initial sales were slow, and not until it was adopted as an advanced mechanics textbook at the University of Cambridge in 1837 did sales pick up dramatically. But it was well-reviewed, and established Mary Somerville's reputation in scientific circles. Naturally she was gratified, but thirty years later she was still riled by the conditions in which she was obliged to write it:

> *A man can always command his time under the plea of business, a woman is not allowed any such excuse … . I was always supposed to be at home, and as my friends and acquaintances came so far out of their way to see me, it would have been ungenerous not to receive them. Nevertheless, I was sometimes annoyed when in the midst of a difficult problem someone would enter and say, "I have come to spend a few hours with you".*

Such annoyance is the lot of most home-working women writers, now as then, but at least Mary Somerville was fortunate, according to her daughter Martha, in having 'a singular power of abstraction':

> *When occupied with some difficult problem … she lost all consciousness of what went on around her, and became so entirely absorbed that any amount of talking or even practising scales and solfeggi, went on without in the least disturbing her.*

This may explain to some extent how she managed to teach her daughters, make marmalade and enjoy a hectic social life while planning her next book, *On The Connexion of the Physical Sciences*, which was to explain these connexions through chapters on astronomy, physics, meteorology and physical geography. She hypothesised on such matters as the strange behaviour of the planet Uranus, suggesting that it might be influenced by another, unseen planet. Neptune was discovered in 1846.

By this time, honours had been showered upon her. She was elected Honorary Member of the Société de Physique et d'Histoire Naturelle de Genève and of the Irish Royal Academy, and in 1835, along with Caroline Herschel, of the Royal Astronomical Society. It has been noted that these were honorary memberships, and that full membership remained the preserve of men, but at least they knocked out one stone in the wall of discrimination. Mary Somerville was also awarded two of the great accolades of nineteenth-century Britain; a marble bust by Sir Francis Leggatt Chantrey to be placed in the hall of the Royal Society of London, and a Civil List pension from the King. She was also pleased to have a ship named after her, with a copy of Chantrey's bust as a figurehead; launched in 1835, the *Mary Somerville* sailed between Liverpool and the East until in 1852 it disappeared, presumably overwhelmed by a typhoon in the South China Sea.

In 1819, when William Somerville had been appointed Physician to the Chelsea Hospital, the family had moved from Hanover Square to a government-owned house near the river. They disliked its low-lying, malodorous situation, and the death in 1823 of their eldest and brightest daughter Margaret, aged barely ten, darkened the memory of the Chelsea years. The bereaved parents tried to find solace in travel in Europe, and through everything Mary continued to work. *On The Connexion of the Physical Sciences* (1834), again published by John Murray, was immediately successful, ran to several editions and sold 15,000 copies in Britain and the United States. It provided sorely needed funds; the Somervilles had lost their savings through poor financial management and, without generous terms and loans from John Murray, who also helped to secure the Civil List pension (raised at this time to £300) they would have had serious financial difficulties. In 1835, William Somerville, now aged 64 and worn out with work and money worries, became seriously ill with what may have been typhoid fever, a disease rife in the London area where human and animal waste from open drains washed into the river Thames.

Advised after a slow recovery to spend the winter in a warmer climate William resigned his appointments and, taking their daughters with them, he and Mary went to Italy. For a couple of years they wandered from Rome to Florence, Paris to London but in 1838 decided to live more or less permanently in Italy. They liked the country and the climate, but perhaps the deciding factor was the lower cost of living; the Brownings would choose to live in Florence for the same reason after their marriage in 1846. The Somervilles enjoyed a nomadic life; they 'took houses' in preference to buying one, but always felt quickly at home, living at different times in Rome, Florence, Venice and Naples, with shorter stays in Perugia, Assisi, Frascati, Lake Albano, Ravenna, Genzano and Bellagio on Lake Como. The book which Mary had begun in London, *Physical Geography*, had to be laid aside due to her husband's illness and the move to Italy, but now, working each day from eight until one o'clock, she completed it for publication in 1848. Acknowledging her debt to Baron (Alexander) von Humboldt (1769–1859) the Prussian philosopher, traveller, geographer and author of the widely read *Kosmos* (1845–52) whom she had met a few years previously, she took an inclusive view of geography, covering the earth's place in the solar system, its water and land formations, mountains, volcanoes, oceans and lakes. She dealt with the effect of elements governing temperature – light, electricity, magnetism. She discussed the distribution of animals, birds and vegetation over the Earth's surface and human impact upon them, issuing a warning that now seems chillingly prophetic: 'Man, the lord of creation, will extirpate the noble creatures of the earth … but will himself for ever be the slave of the cankerworm and the fly.'

Commercially this was Mary Somerville's most successful work and, since in the age of exploration and discovery it required constant updating, it ran to many editions. It was translated into a number of languages, and was considered an essential university textbook until the early twentieth century. Its author was rewarded by election to the American Geographical and Statistical Society in 1857, and to the Italian Geographical Society in 1870, in which year she also won the Victoria Gold Medal of the Royal Geographical Society. But perhaps she cherished as much the generous tribute of the great Baron Humboldt, to whom she had sent a copy:

> *You are queen of regions such as astronomy, meteorology, magnetism … . Only you could have given to your fine literature an original work of cosmology, a work written with the lucidity and the taste which distinguish everything that comes from your pen.*

William Somerville died in Florence in 1860, aged 92, and in 1865 Mary's only surviving son Woronzow Grieg, whom she dearly loved, died of heart failure aged sixty. She was reticent in print about her personal feelings, but these losses must have pained her deeply. She took refuge in work on her last scientific book, *Molecular and Microscopic Science*, and in writing, with unclouded recall, her *Personal Recollections* of a life begun in another century in a small coastal Scottish town. She had lived in the reigns of four monarchs, watched from the gallery of Westminster

Hall the bizarre spectacle of George IV's Coronation Banquet and conversed with Queen Victoria. She could remember the French Revolution and the Napoleonic Wars; the industrialisation of the North, the rise of the British Empire, the Factory Acts, three Reform Acts and the struggle for the unification of the states of Italy. Such events had been the political background of her life, and the foreground the great scientific progress in which she had herself played a part. In her memoir she interwove this tumultuous international narrative with the more intimate concerns of family life and friendships, writing with a blend of simplicity and art which places *Personal Recollections* among the most beguiling memoirs of the nineteenth century. To see the work, however, purely in terms of its charm would be to misunderstand Mary Somerville's motive in writing it. It was also her way of settling the score with those who had scorned her.

Unlike Elizabeth Grant and Eliza Fletcher, who wrote their reminiscences for the family circle, Mary Somerville was a professional who wrote for publication. In an early draft she noted as her two aims: '… to prevent others misrepresenting me after my death, and to encourage other women'. Experience of unfair criticism had made her distrustful, and her struggle to educate herself and be taken seriously in a male-dominated society still rankled. She acknowledged warmly the help and encouragement she had received from enlightened male scientists, but could not but be aware that even they regarded her as an exotic rarity, whose achievement need not modify the general view of a woman's inferior role in society. She knew too, from experience within her own family, that too many women agreed with the men. So she gave credit where it was due, wrote proudly but modestly about her achievements and, as she approached her ninetieth birthday, passionately about the causes she had supported:

> *Age has not abated my zeal for the emancipation of my sex from the unreasonable prejudice too prevalent in Great Britain against a literary and scientific education for women … . I joined a petition to the Senate of London University praying that degrees might be awarded to women, but it was rejected. I have also frequently signed petitions to Parliament for the Female Suffrage, and have the honour now to be a member of the General Committee for Woman Suffrage in London.*

Fifty-six years would pass after the death of Mary Somerville before the Representation of the People Act (1928) would give all women over the age of 21 equal voting rights. It would take considerably longer for all the professions to open their ranks to women entrants; the battle for recognition in medicine, science, law, finance, publishing, universities, the church and the arts was still being fought a hundred years after Mary Somerville died. Concern about unequal representation of women in Parliament and the judiciary is still prevalent today.

In the last years of her life, Mary Somerville lived mainly in Naples, still writing the account of her life which gradually became less a historical record than a journal of the thoughts and feelings of a very old woman approaching the end of her life. Although she had in girlhood abandoned the cold Calvinism of her upbringing and always shunned religious argument, her mathematical researches had failed to shake her belief in the existence of God. On the contrary, she wrote:

Nothing has afforded me so convincing a proof of the unity of the Deity as these purely mental conceptions of numerical and mathematical science which have been by slow degrees vouchsafed to man, and are still granted in these latter times by the differential calculus, now superseded by the higher algebra, which must have existed in that sublimely omniscient Mind from eternity.

She had seen the great wonders of nature, comets, solar eclipses, the aurora borealis, a major eruption of Vesuvius in 1868, yet her thoughts as she prepared for death were of more intimate things. Toward the end of *Personal Recollections* she admitted that, being afraid to sleep alone on stormy nights, she felt some trepidation at the loneliness of transition from human life to eternity. Despite her belief in the 'infinite glories' of an afterlife where she would find her lost husband and children again, she confessed some reluctance to leave the Earth and no longer see the sky and the sea, 'the earth with its verdure and flowers', and most of all 'animals who have followed our footsteps faithfully for years, without knowing for certainty their ultimate fate, though I firmly believe that the living principle is never extinguished'. All her life, Mary Somerville had loved birds and animals; she was horrified by the cruelty they suffered, and revolted by the evil practice of vivisection. Humane attempts to stop such abominations had gained her eager support, and it seemed to her only natural justice that exploited species should share resurrection to a happier life.

Molecular and Microscopic Science was published in 1869, when Mary Somerville was in her ninetieth year. It was respectfully reviewed by scientists barely half her age, but knowledge was rapidly expanding, and to them she was already a figure in history. She herself was her work's harshest critic: 'In writing this book I made a great mistake and repent it. Mathematics are the natural bent of my mind. If I had devoted myself exclusively to that study, I might probably have written something useful ...'. Instead she had to settle for a place among the great scientific expositors of her age. But although she was now deaf and troubled by shaking hands, she went on working, thankful that though her memory for names and places was failing, her faculties were otherwise intact. One of her last letters was to her friend and publisher John Murray, who had sent her a copy of Darwin's *The Descent of Man* (1871). This work 'interested [her] exceedingly', but, she added, 'I cannot as yet pay due respect to the gorilla as my ancestor, [as] I am only reading the first volume.' She went on to report that though easily fatigued, she was happy to say she had not lost her facility in mathematics, and asked Murray to send her Sir William Hamilton's *Lectures on Quaternions*. She was working on a paper about quaternions on 28 November 1872, and died quietly in the early morning of the next day.

Mary Somerville had been much celebrated during her life, and her obituaries were fulsome. The London *Morning Post* called her 'The Queen of Science', and *The Times* 'The first scientific lady of the world'. In the years that followed, she became an icon for young women determined to fulfil her ambition for women's education on a par with men's, and in 1879 she was paid the supreme compliment of having the University of Oxford's first college for women students named after her. In the twentieth century a crater on the moon and an asteroid were named for her, and even more recently she was awarded the ultimate twenty-first-century accolade. Having won a public vote, beating such luminaries as Thomas Telford (1757–1834) and James Clerk Maxwell (1831–79), her image appeared on the Royal Bank of Scotland's first polymer £10 note in 2017. On 2 February 2020 she was celebrated with a Google Doodle [https://www.google.com/doodles/celebrating-mary-somerville].

Such were modernity's acts of homage to a great Scottish scientist and advocate of women's rights, yet on a domestic level genius often unwittingly demands sacrifice. A thought may be spared for the faceless daughters of Mary Somerville, Martha and Mary, to whom she had taught Latin and algebra so that they might be as well-educated as men. In the event, they spent their adult lives drifting round Europe, doomed to fulfil the archaic role of unmarried women, looking after their ageing parents, dabbling in watercolour and wood-carving, standing in the background of other people's lives until they were old themselves. Neither long survived her mother. The younger, Mary, died in 1875, aged 58. Martha lived long enough to edit *Personal Recollections*, interspersed with letters and mainly hagiographical commentary, and to see it published in 1874. She died in 1879, aged 64. There is no evidence that Mary Somerville was troubled by the situation she had allowed to develop, nor that 'the girls' felt aggrieved by the gap between promise and fulfilment. Perhaps it was honour enough to have been the daughters of Mary Somerville.

14

WATERLOO AND
OTHER STORIES

On Saturday the 10th of June, 1815, my brother, my sister and myself sailed from the pier of Ramsgate at three in the afternoon, in company with ... an incongruous assemblage of horses, dogs, and barouches; Irish servants, French valets and steerage passengers too multifarious to mention.

Charlotte Waldie (1788–1859)
A Narrative of a Residence in Belgium 1817

BEFORE THE TWENTIETH century, with its migrations, cheap air fares and vogue for foreign travel, many Scots. both men and women, had lived and died no further than twenty miles from the place where they were born. At least as many were accustomed to an itinerant life, for reasons sometimes religious or recreational, or as students or military personnel. More mundanely, many were driven by economic necessity. Before the Reformation put an end to pilgrimage, Scots had travelled into England to pray at the tombs of St Cuthbert at Durham, St Thomas at Canterbury and the shrine of the Virgin Mary at Walsingham, while pilgrims of both sexes crossed the Channel, en route for Rome, Jerusalem or the great shrine of St James at Compostella in northern Spain. Many pilgrims visited shrines in the hope of miraculous cures for untreatable diseases, others as a penance or to pray for salvation; many simply enjoyed the fellowship, the sense of adventure and collecting commemorative badges to wear on their hats.

Into more recent times, Scottish farm workers, usually accompanied by wives and children moved around Britain seeking seasonal work, while men fished in coastal waters and fisher women annually followed the herring boats as they moved down the east coast from Wick to Lowestoft, gutting and packing the catch for transportation to Europe and even the West Indies. Only with the emigration of Highland families to North America during the early nineteenth-century Highland Clearances did a sizeable number of Scotswomen leave their familiar haunts to start a new and perilous life beyond the Atlantic Ocean. All had tales to tell, and told them orally through traditional song and story, but were impeded by illiteracy from giving enduring accounts of their experiences. The only thing we can be sure

of is that they did not travel for fun. Thus 'travel writing' as a genre was the preserve of the educated, which meant, as usual, the aristocratic and upper middle
classes.

In the early eighteenth century it became fashionable for wealthy young men,
but not of course women, to travel round Europe, accompanied by a tutor, to round
off their education by absorbing the art and culture of the great capital cities and
viewing the ancient ruins of Greece and Italy, familiar from their classical studies.
This refined species of tourism, however, was suddenly interrupted by the outbreak
in Paris of the French Revolution, the subsequent Reign of Terror and the wars, with
their heavy British involvement, which engulfed Europe between 1792 and 1815.
One consequence was that with the Continent closed to all but the most intrepid of
civilian travellers, Scotland, particularly Edinburgh, became a fashionable destination. The vogue for wild 'romantic' scenery, fed by the Ossian poems and Gothic
literature, also drew the more adventurous into the Gaelic-speaking Highlands – to
the economic benefit, if also mutual incomprehension, of both Highlanders and
their guests. Even before the publication of Scott's *The Lady of the Lake* (1810) and
Waverley (1814) kick-started a tourist boom in the Trossachs and the West Highlands, curious travellers were arriving, among them women taking notes – like the
teenaged Eliza Fletcher, whose Highland tour in 1786 became the subject of a self-
derided journal. Others wrote letters home, kept diaries and later wrote memoirs,
forming a large body of essentially private writing. Only a few were professionals,
ambitious to reach a wider audience.

Mrs Sarah Murray (1744–1811) was the English widow of the Hon. William
Murray, member of an aristocratic Perthshire family, when she set out from London
to explore the Scottish Highlands in 1796. By then in her fifties, she had previously
run a girls' school in Bath and published in three volumes *The School*, an imaginary
correspondence between a girl and her mother, but now had something more challenging in mind. Dressed in 'a red leather cap trimmed with brown fur, and the habit
of tartan such as is worn by the 42nd regiment of Highlanders', amiably eccentric
Mrs Murray spent five months travelling through the Highlands, mostly on horseback, covering large tracts of moorland and forest, in the care of guides whose
language she could not speak. Back in London, she wrote and published *A Companion and Useful Guide to the Beauties of Scotland* (1799), before deciding that it
required expansion. So in 1800 she was off north again, this time to the Atlantic
shore and the Hebrides, clambering over slippery rocks in her long tartan skirt,
island-hopping in a small open boat. She visited Fingal's Cave and viewed the
famous whirlpool of Corryvreckan which, on a relatively calm day, was not whirling
fiercely enough to please her. 'I questioned my companions … with earnestness,'
she wrote of one hair-raising voyage, 'if we were in danger of going to the bottom:
Oh! yes, was the answer repeatedly given by both men.'

Home again in the less thrilling ambience of Kensington, Sarah Murray relived her journeys to the wild places, extending and revising her book. *A Companion and Useful Guide to the Beauties in the Western Highlands of Scotland and in the Hebrides* was published in 1803, with a second edition in 1810. This *Companion* began with much good advice to other travellers on the distances between inns and how to judge them; whether to take your own sheets and towels, whether the landlord was civil and the catering good and, most importantly, whether the beds were already occupied by the pests whom she called 'the hopping gentry'. The remainder of the narrative combines a flowing style, a rich sense of humour, courage and a romantic passion for the picturesque; Sarah Murray fell in love with lochs, mountains, rushing rivers, waterfalls, the Caledonian Forest and the steely, unpredictable sea.

*

Elizabeth Isabella Spence (1768–1832), born a generation after Sarah Murray and with some claim to be her successor, published the first of her travelogues, *Summer Excursions*, in 1809, when Scott was on the brink of publishing *The Lady of the Lake*. Two more were to follow in the post-*Waverley* years, when Scotland was basking in its distinction as the prime tourist destination in Europe. Elizabeth Isabella was born in Dunkeld, the only daughter of a physician, but shortly afterwards moved with her parents to England where she passed the rest of her life. The details of her early life are scant, but it is known that her father practised medicine in Durham and later in Guilford, and that both parents were dead before Elizabeth Isabella was 18. It is believed that she was left badly off, lived for a while in London with her maternal aunt and, to pay for her keep, began to write articles and short stories for magazines. She then turned, with moderate success, to novels, publishing three between 1799 and 1807. But if she is remembered at all nowadays, it is as a traveller in the land of her birth, and a perceptive observer of the customs and manners of the Scots. There was one aspect of her writing, however, which made her stand out from the rather too many writers who were rhapsodising on the same subject at the same time. On her last excursion, written up as *Letters from the North Highlands* (1817) and addressed to her novelist friend Jane Porter (1776–1850), she took the unusual approach of marking her journey not by extolling famous men, but by noting associations with the Scottish women writers who had preceded her. Dunfermline was described as 'the dwelling of the author of Clan-Albin' Christian Isobel Johnstone (although the only actual connection is that her husband was once a schoolmaster there). Fort Augustus reminded her of Anne Grant, who had lived in the barracks before marriage took her to Laggan. Riding among the Angus braes, the villages recalled Elizabeth Hamilton and *The Cottagers of Glenburnie*, while in the capital Eliza Fletcher was celebrated as a literary enabler and hostess, 'the Mrs Montague of Edinburgh'. It is a pleasing way of subverting the usual narrative, and satisfying that the male critics of the periodicals were so sniffily unimpressed.

*

By the twentieth century, it was customary to think that while men went to war, the role of women was to stay behind, keeping the home fires burning and, for single women, perhaps joining the forces as support workers, or working in factories and on the land in jobs normally done by men. Historically, however, this division was less apparent; there were recorded instances of women in the seventeenth century disguising themselves as men and fighting on the battlefield. More often they became 'camp followers' who trailed all over Europe in the wake of armies, set up their own encampments and provided services such as cooking, nursing and mending uniforms. Some were prostitutes, but most were soldiers' wives and lovers, who found danger preferable to the anxiety and insecurity of being left behind. Particularly after the formation of Scottish regiments to fight the French, Scotswomen from towns and farms from Moray to the Borders, ignoring the British Army's rule that only four wives from each company were allowed, packed their belongings, gathered their children and set out for northern Europe in the wake of their non-commissioned husbands and sons.

As might be expected, the rule for the wives of officers was different. These upper-class women travelled freely with their husbands, living in hotels and rented houses, enjoying balls, dinners, shopping and drives in the parks of Europe's capitals. So it was that, as the long war against the French Army of Napoleon Buonaparte drew toward its climax in cornfields around the Belgian farm villages of Quatre Bras and Waterloo, twenty miles away the city of Brussels was packed with British nationals of every class, a sizeable proportion Scots. The most vivid fictional account of this time is found in *Vanity Fair* (1848) by W. M. Thackeray (1811–65) and, since he was only four at the time of Waterloo, it is tempting to speculate whether, among the works he used for research, might have been *Narrative of a Residence in Belgium during the Campaign of 1815 and a Visit to the Field of Waterloo*, published in 1817 with the by-line 'by an Englishwoman', who was by birth a Scot.

Charlotte Ann Waldie (1788–1859) was born the daughter of a Scottish landowner and his English wife at Hendersyde Park, an estate on the fringe of Kelso now mainly occupied by new housing and an equestrian centre. In 1822 she would marry Stephen Eaton, a banker in Stamford, Rutland, but in 1815 she was still single and on the verge of a great adventure. The wars that had for long been a deterrent to continental travel had become tedious, and younger civilians, convincing themselves that actual danger was a remote possibility, were now more willing to take risks. Among them were Charlotte Waldie, her brother John and sister Jane, who crossed the Channel to Ostend June 1815. The next day they travelled on to Brussels, cheerfully unaware that Napoleon, escaped from Elba, was at Charleroi, thirty miles away, gathering his Army for the last great battle against the British and their Prussian allies. Charlotte's account of the panic and disorder in Brussels when messengers arrived to call the British regiments to arms is breathlessly high-spirited; as the bugle sounds, the officers rush out from the Duchess of Richmond's famous ball, and the whole city seems to decant itself into the streets. Bagpipes skirl, and Charlotte swings between swooning admiration for the marching High-landers in their kilted splendour, and pity as she watches their sombre farewells to their trembling wives and children.

This self-styled Englishwoman was never more a patriotic Scot than when boasting of the superior courage of her countrymen; of the preliminary encounter with the French she wrote: 'It is a perversion of words to call the troops engaged in the battle of Quartre Bras the English Army ... for several hours [the Highland regiments and the Royal Scots] alone maintained the tremendous onset and the shock of the whole French Army, and to their determined valour, Belgium owes her independence and England her glory.' On 18 June, the day of Waterloo, while her brother, like Jos Sedley in *Vanity Fair*, was out trying to hire horses in case they had to flee, Charlotte and Jane were walking in the streets, recording the ambiva-lence of the Belgians about the outcome, the rumours and counter-rumours of victory and defeat, catching the atmosphere of an undefended city where the thunder of cannon could be heard only twenty miles away. In the aftermath of the battle, the Waldies went sightseeing; returning in sober mood from the devastated battlefield, they fell in with a group wounded soldiers making their painful way back to Brussels. 'Some of them were Highlanders and some of them were Low-landers,' wrote Charlotte, 'and when they found out that I came from Scotland, and lived upon the Tweed, they were delighted. One of them was from the Tweed as well as myself, he said, he "cam' oot o' Peebleshire".'

Sir Walter Scott's account of Waterloo in *Paul's Letters to His Kinsfolk* (1816) is better known, but Scott, who at the age of 44 had never previously ventured abroad, did not arrive in Belgium until late July. He had previously thought that soldiering was a glamorous profession; now he was appalled by the sight of the trampled battlefield with its evidence of carnage – shallow graves, putrefying horses, bloodied flags and discarded weapons. But he could only imagine the action and, having secured some gruesome souvenirs, he moved on thankfully to the victory celebrations in Paris. His book, voiced by a fictional character, was suc-cessful principally because *he* had written it. It could never match the vivacity, drama and youthful tendency to inappropriate laughter that make Charlotte Waldie's narrative both endearing and compelling.

Hilariously, in the circumstances, Charlotte's wild enthusiasm for all things Scottish did not long survive her Belgian adventure. Six weeks after they had left Margate, the Waldies arrived back at the same port, Charlotte with a full notebook and bursting with satisfaction. 'I returned to my country,' she wrote, 'after all the varying and eventful scenes through which it had been my lot to pass, – more proud than when I left it of the name of – AN ENGLISHWOMAN.'

*

After the victory at Waterloo brought peace to Europe, the continent was open to British travellers for the first time in more than twenty years, occasioning a rush of tourists eager for novelty and exploration. As the century passed and movement was facilitated by a network of railways, British communities, predominantly middle-class, became established in cities such as Paris, Rome, Naples, Florence, Venice and Geneva. Some expatriates sought literary and artistic inspiration, some perceived benefit to their health, all enjoyed the stimulus of new scenery and a different perspective on life. Among these was for a time a Scottish family, whose eldest daughter was destined to have a most unusual cultural experience.

Emily Gerard (1849–1905) was born at Ancrum near Jedburgh, but spent her early years at Rochsoles House, a mansion in the parish of Monklands, close to Airdrie in Lanarkshire. Her father, Colonel Archibald Gerard, was descended from a line of Episcopalian divines while her mother, Euphemia Robison, had converted to Roman Catholicism the year before Emily was born. Emily and her two younger sisters were brought up in their mother's faith. Since the Gerards could afford to educate their daughters at home, until she was 14 Emily had seen little of the world beyond the Rochsoles estate. In 1863, however, there came an event which determined her future; the family went for three years to Venice, where for 18 months Emily shared lessons with Princess Marguerite (1847–93), niece of the Comte de Chambord (1820–83), the unsuccessful claimant to the throne of France. She then spent three years at a convent school near Bregenz in the Austrian Tyrol, leaving with a perfect command of German, the language she would need most in the years ahead.

In 1869, aged twenty, Emily Gerard married Miecislas de Laszowski, a minor Polish aristocrat twice her age, then an officer in the Austrian Army. Following his career as officers' wives were obliged to do, she lived for several years in Brӕzum in Galicia; there she had two sons and collaborated with her younger sister Dorothea (1855–1915), who had also married an Austrian Army officer, in writing romantic novels (as E. D. Gerard) based on their experience of Eastern European life and knowledge of Austrian aristocracy. But it is not for these works, strong on atmosphere as they are, that Emily Gerard is remembered today, nor for her reviews of French and German books published in *The Times* and *Blackwood's Magazine*. In 1883, when her husband was appointed to command the cavalry brigade in Transylvania, now in Romania but then the remotest region of the Austro-Hungarian Empire, Emily Laszowska found, in the ancient 'land beyond the forest', the greatest interest of her life.

In the dark woods and among the wind-blasted Carpathian Mountains, with their deep caverns, glancing sunshine, blinding winter snows and spectacular thunderstorms, she found a race descended from invading Huns, Slavs, Magyars and Germans, secluded and untouched by outside influences. In scattered settlements stood ancient wooden churches with high spires and steeply-pitched roofs, and among the mountains isolated castles, clinging to precipices of dizzying height, pushing up their turrets and spires into the restive sky. Both sinister and romantic, this was a landscape to inspire legend and superstition, and Emily Gerard became fascinated by its rich folklore. Talking to the men and women she employed, and those whom she met in town and countryside, she made copious notes of the superstitions that governed every aspect of their lives, the charms used to avoid ill luck; fear of witches and werewolves; arcane theories about healing and the fate of the dead, in all of which they trusted, seeing no conflict with their Eastern Orthodox Christian beliefs.

Most interesting to Emily Gerard was the Transylvanians' fervent belief in the shape-shifting vampire, the *nosferatu* who, usually in the shape of a giant bat, entered sickrooms and tombs to suck the blood of the dead, creating new vampires, the 'undead' who could only be finally annihilated by opening the coffin and driving a stake through the corpse. 'In very obstinate cases of vampirism,' wrote Emily Gerard, 'it is recommended to cut off the head, and replace it in the coffin with the mouth filled with garlic, or to extract the heart and burn it, strewing its ashes over the grave.' If these bloody rituals sound familiar to modern readers, it is unlikely to be because they have read either 'Transylvanian Superstitions', a long article by Emily Gerard published in 1885, or *The Land Beyond the Forest* (1888), her more comprehensive work on the subject. Other writers had previously published fiction based on the vampire legends, notably John Polidori (1795–1821) in *The Vampyre* (1819) and Sheridan Le Fanu (1814–73) in *Carmilla* (1872). But it was Bram Stoker (1847–1912), who in *Dracula* (1897) produced what is still – despite its weak characterisation, old-fashioned emphasis on English upper-class manliness and sexist stereotypes – the most famous of occult tales. Stoker claimed to have spent seven years on research, but need scarcely have bothered. The most blood-curdling elements in *Dracula* are all drawn from material he lifted straight out of Emily Gerard's *The Land Beyond the Forest*. The copy he used, heavily annotated in his own hand, is still held in the London Library.

In 1885, Mieceslas de Laszowski retired from the Austrian Army and settled with his Scottish wife in Vienna. It has been suggested that their marriage was unhappy but, whether or not, they died within a fortnight of each other in 1905.

15

IN GOLDEN LANDS

This is rather exciting, for I have had an unusual journey, and my circumstances are unusual, for Mr Low, the Resident, has not returned, and not only am I alone in his bungalow in the heart of the jungle, but as far as I can learn I am the only European in the region.

Isabella Bird (1831–1904)
The Golden Chersonese and the Way Thither 1882

EMILY GERARD'S TRAVELLING to the most remote area of Europe had been dictated not by personal preference, but by the exigencies of her Austrian husband's career. Similarly British Army wives were obliged, in the heyday of Empire, to spend years of their lives in exotic locations from North Africa to the South Seas. Employed both as peacekeepers and defenders of British interests, Scottish and English regiments were sent routinely to countries all over the globe, but had a particularly strong presence in India. Because of its great wealth, this exotic sub-continent was known as 'the jewel in the Crown' of Queen Victoria, who assumed the title 'Empress of India' in 1876. A whole literature, factual and fictional, has evolved about 'British' India, to which Scotswomen, mostly the wives of Army officers and colonial civil servants, contributed their personal experiences of life and interaction with Indians. Probably the best known nowadays is the poet and novelist Violet Jacob (*see* chapter 17), who kept a diary and wrote long letters from Mhow in central India to her mother in faraway Angus, learned Hindi and fulfilled the caring duties of an officer's wife. She was not, however, greatly inspired to use these experiences in her fiction.

More prolific and famous in her time was Flora Annie Steel (1847–1929), born Flora Webster at Harrow-on-the-Hill, Middlesex, into a family of eleven 'healthy strong Scottish children, half Lowland, half Highland'. Financial difficulties required the Websters' relocation to Scotland, and from the age of nine Flora was brought up in Forfar, where her father became Sheriff Clerk. As so often in middle-class families, money was scraped together to send the boys to boarding school; Flora's brothers went to Harrow and, since she alone among her sisters was of an age to have a governess, employing one was dismissed as an unwarranted expense. Left to educate herself, like Mary Somerville she was fortunate that her father had a well-stocked library, containing works of history, philosophy, poetry, and fiction. There were even some textbooks which her father had inherited from a medical relative; these would prove useful to Flora later on.

Aged twenty, Flora Webster married Henry Steel, an engineer and civil servant in India, and for the next 22 years lived with him in the Punjab. For much of that time their home was in the remote district of Kasur, in a house converted from an ancient tomb, which might have spooked some tenants, but of which she writes in her autobiography, *The Garden of Fidelity* (1929): 'I loved the old echoing dome ... It was all so dim and mysterious, so dignified, the echoes might have reached high heaven.' She recalls with an old woman's unclouded memory of youth the India she saw during months spent 'camping' as she accompanied her husband on tours of inspection of his district, her appreciation of startling scenery, colour, contrast, flowers, animals, above all people.

It was usual in 'British' India at that time for English 'memsahibs' to spend languid afternoons drinking tea and exchanging gossip, but that was not Flora Annie Steel's style. Setting herself to learn the language of her Indian neighbours and understand their customs, she soon perceived failings in the colonial admin-istration and resented its neglect of young boys' and particularly women's welfare and education. Sharp-eyed and outspoken, she pestered officials with embarrassing questions, causing one of her husband's senior colleagues to ask him why he didn't keep his wife in order. To which Henry Steel responded by inviting his colleague to take her himself for a month, and see if he could do better. Perceiving that the poor English skills of teenage Punjabi boys would hinder them in later life, she began to teach them, rewarding progress and good behaviour with music, singing and playing the piano to amuse them after lessons. She was shocked, at this time, to discover in the class a distraught 15-year-old father, whose twelve-year-old wife had just lost her first child. It was around this time that she also set up shop as a pharmacist, dispensing medicines from a chest she had thoughtfully brought with her from Scotland.

According to her autobiography, the birth of her daughter Mabel – 'because a baby is always a good ambassador' – gave Flora Annie an entrée into the society of her female Indian neighbours. She found that women, confined by religious con-vention to the seclusion called 'purdah' and so denied treatment by male doctors, were often in poor health and alarmingly ignorant of ailments in their children. Armed with her medicine chest and the medical texts she had also transported from Forfar, she began to instruct them in how to dose their children with 'castor oil, grey powder, rhubarb and ipecacuanha' – not among the most dangerous of Victorian remedies, since their main effect was laxative. She gained kudos from her success in nursing a young mother through puerperal fever, and gradually won the women's trust. Realising that their principal deprivation was educational, she set herself with typical energy and determination to alleviate it

During the 1870s, with a mixture of hospitality, charm and the appearance of seeking co-operation, she muted the disapproval of Muslim and Hindu male hierarchies where she could, and when she couldn't went ahead anyway, succeeding in establishing schools to teach Punjabi women numeracy, literacy and elementary childcare. She wrote primary school textbooks, some of which were illustrated by John Lockwood Kipling (1837–1911), father of Rudyard Kipling (1865–1936) and finally, in 1884, was rewarded for her efforts. In 1895 she was offered the position of Inspectress [*sic*] of Girls' Schools in the region between Delhi and Peshawar, an area covering 141,000 square miles. A self-styled autocrat with boundless confidence and energy, she loved the job – and got results.

Henry Steel retired from the Indian Civil Service in 1889. Back in Britain, for the first time Flora Annie found herself with time to write and, with the exception of *Tales of the Punjab*, which she had completed in India, all her creative works were written far from the great subcontinent that had inspired them. Of her fiction, *On the Face of the Waters* (1896), a powerful and unusually impartial novel about the contentious Indian mutiny of 1858, is arguably the most enduringly resonant, while *The Garden of Fidelity*, courageous, humorous and finished just before her death in 1929, holds a place among the great memoirs of nineteenth-century colonial life. Racial prejudice was endemic in Victorian Britain, and Flora Annie Steel was not free from it. Taking for granted the superiority of European culture and the rightness of British rule, she was nonetheless a fearless critic of its methods, and, far ahead of most of her contemporaries in prophesying that India would become an independent state. More immediately, at the end of her own life, she knew she had battled the patriarchal authority that denied Indian women their right to health care and education, emerging victorious. Yet it may be that for others her high-profile public life had masked her acute sensitivity to the beauty of India and its ineffable sense of mystery, which would haunt her and influence her spiritually for the rest of her days. In a moving passage describing her departure from Bombay (Mumbai) in 1889, she observed that the ship was moving slowly through a writhing belt of wrack:

> *Ancient travellers have it that the belt is of sea serpents, set to guard the treasures of Hindustan. We moderns know it as seaweed set in motion by the movements of the microscopic animalcule by which it is infested. I am not sure which is right, but of this I am certain, that those travellers who, looking down through the blue water at the brown, snaky coils, can see nothing but seaweed had better not go to India. They will see nothing there.*

Amusingly, amid all her travel books, novels and retellings of Indian and English folklore, Flora Annie Steel's bestseller belongs to a more mundane genre. In a twist that recalls Christian Isobel Johnstone's 1826 success with *The Cook and Housewife's Manual* 'by Mrs Margaret Dods of the Cleikum Inn, St Ronans', which outsold all her other books put together, Flora Annie Steel's *The Complete Indian Housekeeper and Cook* (1888), co-authored by fellow-memsahib Grace Gardiner, went into many editions, becoming a bible for insecure young British women struggling to cope with the responsibility of running a large household in India. It is easy to see why. Confident and opinionated, its subjects range from the duties of servants and kitchen hygiene to first aid, advice on clothing, growing vegetables and teaching Indian chefs to cook solid British meals. The best advice for an English memsahib, the novices were told, was to display dignified authority – and learn Hindi, the better to order one's servants about.

After India, the Steels first settled in Aberdeenshire and later moved to North Wales, then Shropshire. Henry Steel died in 1923. In the last year of her own life, Flora Annie Steel visited Jamaica, where her family owned property, then went to Oxford, where she spent some days reading about transcendentalism in the Bodleian Library. According to her daughter's account, she died 'suddenly and splendidly' in Gloucestershire on 12 April 1929, aged 82.

*

Although they were a rarer breed, there were some women in the nineteenth century, unencumbered by children and with a sense of adventure. who needed no husband to direct their travels. They were not perhaps consciously feminist but, being of independent mind and with money at their disposal, they could afford to defy convention and venture into territories which, fifty years previously, even male adventurers would have feared to enter. Prominent among this group were two women with strong Scottish connections, Isabella Lucy Bird (1831–1904) and Constance Frederica Gordon Cumming (1837–1924). The fact that Isabella Bird is better known in the twenty-first century is largely due to the decision of feminist publishers, notably Virago Press, to reissue her work in the 1980s and 1990s, at the expense of Constance Gordon Cumming, a writer and artist equally popular in her day.

Isabella Bird, like Eliza Fletcher a generation before, was not a Scot by birth, but her long residence in Edinburgh and on Mull, her brief marriage to a Scottish doctor and her dedication to Scottish causes have, it is widely agreed, given her honorary status. She was actually born at Boroughbridge, near Harrogate in Yorkshire, into a fairly well-off family; her father, Edward Bird, who had been a lawyer in India until the climate broke his health, was now a vicar in the Church of England, and her mother, Dora Lawson, the daughter of another clergyman. The Birds belonged to the Evangelical wing of the Church, and Isabella and her younger sister Henrietta were reared in a household dedicated to Christian endeavour and charitable pursuits – responsibilities they carried throughout their lives. After spells as vicar of Tattenhall in rural Cheshire and in the city of Birmingham, the Rev. Mr Bird moved his family to the parish of Wyton, now in Cambridgeshire.

Isabella was an ailing child who caused her parents much anxiety; visits to the English seaside and holidays in the Western Isles of Scotland failed to strengthen her and when, aged 18, she underwent spinal surgery she was left depressed and in great pain. Before the advent of modern medicine, the supposedly therapeutic effect of travel, particularly sea voyages, were seized on by Victorian doctors and patients alike. Accordingly in 1884, financed by her father and in the company of some distant cousins, Isabella sailed to New York where, ditching the cousins, she travelled on alone in the area of the St Lawrence River and the Great Lakes. She stayed happily in insanitary hotels, ate nauseous meals with dirty cutlery and thoroughly enjoyed the raucous but good-humoured company of her fellow passengers on coaches, trains and steamboats. The poor health that had plagued her at home seemed to fade in these heady, independent days. The degree to which her symptoms were psychosomatic is impossible to gauge; it is only certain that for the rest of her life she only felt truly alive when travelling the world, meeting new people, enduring hardship in dangerous places and revelling in hair-raising situations. On her return from North America, she used the letters she had written home to construct *The Englishwoman in America*, published to good reviews by John Murray in 1856.

In 1858 Edward Bird died, and Isabella moved to Edinburgh with her mother and sister. After the death of Mrs Bird, Henrietta, no doubt remembering family holidays in the Hebrides, bought a cottage at Tobermory on Mull, where the sisters spent part of each year. Like many visitors, they had been shocked by the devastation of island communities by potato blight in the 1840s and emigration in the wake of the Highland Clearances; as evangelical Christians they engaged in missionary work and gave generously towards the relief of the poor. It was not until 1872, again ill and depressed, that Isabella once more set sail. Her intention was to visit New Zealand, but when the ship reached the Sandwich Islands (Hawaii) she went ashore – and stayed for six months. During this visit she learned to ride astride like a man (donning bloomers and a divided skirt in an attempt still to look 'ladylike'), rode among the terrifying gulches of the island's north coast and climbed two active volcanoes, Kilauea and Mauna Loa. Later she would describe her adventures in *Six Months in the Sandwich Islands* (1875), writing of Kilauea:

> As we ascended, the flow became hotter under our feet, as well as more porous and glistening. The crust became increasingly insecure ... I fell through it a number of

times, and always into holes full of sulphurous steam, so acid that my strong dog-skin gloves were burned through ... [Looking down from the crater's edge] ... we were speechless, for a new glory and terror had been added to the earth. It is the most unutterable of things ... . There were groanings, rumblings and detonations, rushings, hissings and splashings, and the crashing sound of breakers on the coast, but it was the surging of fiery waves upon a fiery shore.

During the following years, Isabella Bird's life settled into a pattern. During long, arduous voyages and overland journeys to the Rocky Mountains in Colorado, Japan, Malaya, Tibet, Persia, Korea, China, Turkey and Kurdistan, she recorded her experiences – including being attacked by a mob in China who called her a 'foreign devil' and tried to burn down the house in which she had taken refuge – in minutely detailed letters to Henrietta, which at home between expeditions she revised for publication in book form. Nowadays she is best known for *A Lady's Life in the Rocky Mountains* (1873), with its intriguing love interest involving the 42-year-old 'lady traveller' and a swashbuckling desperado named James 'Mountain Jim' Nugent, and *Unbeaten Tracks in Japan* (1880). Widely praised for its close observation of landscape and culture only a decade after Japan had stopped refusing entry to foreigners in 1868, *Unbeaten Tracks* established Isabella Bird as a genuine explorer rather than a tourist, and is still well regarded among historians and geographers of the East in the nineteenth century.

For the modern reader, however, accustomed to a different kind of travel narrative, the book's detailed description of every habitation, inn, temple, forest, seashore and cliff can become exhausting, and suggests an inability to select material. The method was, however, intentional. Since the mid-twentieth century, improvements in the presentation of visual images, in photography and film, have become evermore sophisticated, making much verbal description redundant. Although Isabella Bird made some sketches and took photographs which still fascinate (she published a selection, *Chinese Pictures*, in 1900), inevitably her grey images are static, only moments in time imperfectly recorded. For the accurate description she thought essential, the only medium available was the written word.

Isabella Bird broke new ground as a woman explorer and travel writer, and she remains a vital source for anyone curious about the landscape and cultures of newly discovered lands. She was inquisitive and fearless, and had a strong sense of the ridiculous; when she fell into a disused bear pit in Japan, she could hardly climb out for laughing. So it is a pity that occasionally her work is marred by the Victorian assumption that European civilisation was exceptional and Christianity the only truth, thus justifying the whole apparatus of colonial rule. This mindset is sharply illustrated by her remarks about the Ainu people, a bear-hunting tribe of East Asian origin who had settled in Hokkaido, a region in northern Japan recently brought under the control of hostile Japanese authority. Despite their genial hospitality, beautiful manners and benevolence to one another, (traits also observed among the aboriginal people of Australia), their European guest called the gentle Ainu people 'savages' of 'low intellect', disapproved of their religion and disparaged their peaceful way of life – though, to be fair, she was no more flattering about her neighbours on Mull, of whom she remarked: 'The Highlanders have some very charming qualities, but in cunning, moral timidity and plausibility, they remind me of savages of a rather low type.' Seen alongside modern sensitivity to ethnic minority cultures, these remarks suggest that the past is indeed a foreign country.

For the non-academic reader of today, perhaps the most accessible of Isabella Bird's writings describe her interaction with individuals she met – 'Mountain Jim' in Colorado; her umbrella-wielding companion, Miss Karpe, on the crater of Kilauea; the eccentric British Resident Mr Hugh Low in Malaya; the splendidly named Moravian missionaries Dr Karl Marx and Dr Redslob in Kashmir – all live on the page as if 130 years do not lie between us and them. At least they all spoke her language. To the Japanese, completely ignorant of Europeans, she was as exotic as they were to her, and their hospitality and good manners were tempered by curiosity and astonishment. Her relationship with her Japanese guide, Ito, is described with a mixture of amusement and exasperation; it is no surprise that this fastidious young man, who had joined her to improve his English, was much less keen on the discomfort of life on unbeaten tracks than she was.

Some of Isabella Bird's most engaging writing about animals is to be found in *The Golden Chersonese and the Way Thither* (1883), an account of her travels in the Malay Peninsula. It was here that she had her first uncomfortable ride on a recalcitrant elephant, and found herself alone, apart from a native servant, in a deserted bungalow in the middle of a tiger-frequented jungle. On the first night her dinner companions were two apes, the semi-tame familiars of the absent colonial administrator with whom she had arranged to stay. The large ape she found unappealing, but the smaller one, a Borneo ape or 'wah-wah' named Eblis, 'before very long emigrated from his chair to the table, and, sitting by [her] plate, daintily helped himself from it'. 'What a grotesque dinner party!' she added cheerfully. 'What a delightful one! ... . Shall I ever enjoy a dinner party so much again?' Her descriptions of Eblis, 'this lovable, infatuating little semi-human creature' who took her pen and spoiled her letters, hanging round her neck and uttering affectionate little cries of 'Ouf! Ouf!', are among the most tender and humane she ever wrote.

In 1880 Henrietta Bird died, and the following year Isabella, grieving and perhaps daunted by the prospect of lonely old age, married Dr John Bishop (c. 1841–86), who had attended Henrietta in her last illness. From this time she was called 'Mrs Bishop'; she would never have referred to herself as 'Bird Bishop', an American usage unfamiliar in Britain until recent years. The marriage seems to have been happy but, despite Dr Bishop's being ten years younger than his wife and seemingly likely to outlive her, he died in 1886 from a lingering infection contracted on the wards of Edinburgh Infirmary. His 55-year-old widow dealt with her grief by taking a course in nursing and resuming her travels. Her fortune increased by inheritance from her husband, she first founded a hospital in his memory at Leh, near Srinagar in Tibet, then one at Amritsar in the Punjab in memory of her sister. From this time onward, she regarded herself primarily as a missionary, and her travels through India, Tibet, Persia, Kurdistan, Korea and the Yangtze Valley were marked by evangelical zeal.

In 1890, Isabella Bishop received an Honorary Fellowship of the Royal Scottish Geographical Society, followed in 1892 by a Fellowship of the Royal Geographical Society in London, which had only recently agreed to admit 'lady members'. Unfortunately this distinction soon turned sour; the admission of women was opposed by the stuffier male members, and discontinued for twenty years. Mary Somerville would have sympathised.

Isabella Bishop's final expedition to Morocco took place in 1901, when she was seventy but, her strength declining, the book she had planned was never written. Since her husband's death she had been unable to settle either in Edinburgh or Tobermory, and her last sad years were spent in rented rooms and finally in nursing homes. But she died in her own house in Edinburgh's Melville Street on 7 October 1904, without abandoning her dreams. Among her belongings were found the trunks she had packed for another journey to China.

*

The only other Scottish woman travel writer to equal, at least in her own time, the popularity of Isabella Bird was Constance Frederica Gordon Cumming, known to her family and friends as 'Eka'. She was friendly enough with Isabella Bird to ask her to read her first book in proof, but there is not much evidence of intimacy. Eka Gordon Cumming was one of twelve children born to Sir William Gordon Cumming, 2nd Baronet and Chief of Clan Comyn (also spelt Cumming) of Altyre near Forres and his first wife, Eliza Maria Campbell; by his second marriage Sir William would become father to another three. Eka's early childhood was spent in the Highlands but, after her mother died when she was six, her home was with her eldest sister in Northumberland. In term time, until she was 16, she attended Hermitage Lodge School in Fulham, London.

Her much older brothers had proved adventurous, one travelling in Canada, and one in Africa; one became a tea planter in Ceylon (Sri Lanka) and another an Army officer in India. It would have been strange if their letters home had not aroused some degree of wanderlust in a sheltered young woman, but the conventions of the time made independent travel problematical. She taught herself to paint in watercolour, with some advice from her father's friend Sir Edwin Landseer (1802–73), Queen Victoria's favourite painter, but until 1868, when she was 31, a painting holiday in the Western Isles was the closest she had ever come to visiting a wild place. In that year, however, Eka Gordon Cumming was invited to visit her younger half-sister Emilia Sergison, married to an Army officer in India, and after some dithering decided to accept. The outcome she described as 'a year of enchantment', which led to her first publication, *From the Hebrides to the Himalayas* (1876). By then her 'year of enchantment' had given her a taste for more. She spent 'two happy years' in Ceylon and for the next twelve, carrying notebooks and paintbox, she was almost constantly in strange lands or on the sea, visiting Australia, Fiji, Hawaii, Egypt, California, Japan and China. Sometimes she travelled alone but, given her aristocratic connections, quite often as the guest of state governors and high officials of the British Empire. As a close friend of Sir Arthur Hamilton Gordon, son of the Earl of Aberdeen and newly appointed Governor of Fiji, she was invited to travel there in 1874 with his family via Singapore, the Torres Strait Islands, Brisbane and Sydney. At Brisbane the party was joined by Sir Arthur's new private secretary Alfred Maudslay (1854–1931), who would later become a distinguished archaeologist. In a letter to his sister, Maudslay gave a candid description of his boss's guest:

> *Miss Gordon Cumming … is a very tall, plain woman, a regular globe-trotter, wonderfully good-tempered, no tact, very pushing when she wants something done, and yet one of the best creatures in the world … . She is sufficiently clothed in suits of brown holland and blue serge and wears an enormous pith hat.*

Her 'wonderful good temper' was remarked on throughout her life; affable, determined and aristocratically self-assured despite her plainness of person, she has been described as 'less an explorer than a tourist on the grand scale'. Maudslay went on to remark that she had 'written travel books in two large volumes' which he had not been tempted to read; he was more interested in her art, expressing qualified admiration (he thought that she overpainted, not knowing when to stop) and remarking that her *raison d'être* was to wander the world 'and see things and paint them'. This might lead one to suppose that she saw herself more as an artist than a writer; more probably she saw the roles as complementing each other. Although both she and Isabella Bird were curious and dauntless observers of landscape, architecture and human behaviour in the countries they visited, their recording methods were not really comparable. The painstaking detailing of Isabella Bird has been rightly appreciated, but Eka Gordon Cumming's style is more economical, probably because she was less reliant on words. Hers was primarily a visual imagination, and the use of her paintings as illustration meant that she could cut explanatory corners.

She was also skilled in evoking atmosphere through the use of other people's art as an imaginative reference. In 'Across the Yellow Sea', an article published in *Blackwood's Magazine* in 1880, she wrote of a voyage she had taken on a small Danish trading brig from Chefoo (Yantai) on the Shendong Peninsula in China to Nagasaki in Japan, during which for a week the ship was becalmed and wrapped in a clammy shroud of fog:

> *Not one sail did we sight in all these seven days; but when the mist was most dense and brooding silence which we could almost feel seemed to rest upon the waters, a large skeleton junk floated noiselessly past us, its great black ribs looking weird and spirit-like like one of Gustave Doré's strange fancies. There could be no doubt that all her crew had perished, – at all events no living thing remained upon her.*

Gustave Doré (1832–83) had in 1878 published a set of 38 disturbing engravings for an edition of Coleridge's great poem of the supernatural, *The Rime of the Ancient Mariner*, and the apt association of the spectral ship of the well-known engravings with the skeleton junk loose in the ocean saves the need for lengthy description. Many of the places visited by Eka Gordon Cumming – California, Hawaii, India, China and Japan – had also been visited by Isabella Bird. Often the watercolours of one of these near-contemporaries might fittingly have illustrated the writing of the other.

In *Across the Yellow Sea*, Eka Gordon Cumming, like Isabella Bird a committed Christian, went on to write of the terrible fate of early missionaries in Japan, where both Buddhists and Christians were, as recently as the late eighteenth century, subjected by Japanese rulers to torture, death by burnings, impalement and crucifixion. In an essay published in the *British Quarterly Review* in 1885 titled 'The Offerings of the Dead', she also spoke out against widespread female infanticide in China, blaming the cult of ancestor-worship which prescribed that only sons could perform rites necessary to the repose of the dead. But she was too broadminded to suggest that Christians had always behaved perfectly, and showed a rather modern interest in the way that similar superstitions and folklore were shared by different religions across the world. The healing rites at the 'Clootie Well' at Munlochy in Presbyterian Ross-shire, she pointed out, were also found in Catholic Ireland, at Muslim religious sites in Constantinople (Istanbul) and Jerusalem, and in Buddhist Ceylon. She seems to have felt strongly drawn to China, and it was appropriate that on a visit to Peking (Beijing) she found a cause which she would support for the rest of her life. In 1879 she met William Hill Murray (1850–1931), a Scottish missionary who had founded China's first School for the Blind. She was impressed by a Numeral Type System, comparable to Braille, that Murray had invented, enabling blind people to read by touching raised numbers, representing the 408 syllables of Mandarin Chinese. In 1900 she published a book which explained and promoted Murray's invention.

When her travelling days were over, Eka Gordon Cumming settled at College House in Crieff with her widowed sister Eleanora Grant. She continued to write travel books and articles, and arranged temporary exhibitions of her paintings at Kew Gardens in London, Glasgow and Liverpool. She failed, unfortunately, to find a permanent home for her vast collection; the largest segment was eventually housed, due to the diligence of a group of friends including Alfred Maudslay, at Cambridge University Museum of Archaeology and Anthropology, along with her collection of Fijian artefacts. Some paintings were given away to friends and family members; since she had, she remarked in *Memories* (1904), 'started in life with fifty first cousins, about twice as many second and third cousins, and collaterals without number', many beautiful works, barely appreciated, were thus lost for a time. Only quite recently have some begun to reappear at auction, where they now command prices that would surely have gratified her. Her humorous, bright and humane writing, dismissed in her lifetime by uppity male critics like the American Henry Adams (1838–1918), who absurdly described it as 'a collection of anecdotes, without much interest', deserves a similar revival.

Constance Frederica Gordon Cumming died in Crieff on 4 September 1924 aged 87, and was buried nearby at Ochtertyre where, with so many cousins, she unsurprisingly had family connections.

16

TURNING
THE CENTURY

Nature has unmistakeably [sic] *given to women a greater brain power. This is at once perceivable in childhood. Yet man deliberately sets himself to stunt that early evidence of mental capacity, by laying down the law that woman's education shall be on a lower level than that of man's. I maintain to honourable gentlemen that this procedure is arbitrary and cruel, and false to Nature. I characterise it as Infamous.*

Lady Florence Dixie (1855–1905)
Preface to *Gloriana* 1890

THE PATRONISING DISMISSAL of Susan Ferrier's writing by Matthew 'Monk' Lewis in 1817 and the similar contempt shown for Constance Frederica Gordon Cumming's by Henry Adams sixty years later might suggest that in the interval nothing had changed. In fact, a lot had changed. Critics like Lewis and Adams had become less numerous; the quality of Susan Ferrier's work, the wide popularity of Margaret Oliphant's and the emergence of new talent had demanded more impartial and respectful reviews. Editors of the powerful literary journals had became more willing to accept contributions by women, and women themselves were emboldened to speak out on subjects previously regarded as the sole preserve of men. As early as 1841, Edinburgh-born Margaret Mylne (1806–92) published a thoughtful article titled 'Woman and her Social Position' in the influential *Westminster Review*; in it she traced instances of gender equality in European society, and called for women 'who exercised the duties of citizens' to be granted the right to vote in elections to Parliament. In 1866, she was a signatory to the petition, organised by John Stuart Mill and headed by Mary Somerville, to extend the franchise to women which, although summarily dismissed, was the most significant indication so far that women had had enough.

In the following decades, while women continued to be excluded from male colleges and became more irritated than thrilled by the award of 'honorary fellowships' to male societies, all their dissatisfaction was demonstrated in the life of one Scotswoman, of aristocratic birth but sympathetic to the aspirations of all her sex. Lady Florence Dixie (1855–1905), feminist, writer, traveller, political campaigner,

vocal supporter of Irish Home Rule and enthusiast for women's sport, used a privileged position to speak up for the voiceless, and packed into a short life more
activity than most people manage if they live almost twice as long.

Florence Dixie née Douglas was born in Dumfriesshire at Kinmount House,
Cummertrees, the family seat of her father, the 8th Marquess of Queensberry and
his wife Caroline Clayton. She had four elder siblings and a twin, Lord James Douglas, a loving but weak child who relied too much on his sister's robust good nature.
Florence was only five when her father died, probably by suicide; in the aftermath
her mother converted to Roman Catholicism, decamped to Paris to escape the
wrath of her fearsome Protestant mother-in-law and brought her younger children
up in her new faith. Florence was sent to a convent school where she rebelled
against the Church's dogmatism, and hard discipline did nothing to reconcile her
to any religious belief. In 1875, aged 19, she married Sir Alexander Beaumont Churchill, 11th Baronet Dixie, known as 'Beau', with whom she might have been happy,
had it not been for an out-of-control gambling habit of which she had previously
been unaware. Within months of her marriage, she was writing mournfully:

> It was a great blow to me to find that the last remnant of a once splendid fortune
> must go to pay [this] debt. Beau has been so accustomed to have heaps of money
> at his command that he cannot understand that it is all gone. By selling Bosworth
> [Dixie's family house and estate in Leicestershire] … these debts could be met.'

The estate went, but the marriage endured; two sons were born and in 1877 Florence published, to disappointingly little profit, her first book, *Abel Avenged; A
Dramatic Tragedy*.

She had better luck with the second. In 1878, in order, she said, 'to flee from
the strict confines of Victorian society', but more probably from angry creditors,
she and her husband and brother James crossed the Atlantic to South America,
where they travelled, mostly on horseback, in the vast territory of Patagonia. Florence Dixie's account of this adventure was published on her return as *Riding
Across Patagonia* (1880), and it was a bestseller. By this time, however, she was
moving on. In 1881, she managed to talk herself into an appointment as a field
correspondent of the London *Morning Post* and, no doubt after much pulling of
strings, was sent to cover the aftermath of the Anglo-Zulu War in South Africa.
The first woman journalist to report from a war zone, she interviewed the Zulu
King Cetshwayo, whose detention by the British she opposed; on her return she
wrote two books, *A Defence of Zululand and its King* (1882) and *In The Land of
Misfortune* (1882), which are credited with helping Cetshwayo to regain his throne.

As a passionate campaigner for women's equality, with strong views on their
education, dress, inheritance rights and the iniquity of the law that forced divorced

women to cede guardianship of their children to their former husbands, Florence Dixie's name frequently appeared in the correspondence columns of British newspapers. She also contributed to feminist literature a quixotic novel titled *Gloriana; or the Revolution of 1900* (1890), which tells the improbable tale of a young woman named Gloria de Lara who, horrified by the unfair treatment of women, disguises herself as a man and adopts the name Hector L'Estrange. Becoming a Member of Parliament, 'Hector' leads a revolutionary party named The Women's Volunteer Company, is involved in violence, accused of murder, and outed as a woman. Fortunately these trials prove temporary; the book ends with Gloria elevated to heroic status and, a century later, reverently remembered as the enabler of the peaceful, prosperous egalitarian utopia existing in 1999.

Florence Dixie's personal life was marked by tragedy. Her twin brother James, emotionally dependent on her into adulthood, had inherited the mental illness occasionally evident in the Douglas family and, after a disastrous marriage and spells of increasingly manic behaviour, cut his own throat in 1891. During the following decade her unpleasant and vengeful eldest brother John Sholto, 9th Marquess of Queensberry, attracted much public opprobrium for his role in the downfall of Oscar Wilde (1855–1900), her husband continued to run up alarming debts and she herself prematurely developed crippling arthritis.

None of these misfortunes, however, affected her ardour for the causes she believed in. She joined the National Union of Women's Suffrage Societies, wrote a book, *The Horrors of Sport*, arguing against the hunting of wild animals, endured an assassination attempt due to her outspokenness about Irish affairs and fearlessly aired her atheist opinions. In her preface to *Gloriana*, where her spikiness might seem to tip over into absurdity, she was gleefully using her gift for riling men. In 1895 she riled them further by becoming the first President of the British Ladies Football Club.

Forced to move house a number of times due to her husband's gambling debts, in the later years of her life Florence Dixie found shelter at Glen Stuart, a house on the Kinmount estate on the Solway coast, where she died of diphtheria on 7 November 1905, aged fifty. Although she is known to have been buried in the private enclosure of the Queensberry family at nearby Gooley Hill, in obedience to her funeral instructions no religious rites were observed, and no monument marks where she lies.

*

Because of her aristocratic birth and the opportunities it afforded her, as well as her charisma and literary talent, in some ways Florence Dixie was a one-off. Yet her passions and preoccupations were shared by women of less celebrity, and her best personal attributes may have been her solidarity and enthusiasm for a common cause. When invited to become President of the British Ladies Football Club, she had agreed on condition: that the players 'should enter into the spirit of the game with heart and soul', and she lived her life on the same principle. Her aims, however, were far from unique.

The last thirty years of the nineteenth century showed a marked change in British and American women's thinking about their place in society. Younger women, tired of being 'ladylike', were voicing exasperation rather than just feeling it. Elementary education, made compulsory in Britain by the Education Act of 1880, gave more women access to print media and, egged on by feminist writers including the Glasgow poet Marion Bernstein and Scottish prose writers Felicia Mary Skene (1821–99) and Charlotte Stopes (1840–1929), through reading to the new delight of forming heterodox opinions. Most importantly, there was a growing perception that the way forward lay not in the crying of lone voices, but in the power of group action. Women of all social classes began to realise what had long been apparent to a few; to progress further towards their goals, they must break in to the ultimate citadel of male power and privilege, the House of Commons in Parliament.

The National Society for Women's Suffrage was founded in 1867, and between 1890 and 1919 was headed by Millicent Fawcett (1847–1929), a keen suffragist who believed in reasoned argument rather than direct action. By the turn of the century, however, many women were becoming impatient with this approach, and in 1905 a breakaway society, the Women's Social and Political Union (WSPU), was founded in London by Emmeline Pankhurst. Across Scotland branches were quickly established, not only in the cities but as far afield as the Western and Northern Isles. A strategy of civil disobedience was decided on; the tactics of the 'Suffragettes' – including chaining themselves to street railings, setting fire to postboxes, smashing windows and setting bombs to damage public buildings – are well documented, as are the barbaric and disproportionate punishments inflicted upon them.

A strong advocate of this type of direct action was Helen Archdale née Russel (1876–1949), born at Nenthorn near Kelso to Helen de Lacey Evans, who had been a student of the pioneering feminist Dr Sophia Jex-Blake (1840–1912) and Alexander Russel, editor of *The Scotsman*, who had supported Jex-Blake's successful campaign for admission to the Medical School at the University of Edinburgh. Helen was educated at St Leonard's School at St Andrews, founded in 1877 with the aim of giving girls the educational opportunities previously reserved for men, and at the University of St Andrews where she was among the first women graduates. In 1901 she married a professional soldier, Theodore Montgomery Archdale, with whom she spent time in India, although little is known of her experience there. It is clear, however, that despite the birth of three children, the marriage was not successful. It seems likely that Helen's outspoken feminism clashed with the establishment view of a senior Army officer.

By 1908 Helen Archdale was back in Edinburgh and in October 1909, now a member of the WSPU, took part in a huge pro-suffrage demonstration in the city centre. Later that month, she was arrested in a disturbance at the Kinnaird Hall in Dundee during a meeting where the local MP Winston Churchill was scheduled to speak. Arrested with four others, she went on hunger strike, but was released after four days of a ten-day prison sentence. Undeterred, she moved on to London, where in 1911 she was again arrested and sentenced to two months in prison for breaking windows – her daughter Betty (1907–2000) later remembered picking up stones in the street for her mother to throw. On her release, she and her husband parted, probably with mutual relief, and Helen went to work on the WSPU news-paper *The Suffragette*. It may be that as a journalist she achieved more sympathetic understanding for the Women's Movement than she did as a smasher of windows; she later became the influential editor of the initially leftist magazine *Time and Tide*, founded by her partner Margaret Haig Thomas, Lady Rhondda, with whom she moved in after separating from her husband. She also contributed articles on women's issues to *The Times*, *The Scotsman* and the *Daily News*.

It is hardly surprising that the socially divisive period of the suffragettes, which lasted from 1905 until 1918, produced more intense journalism than good fiction; an exception in Scotland being the well-regarded novels of the Findlater sisters Mary (1865–1943) and Jane (1866–1946), joint authors of *Crossriggs* (1908) and *Penny Moneypenny* (1911). The suffragette movement proved one of the great catalysts of change in the public perception of women, pushing the image of female subservience, all too common in Victorian society and literature, firmly into his-tory. It was, however, cut short by another catalyst for change which was also a cataclysm, the outbreak in 1914 of the First World War.

*

There is no doubt that the conduct of women, during the 'Great War' that con-vulsed Europe in the years 1914–18, changed the attitude of many men towards their capabilities, though it is a mistake to think that it led directly to their enfran-chisement. Although an Act of Parliament of 1918 gave votes to women over the age of thirty, subject to the educational and property qualifications already required for men, its primary aim was to extend the franchise to soldiers returning from the War. Not until 1928 would women's rights be equalised. On the outbreak of war, however, the battle for suffrage rights was put on hold, and women for the first time went to work in agriculture, munitions factories, transport, warehouses and hos-pitals. Among women in Scotland the icon of this period, and an enduring legend, was Elsie Inglis (1864–1917), born in India but educated and trained as a doctor in Edinburgh. She was also a prominent suffragist and author of an unpublished novel titled *The Story of a Modern Woman*, written around 1904 and found in manuscript after her death in 1917. But it was not as a novelist that Elsie Inglis was destined to be remembered. She had already had a distinguished career as a physician and surgeon when in 1914, aged fifty, she defied the famous advice from the Home Office in London that she should 'go home and sit still'. Instead, with the approval of the governments of France and Serbia, she raised enough money to found the Scottish Women's Hospitals, which cared for badly wounded soldiers close to the battlefields in France and eastern Europe. The first contingent of nurses who left Edinburgh were Scots, but women of other nationalities were inspired to join them; as doctors, nurses, ambulance drivers and orderlies, they worked in makeshift hospitals and field stations, performing operations, enduring severe hardship, coming under enemy fire and developing the solidarity of common purpose.

Many searing eye-witness accounts, novels and poems, meditations on the horror and futility of modern conflict were written during and after the 'Great War', but inevitably they were the work of the men who endured them. Women who also served, particularly doctors and nurses, were writing too, but their writing was more likely to be official reports, pleas for donations, informal diaries and letters to their families. In recent years these have been discovered, curated and some published; forming an important part of our national record. The research of Eileen Crofton for *The Women of Royaumont* (1997), an account of the foundation and running of the Scottish Women's Hospital at the Abbaye de Royaumont thirty miles from Paris, produced many examples of this enlightening but functional kind of prose. Even deeply moving personal diaries such as those of Mary Lee Milne (1873–1945), a minister's widow from Selkirk who, aged 43, joined Dr Inglis in Southern Russia as cook to a unit of 75 doctors and nurses, were never intended as 'literature'. Neither the Women's Movement nor the War produced much other than necessary writing. Women were exhausted and preoccupied with other matters. It was left to a young Scottish woman who did not arrive in France until just before the Armistice was signed in November 1918, to write a memoir of her experience in the aftermath of the War so vivid that it still pulses with life more than a century after the events it describes.

Christina Keith (1889–1963) was born in Thurso, a small town on the far north coast of Scotland overlooking the Pentland Firth, the eldest of the eight children of Peter Keith, a solicitor, and his wife Catherine Bruce. Her parents were themselves well-educated, and had high aspirations for their daughters as well as their sons. Christina was educated first at the Miller Institute, the forerunner of Thurso High School, leaving aged 14 to board, like Helen Archdale, at St Leonard's School in St Andrews. Finally she moved to a small girls' school in Abercromby Place, Edinburgh, which specialised in preparing its pupils for university entrance. Gaining a place at the University of Edinburgh, first open to women students in the year of her birth, she chose to study Latin and Greek, subjects usually considered the preserve of men. Thus she entered the academically privileged world which for women a generation earlier had been no more than a dream.

Her choice of subjects suggests that Christina Keith was already aiming for an academic career. She had to learn Greek from scratch, but still graduated in 1910 with First-Class Honours in Latin, Greek and Classical Archaeology and, funding herself by winning scholarships, spent some months studying sculpture at the British School at Rome. She next enrolled at Newnham, a women's college in Cambridge founded in 1871, where she was again placed in the First-Class Honours list, but was not allowed officially to graduate; astonishingly, women students at Cambridge were not awarded degrees until 1948. Nonetheless, by June 1914 Christina Keith's scholarly distinction had secured her a lectureship in the Classics department of Armstrong College in Newcastle, a division of Durham University. There, as her brothers joined the armed forces, students left to enlist and war engulfed Europe, she spent the next four years. In 1918, she applied successfully for a post as tutor in Classics at St Hilda's College, Oxford but, just as she was about to re-enter the female ambience she had known in Cambridge, an opportunity arose for what would prove the great adventure of her life. That such an experience could have occurred with the encouragement of parents, and without stumbling-blocks devised by disapproving men, shows how greatly the traditional view of female dependence had already shifted as the nineteenth century segued into the twentieth.

When Christina Keith died in 1963, among her papers was found in manuscript a short book, written under the pseudonym 'A Fool in France' which, with the remembered excitement of youth yet a sophisticated mastery of narrative, tells the story of a six-month interruption in a scholarly life. In July 1918 the British Army, aware that a great number of young soldiers were soon to return to civilian life lacking the education and skills needed to make them employable, devised an enterprise which aimed to fill fruitfully the impatient months between the end of combat and demobilisation. The Young Men's Christian Association (YMCA) was charged with organisation, and the Principal of Armstrong College, Sir Henry Hadow (1859–1937) was appointed as the Army's Director of Education. Volunteer teachers were required and Christina Keith, probably recruited by Sir Henry and with permission to delay her Oxford appointment, decided to apply; thus she was catapulted from the rarified ambience of a university department into an environment disordered, uncomfortable and demanding beyond any she had ever known. Fortunately, gifted with humour, tolerance and an easy acceptance of life as she found it, she rose to the challenge with courage and grace.

The first part of 'A Fool in France', as she chose to call herself, is written with a verve and hunger for new experience which recalls the jaunty tone of Charlotte Waldie's setting out for Belgium and the battlefield of Waterloo a century before.

Christina tells of adventures and near-catastrophes, of a night spent alone in a spooky house in a forest, of her time in classrooms and canteens where she learned to live alongside people of many backgrounds, of fleeting friendships, flirtations with young officers and the unjudgemental relationships she made with the private soldiers who became her pupils. As well as teaching, she spent time working in the Army canteens erected around her base in Dieppe. She shared the celebrations when the Armistice was signed, made shortbread – probably for the first and last time in her life – and triumphantly organised a Christmas dinner for 16 officers with wine and decorations, despite a local dearth of turkeys and plum puddings. For all the privations, she was loving every minute of it.

In the second part of the book, which again recalls Charlotte Waldie distressed by horrors on the field of Waterloo, the relish for adventure is undiminished, but laughter falters and the tone darkens. Christina Keith was reluctant to return home without a sight of the battlefields where her brother and so many of her contemporaries had fought, but the terrain was dangerous and sightseeing discouraged. As her time in France dwindled, however, she applied for permission to travel through the area of the river Somme, the 'Flanders Fields' where the most bloody engagements of the European war had been so recently waged. Persistence succeeded; after a frustrating delay she eventually secured a permit for two, and accompanied by an unnamed English 'Hut Lady' (the title given to volunteer workers in the Army recreation centres), she travelled 'up the line' by train through the ruined towns of Amiens, Albert, Arras and Cambrai, names for ever associated with the tragedy of the trenches, appalling loss of life, hastily dug graves and the senseless destruction of war.

The photographs we know are desolating enough, but Flanders was seen by Christina Keith in the raw aftermath of its destruction, and her descriptions haunt the imagination. After a night journey through broken countryside beyond ruined Albert, alarmed by 'scarred and shapeless things' seen from the window of the slowly moving train, she fearfully asked a soldier in the compartment what they were. Trees, she was told. 'Thiepval Wood and the dawn. The hour when the boys stood to.' The horror of these terse words, recalling 1 July 1916, the first day of the Battle of the Somme and the last dawn that thousands of the boys would ever see, profoundly affected Christina. 'Every time I call up the picture of Thiepval Wood and what had been its trees,' she wrote later, 'I see again the patchy light falling cold and grey and the desolation that overwhelmed me.' All around lay a landscape of churned ochre mud, where frightened French refugees peered furtively from abandoned dugouts, and groups of hastily made wooden crosses marked young men's graves – gently described by a group of nurses at a base hospital not as 'military cemeteries' but as 'the places where the boys are'. Then at the Vimy Ridge battlefield, where only a year previously 3,650 Canadian and British troops had died, in the unbroken silence and in a desolate land Christina Keith found and picked a flower. 'It was the commonest little yellow thing, which grows in unnoticed thousands at home,' she said, 'but I held it reverently and greedily, and the Hut Lady looked at it too.'

It is not known for certain whether Christina Keith tried to find a publisher for her book, though her care not to mention its *personae* by name may indicate that she had it in mind. Perhaps in the flood of war memoirs struggling for publication in the 1920s, it was simply overlooked. In the autumn of 1919 she returned from the deserted camps of northern France to Oxford and her delayed tutorship at St Hilda's; a photograph taken soon afterwards in a leaf-strewn garden shows her smiling demurely and beautifully dressed among her colleagues, five formidable academic ladies in large hats, furs and highly polished shoes. It is not known either when exactly she wrote the account of her time in France, although its fresh and vivid recall suggests that she felt some urgency to set it all down. Whatever the facts, almost a century passed before it came to the attention of her great-niece, the Scottish writer and historian Flora Johnston. Introduced and edited by her, it was published in 2014 as *War Classics: The Remarkable Memoir of Scottish Scholar Christina Keith on the Western Front*, to coincide with the centenary of the outbreak of the Great War.

Christina Keith spent all her working life at St Hilda's, teaching and tutoring young women in Latin and Greek. She also taught inmates at Oxford Prison, having long since proved her ability to engage the attention of uneducated young men. She remained unmarried and, retiring in 1942, turned north again. The last twenty years of her life were spent in her native Caithness, with its biting winds, mutable skies and fitful sunshine, and the small town of Thurso with its face to the sea. She wrote newspaper articles, mostly on topics suggested by local history, and a biography of Robert Burns, *The Russet Coat* (1956). Her biography of Sir Walter Scott, *The Author of Waverley*, was published posthumously in 1964.

17

MY OWN
COUNTRY

Laddie, my lad, when ye gang at the tail o' the plough
  An' the days draw in,
When the burnin' yellow's awa' that was aince a-lowe
  On the braes o' whin,
Dae ye mind o' me that's deaved wi' the wearyfu' south
  An' its puir concairns
While the weepies fade on the knowes at the river's mouth
  In the Howe o' the Mearns?

Violet Jacob (1863–1946)
Songs of Angus 1915

WHEN CHRISTINA KEITH returned to Britain in 1918 from her eventful six months in France, it was to a country where the tranquil transition from the nineteenth to the twentieth century was a distant memory, soured now by grim reality. Soldiers coming home from 'the war to end wars' found promises of employment and prosperity unfulfilled; new war memorials revealed the cold statistics of loss, and the words 'For King and Country' became bitter in the mouths of the bereaved and the scarred young men who believed that their country had let them down. The Russian Revolution of 1917, which saw the execution of the Tsar and the rise of Communism, followed by the establishment of the Weimar Republic in Germany, had profoundly shaken the political structure of Europe. Social divisions widened, and there came a despairing perception that though the conflict with Germany had stalled, there might be a second episode to come. A worse dictator than Kaiser Wilhelm was waiting in the wings.

Against such a background, it was inevitable that forms of cultural expression would change in art, architecture, music and drama as well as writing, as young artists struggled to reflect the new reality of a broken world. This was bad news for late Victorian writers such as J. M. Barrie and Annie S. Swan (1859–1943), whose couthy tales of humble Scottish country life seemed cloying and irrelevant to a battle-hardened generation. Sadly, more significant novelists, Margaret Oliphant and Robert

Louis Stevenson among them, also suffered a prolonged eclipse. The break with the past occasioned by the War was, nonetheless, beneficial, since it enabled the 'Scottish Renaissance' (1920–c.45), a vigorous flowering in art, architecture, drama, music and, particularly literature. The emergence of 'Lallans', a 'synthetic Scots' hybrid language drawing on regional dialects and largely invented by the influential Christopher Murray Grieve, aka 'Hugh MacDiarmid' (1892–1978), was particularly significant in poetry, as was the new realism in fiction foreshadowed by George Douglas Brown (1869–1902) in *The House with the Green Shutters* (1901). In different forms, this change of approach would strengthen the novels of Neil M. Gunn (1891–1973), Lewis Grassic Gibbon (1901–35) and A. J. Cronin (1896–1981).

The post-war period also brought new opportunities for women writers; Catherine Carswell, Nan Shepherd and Naomi Mitchison (1897–1999) would all publish their first novels in the 1920s. Outspoken on social and political issues and unafraid to explore personal emotions and sexuality, these writers were the beneficiaries of the feminists and suffragists who had fought for women's rights in the previous generation. From them they inherited a freedom unthinkable for women like Mary Brunton and Susan Ferrier a century before, obliged to pussyfoot in a hostile male world, and write in the shadow of Calvin. It is easy, nonetheless, to overstate progress. In a significant publication, *Modern Scottish Poetry: An Anthology of the Scottish Renaissance 1920–1945* (1957), edited by Maurice Lindsay, thirty men are featured and six women, only one of whom, Helen B. Cruickshank (1886–1946), was closely identified with the 'Scottish Renaissance'.

Among Lindsay's choices, however, was one who may be regarded as the most substantial and enduring contributor to Scottish women's writing on both sides of 1900, but who does not fit easily into the narrative of progressiveness. Violet Jacob (1863–1946), was a generation older than the young mould-breakers of the post-war years and, although at the dawn of the movement her vernacular poetry was admired, even by more radical poets, she was never in thrall to modernity. Sidestepping MacDiarmid's literary Lallans in favour of traditional dialect, and substituting for gritty realism a more lyrical vision of the past, she rather provided a counterbalance to the eager push for innovation.

Violet Jacob, diarist, novelist and poet, was born Violet Augusta Mary Fredericka Kennedy Erskine at House of Dun, a mansion built near Montrose in the 1740s for her ancestor David Erskine, Lord Dun (1670–1758). Her mother, Catherine Jones, was a Welsh gentlewoman from Carmarthenshire and her father, Captain William Kennedy Erskine, Laird of Dun (1828–70) was the son of Augusta FitzClarence (1803–65), an illegitimate but acknowledged daughter of King William IV (1765–1837). Violet was related to the Erskines, Earls of Mar and to the Kennedys, Marquesses of Ailsa and, with such a background, it might seem surprising that she grew up with such an extensive command of the 'Doric' dialect of Angus and the Mearns. A farm worker at Dun is said to have explained that 'as a bairn she was aye in and oot amo' the ploomen's feet at the Mains o' Dun.' In time, her acquisition of an alternative language would serve her well. Even the hypercritical Hugh MacDiarmid, who published her writing in *Northern Numbers* (1921–23) and *Contemporary Scottish Studies* (1925–27) called her 'by far the most considerable of contemporary vernacular poets', and linked her to earlier aristocratic women poets, Jane Elliot of Minto and Carolina Oliphant, Lady Nairn.

In 1894, aged thirty, Violet Kennedy Erskine married Arthur Otway Jacob (1867–1936) an Irish officer serving in a British regiment, the 20th Hussars. Their only child, Arthur Henry Augustus Jacob (1895–1916), known as 'Harry', was born the following year in the Army base at Colchester in Essex. Almost immediately afterwards, the family moved with the regiment to the garrison at Mhow in central India. Before leaving Dun, Violet promised to write regularly to her widowed mother in Angus, and the letters she sent, along with the extensive diaries she kept for her own record, form a detailed account of what was probably the happiest period of her life.

Like Flora Annie Steel, Violet Jacob was strongly attracted to India. Her diaries (written, she explained later, so that 'If I live to be old, I … shall be able to look back on the sights and sounds of this – to me – beloved country and the good days we had in it, and even on its trivialities…') are crammed with her impressions of a golden landscape, exotic animals, trees and temples, word pictures enhanced by bold illustration. Like Constance Frederica Gordon Cumming she was an artist, with a particular gift for painting flowers; five volumes of her Indian flower paintings remain in the collection of the Royal Botanic Garden in Edinburgh. She was also attracted to the people of India, learning some Hindi (as Flora Annie Steel advised in her *Complete Indian Cook and Housekeeper*), riding alone across the burning plains, visiting mosques and temples to observe their rituals. She developed an interest in Indian folklore which she shared with her small son.

Yet it is hard not to wonder whether the fascination with exotic locations and customs which Violet Jacob felt, arose from what she described as their 'weirdness', rather than their emotional impact. The diaries give no clue, for however profound her understanding of the psychology of her fictional creations, she was a woman of her class and time, and her own intimate feelings were strictly private. Her diary entries are informative but not confessional, and if she was moved spiritually by her encounters with unfamiliar locations and religious beliefs, she did not say so. Hers was an observer's account; the diaries contain no indiscretions and certainly no criticism of the social and political scene. Indeed, apart from responsiveness to the visual beauty of India, she seems to have had little in common with Flora Annie Steel, who loved the country passionately but had a burning desire to change it. Violet Jacob felt no such imperative. Despite her untypical behaviour – travelling without an escort, smoking and wearing trousers on her expeditions – she was a British Army officer's wife, a representative of the ruling class, and seems not to have questioned the propriety of the Raj. She did her duty, volunteering as a nurse at the military hospital at Mhow, caring for sufferers from plague, enteritis and malaria, but almost all the Indians she knew were either her servants or members of the princely caste, whom she met through her husband's diplomatic contacts.

Nor did her experience in India greatly influence her subsequent writing. Her first published volume of poetry, *Verses* (1905) contains nine 'Poems of India', and though three short stories, 'The Black Man's Hand', 'The Fringe of the Jungle' and 'Other People's Gods' appeared in *The Fortune Hunters and Other Stories* (1910), they were a negligible part of her literary legacy. When in the early 1930s she raked out her Indian diaries, retrieved paintings and letters and had them typed and bound with a cover of her own design, she was packing up a dream. Long before 1930 the landscape in her mind had relocated, slipping away from the glaring plains, mysterious shrines and 'low hot moons' of India to the damp sky and blustering winds of north-east Scotland, and 'the knowes at the river's mouth in the Howe o' the Mearns'.

Until the Jacobs returned from India to England in 1900, Violet's only published work had been *The Bailie MacPhee* (1888), a comic narrative poem co-authored with a friend, the architect Walter Douglas Campbell (1850–1914). But she had not given up creative writing and, while still in India, had begun to write a novel. So strongly is Violet Jacob now associated with Angus and the Mearns of Aberdeenshire that it is easily forgotten that she was brought up, after her father's early death, by a Welsh mother, and loved the culture and landscape of Wales. Her first novel *The Sheep-Stealers* (1902), which she began in India, is set in 'a tract of country lying at the foot of the Black Mountain, which rises just inside the Welsh border', and is dedicated to her mother. In this remote place which 'made a kind of intermediate stage between the grandeur of the Twmpa (as the highest summit was called) and the parish of Crishowell with its farmyards and hayfields', is played out the dramatic tale of two young men, Harry Fenton the Squire's son, and Rhys Walters, a farmer forced to go on the run when, in a protest against exorbitant road tolls, he is falsely accused of shooting the tollkeeper.

The central tragedy of the book is the infatuation of both these men for a vain, avaricious young woman, Isoline Ridgeway, who cares for neither but destroys them both by marrying one and driving the other to suicidal despair. The book has a fine cast of supporting characters – Rhys Walters's fanatically religious, unloving mother; the vicar's impudent servant Howlie Seaborne, whose smile 'owing to his rabbit-teeth was almost vertical', but who is capable of heroism; the repulsive 'Pig-driver' James Bumpett, who shelters Rhys only to force him into the crime of sheep-stealing; George Williams, a drifting 'hedger and ditcher' turned criminal, who is the only person in the book redeemed by love. Violet Jacob is an impartial narrator. The protagonist Rhys Walters, socially marginalised by a lie, is neither heroic nor venal; circumstances dictate his actions, and seal his fate.

Yet despite the strength of the plot and the credibility of the characters, perhaps the most memorable aspects of *The Sheep-Stealers* are its evocation of a border region both physical and of the imagination, where ghosts were seen and 'shrines of horror' lay scattered over the bleak countryside, and the obdurate presence of the Black Mountains. In a later novel, *The History of Aythan Waring* (1908), set in the same area, Violet Jacob describes the mountain as 'looming over and dominating the country; a presence sinister and still, brooding changeless, like a foreboding in a troubled heart'. Rarely crossed even by the 'hill folk', this barrier holds the small community in and the wider world out, its immutability scorning the futility of human struggles in the face of indifferent nature. In some ways, *The Sheep-Stealers* rehearses aspects of Violet Jacob's later Scottish fiction; the importance of landscape, the sense of history intruding into the present, the unjudgemental presentation of character and bestowal of dignity on the poor and dispossessed. For a Scottish reader, all that is missing in *The Sheep-Stealers* and the *The History of Aythan Waring* is the rich, flexible dialect of the north-east which the author had learned in the farmyard at Dun, and would use elsewhere to such effect.

The Sheep-Stealers was followed in 1904 by *The Interloper*, the first of Violet Jacob's Scottish novels. Set like *The Sheep-Stealers* in the opening years of the nineteenth century, the story unfolds in the Angus countryside where 'the dark ploughfields stretched sombre, restful, wide', and in the small coastal town of Kaims, in actuality Montrose. Central is the story of the 'interloper' Gilbert Speid, who comes as a stranger from Spain to claim his right of inheritance to the house and estate of Whanland; finding in an attic a portrait of his mother, who died when he was born, he sets out to uncover his own backstory. After encountering his neighbour, the brusque, eccentric Lady Eliza Lamont, Gilbert falls in love with her niece Cecilia Raeburn, and sets in motion the revelation of a tragic love affair of an earlier generation. The narrative is memorable for its account of small-town relationships and rivalries in Kaims, and its vivid, if arguably too large, cast of minor characters. It is enriched by vigorous vernacular speech, especially in the mouths of the itinerant fish-seller, Granny Stirk 'The Queen of the Cadgers' and her grandson Jimmy, who support Gilbert in his wooing of Cecilia and in his search for his true identity. Violet Jacob is at home in this gentle book; atmosphere and landscape are tenderly realised, yet for all its excellence in parts, its regret for the past is only melancholic. Although well received on its publication, it lacks the tragic inevitability of the novel that preceded it, or the one to follow.

The historic internal divisions of Scottish society, and its bitter religious antagonism, were recurring themes in nineteenth-century fiction. Sir Walter Scott's *Old*

Mortality (1816), *The Bride of Lammermoor* (1819) and *Redgauntlet* (1824); James Hogg's *The Brownie of Bodsbeck* (1818); John Galt's *Ringan Gilhazie* (1823) and Robert Louis Stevenson's *Catriona* (1893) all deal with the conflict in Church and State in the two preceding centuries, which tore apart families with irreconcilable loyalties and gnawed at minds disordered by the heaven-and-hell teaching of Calvin. It is no surprise that all of these books were authored by men; war was a subject generally repugnant to women, who in the nineteenth century had other preoccupations and battles to fight. Not until after 1900 did a woman writer have the confidence to venture into this masculine territory, and it seems almost inevitable that she was Violet Jacob, whose *Flemington*, published in 1911, drew its inspiration from House of Dun and the history of her own family.

On one level, *Flemington* is a historical adventure story in the tradition of Scott, Stevenson and Violet Jacob's contemporary John Buchan (1875–1940) but, writing from a woman's perspective, she seems to have found heroic exploits less interesting than the psychology of her characters. She deliberately avoided Scott's habit of building his story around actual figures from history, noting in a brief preface that *Flemington* was not a historical novel, since none of its characters were 'real' people. No doubt this gave her more scope for probing motives and inner conflicts, but she could hardly have denied that it is a novel of history. The 1746 Battle of Culloden, fought between the Jacobite supporters of the displaced Stuart kings and British government forces, its crushing defeat and humiliating aftermath, are wounds in the Scottish consciousness to this day. The setting of the story is again chiefly the braes of Angus and the town of Montrose; House of Dun is represented as Balnillo House, the residence around the time of Culloden of retired judge David Logie, Lord Balnillo – a version of Violet's ancestor David Erskine, Lord Dun. Although owing his position to the Hanoverian government, Lord Balnillo is a Tory with barely concealed Jacobite sympathies. His companion as the story opens is his much younger brother James Logie, a professional soldier who, despite having fought for the Hanoverians, claims to have been a Jacobite sympathiser since he was 15.

To this house and to these politically equivocal people comes on a winter night, as the result of a carriage accident, an unexpected guest, a young man named Archie Flemington. Brought up by his grandmother, the ironically named Christian Flemington, a bitter, unforgiving former Jacobite now turned Whig, Archie presents himself at Balnillo as a portrait painter. In fact, under the influence of his grandmother, he is a government spy in pursuit of James Logie. Thus *Flemington* is a novel of conflict on several levels, setting two political visions, two families, two individuals against each other, and its protagonist is a young man torn between two impulses within himself. Archie Flemington is a Whig, sworn to betray James Logie to the Hanoverian authorities but, as reluctant respect deepens into mutual friendship, he finds his position increasingly painful and difficult to sustain. This dilemma and its consequences drive a taut narrative, played out first on the damp winter braes of Angus and the dreich mudflats of the Montrose Basin, and later on the January retreat from Culloden, the field of blood and broken dreams. There is nothing in this vision of Scotland of flag-waving patriotism, only the tragic consequences of division, of individuals and a country torn apart.

Inhabiting this real landscape is a cast of imaginary characters among the most vivid in Scottish fiction: the calculating, self-protective Lord Balnillo; James Logie, the 'honourable soldier' who is privately generous but chillingly motivated, after his wife's death 'not to be killed, but to kill'; Madam Christian Flemington, a cold, vengeful bully, yet with some remnant of charisma and sense of humour; Archie himself, who loves, betrays, repents and is redeemed through death. There is one other character, however, outside the upper-class ambit of the Flemingtons and Logies, who in life and death has as great a power as any to grip the imagination. This is the Scots-speaking gaberlunzie piper 'Skirling Wattie', legless but with 'the head of Falstaff and the shoulders of Hercules', who rides the Angus countryside in a cart pulled by a team of dogs, carrying seditious letters. Violet Jacob creates Wattie without sentiment; he is grotesque, morally corrupt and capable of betrayal, his coarseness countered only by his enchanting singing voice. Yet with her gift of sympathy for the marginalised, she also shows how the harshness of the beggar's life has made him what he is; his cruel disability, his homelessness, his hunger, his friendlessness apart from his leading dog, the nameless 'yellow cur', symbol of love and loyalty without judgement. So powerfully is this dangerous, pitiable character drawn, that his death is as harrowing as that of a better man. It would be hard to disagree with the judgement of John Buchan who wrote to Violet Jacob that *Flemington* was 'the best Scots romance since [Stevenson's] *The Master of Ballantrae*'.

On 16 July 1916, Arthur and Violet Jacob's only son Harry, a twenty-year-old lieutenant in the Royal Fusiliers, died during the first Battle of the Somme, and was buried at Étaples. A memorial plaque placed by his heartbroken parents in the church at Dun states that their son's love was 'their joy', and records their 'undying pride' in his courage. A friend later wrote that at this loss 'a spring broke in Violet', and although in the many years of life left to her she continued to write, she never produced another full-length novel. It was as if her energy could only be sustained in shorter bursts, and the end of the Great War in 1918 marked the end of her most intensely creative phase. Short stories and poems became her favoured forms.

In 1922, when she had been living for nearly thirty years far away from Angus, Violet Jacob published *Tales of My Own Country*, which blend an exile's yearning for a loved landscape with a vigorous invention of characters and recall of their living language. There were lofty critics at the height of the 'Scottish Renaissance' movement who tried, on the evidence of these stories, to place Violet Jacob among the 'Kailyarders' – a misreading as tendentious as it was insulting. There is nothing couthy or sentimental here, only a mirror held up to the insecurity and hardship of lives endured stoically, and leavened with occasional epiphanies. Violet Jacob's 'own country' was less Scotland than Angus, and she wrote of what she knew; an unstable landscape, capriciously beautiful, wind-raked, indifferent to human endeavour and never far from the sea. Tales such as 'Thievie', 'The Disgracefulness of Auntie Thompson' and 'Anderson' have more in common with Lewis Grassic Gibbon's stories of the Mearns, collected posthumously in *A Scots Hairst* (1967), than with any of J. M. Barrie's couthy *Auld Licht Idylls* (1888).

Violet Jacob was a woman of quiet religious faith, who could see in the setting sun 'a region between which and humanity stood the narrow portal of death'. In a few of her most atmospheric stories such immanence is central; in their chilly sense of an invisible but contiguous world they are reminiscent of Margaret Oliphant's *Tales of the Seen and Unseen*. In 'Annie Cargill', the ghost of a woman long dead and buried in a grave oppressively shrouded with yews, rises in horrible form to smite an old man who in youth had spurned her. 'The Yellow Dog', which may be the embodiment of an evil spirit, whirls around a farmer, misleading him on a lonely road and disappearing suddenly at the place where later the farmer will be found dead.

In the period immediately following the fading of the 'Scottish Renaissance', which coincided with her death in 1946, Violet Jacob's *Tales of My Own Country* went out of print, along with most of her other work. For the next forty years, if she was remembered at all, it was for few anthologised poems, mostly drawn from her 1915 collection *Songs of Angus*. The revival of her prose works came late in the twentieth century, with the new wave of interest in feminism and feminist publishing, specifically of Scottish texts. Young women scholars admired her portrayal of strong, transgressive women who refused to adhere to the expectations of a male society – Christian Flemington; Auntie Thompson; Gilbert Spied's mother Clementina; the eponymous 'Euphemia'. Equally attractive was the author's sympathy with less assertive women, those whose development was hampered, not so much by male aggression as by male incomprehension of their ambition to be other than they were. Yet there was also an unspoken warning in Violet Jacob's writing about women; the saddest are those who, offered the opportunity to change their lives, lack the resolve to embrace it.

In the late novella *The Lum Hat*, collected and republished by Ronald Garden in *The Lum Hat and Other Stories: Last Tales of Violet Jacob* (1982), Christina Miller, the indulged daughter of a provincial bank manager, marries a sea captain and goes with him on a voyage to Australia. Unprepared for marriage and shocked by her husband's rough manners on board, she leaves him and runs back to the stuffy comfort of her father's house. Subsequently her husband dies; for a second time Christina has the chance of fulfilment through love and marriage, but at the last moment refuses, opting for the choking familiarity of small-town life with her ageing father. Violet Jacob was too subtle a writer to take the story beyond this point but, contemplating her future, the price of Christina's failure of courage is clear enough.

Violet Jacob wrote and illustrated books for children, and a history of her family, *The Lairds of Dun* (1931). But her continuing love was poetry, which she wrote throughout her life, initially in English and, like many young writers of her time, leaning rather too heavily on the already outdated poetic vocabulary and prosody of the Victorian Alfred, Lord Tennyson and Elizabeth Barrett Browning. It was only with *Songs of Angus* that she turned away from such models and found her true voice in the language that she used to such effect in her fiction, the rich dialect of the north-east of Scotland. Here she discovered the perfect medium through which to convey the nostalgia of the exile, grief, death and the spirit of place. *Songs of Angus* contained her most celebrated poems: 'Tam i' the Kirk'; 'Hogmanay'; 'The Wild Geese' and 'The Howe o' the Mearns'. The haunting 'Craigo Woods', is an elegy marked by her gift for juxtaposing homely images, the 'stookit corn' and 'braw reid puddock-stules', with the suggestion of less palpable presences:

> Craigo Woods, i' the licht o' September sleepin'
>   And the saft mist o' the morn,
> When the hairst climbs tae yer feet, and the sound o' reapin'
>   Comes up frae the stookit corn,
> And the braw reid puddock-stules are like jewels blinkin'
>   And the bramble happs ye baith,
> O what do I see, i' the lang nicht, lyin' and thinkin'
>   As I see yer wraith – yer wraith?

As time passed death, with the possibility of an afterlife, would become a persistent theme of Violet Jacob's poetry. By 1918, when *More Songs of Angus and Other Poems* was published, her son was dead and the volume, dedicated to him, contains painful memorials. She had been reticent about her emotions in her diaries. In poetry she could channel them through invented personae – homesick exiles, young lovers, shepherds, tinkers, soldiers, old women – but even with intermediaries it is evident that the grief, nostalgia and need for faith are her own.

> I canna see ye, lad, I canna see ye,
> For a' yon glory that's aboot yer heid,
>   Yon licht that haps ye, and the hosts that's wi' ye,

Aye, but ye live, an' it's masel' that's deid ...
  But gin ye see my face or gin ye hear me,
I daurna ask, I maunna seek tae ken,
  Though I should dee, wi' sic a glory near me,
By nicht or day, come ben, my bairn, come ben!

In the mid-twentieth century, with its gleeful literary iconoclasm, younger poets and critics had no time for this kind of poetry; it was to them simplistic, sentimental, and irrelevant to the quest for new forms that reflected the complexity of modernity. But Violet Jacob was indifferent to such opinions, for she knew her strengths and she knew her people. Her ambition was to make poetry out of land, sky and sea, to record the flexible, robust language of the lowland Scots before it was diluted by foreign influences, and to explore the real and symbolic borderlands in which she had passed her life. In a preface to *Songs of Angus*, John Buchan summed up:

> *It is the rarest thing, this use of Scots as a living tongue, and perhaps only the exile can achieve it ... . The dialect is Angus, and in every song there is the sound of the east wind and the rain. Its chief note is longing, like all the poetry of exiles, a chastened melancholy which finds comfort in old, unhappy things as well as the beatitudes of youth. The metres are cunningly chosen, and are most artful when they are simplest; and in every case they provide the exact counterpart to the thought.*

In Scotland today there is a renewed anxiety that although, as Buchan perceived a century ago, 'the various accents remain, the old words tend to be forgotten, and we may be in sight of the time when that noble speech shall be degraded to a northern dialect of English'. If so, the poetry of Violet Jacob, at the end of a line stretching back to the lyrics of Robert Burns and the Scottish novels of Sir Walter Scott, will remind us of how much we have lost.

In 1920 Arthur Jacob retired from the Army and moved with Violet to Ludlow, in the heart of the countryside immortalised by A. E. Houseman (1859–1936) in *A Shropshire Lad*. They were often away from home. A visit to India in 1922 was more painful than pleasant; they met old friends but were haunted by memories of their young son. They spent time in France and Italy, hoping that the climate would alleviate Arthur's chronic asthma, and in the summer went north to Dun where, servants now in short supply, Violet had the novel experience of doing the washing-up. She published two poetry collections, *Bonnie Joann and Other Poems* (1921) and *Northern Lights and Other Poems* (1927), and received an honorary LL.D. from the University of Edinburgh in 1936, the year in which her husband died. 'I hardly know how to stand up to life now,' she wrote to her friend the Brechin artist David Waterson (1870–1954), 'but I will try. I have lost what was more than life to me.'

After this last loss, the exile finally went home. Violet Jacob moved back to Angus, which she had left on her marriage in 1894. She spent the final years of her life at Marywell House, near Kirriemuir, publishing in 1944 *The Scottish Poems of Violet Jacob*, a retrospective collection dedicated to the memory of 'The Comrade Beyond'. She died in September 1946, aged 83, and was buried beside her husband in the graveyard at Dun Parish Church.

18

POSTSCRIPT

Shout, shout, up with your song,
  Cry with the wind, for the dawn is breaking;
March, march, swing you along,
  Wide blows our banner, and hope is waking.

Cicely Hamilton (1872–1952)
The Song of the Women 1911

BY THE END of the nineteenth century, as the reasonable culture of the Enlightenment gradually pushed Calvinism's most restrictive beliefs to the fringes of Scottish society, some of the problems experienced by early women writers had been eased. Their initial anxiety to justify their novels by moral messaging had faded with Calvin's shadow; their writing was more confident, they were exploring different genres and were less afraid to reveal their identity and claim their work as their own. Many were travelling, crossing borders and seeing other ways of life; one of the most striking things about the novels of Margaret Oliphant, the letters of Jane Welsh Carlyle and the memoirs of Mary Somerville, for instance, is how easily their authors fitted in to English society without losing an iota of their Scottish identity. By this time, the bitterness of the post-Union Jacobite eighteenth century was history, and the revival of nationalism in the twentieth still far in the future. Bonded by trading partnerships and the willing participation of Scots in the British Army and Empire, the nineteenth may be seen as the only truly British century.

So for women writers some progress had been made. Their readership had been expanded by better education for women, and it was no longer unthinkable for a woman to be a novelist, a journalist, even a newspaper editor or correspondent. Not unthinkable but, unfortunately, still rare. The traditional, Bible-based teaching of Calvin that in a social group 'the head of the woman is the man' had taken longer to fade than the fear of hellfire; the traditional female roles of housekeeper and childminder suited men too well, and for women writers equal recognition was still a far-off dream. They were accorded fewer serious reviews, and given paltry attention in academia. Like women scientists, mathematicians and explorers, the best they could hope for was to be treated as honorary men. And despite the excellence of post-Great War women novelists such as Nan Shepherd, Naomi Mitchison and Willa Muir (1890–1970) there is evidence that this sexist perception lingered well into the twentieth century.

Nowhere was the continuing bias in favour of men's writing more shamelessly apparent than in *The Scottish Tradition in Literature*, a survey of the Scottish canon by a German scholar, Kurt Wittig, published in 1958 by Oliver & Boyd, one of the great Edinburgh publishers now sadly defunct. The book, which was generally accepted as the most comprehensive study of the subject to date, began with a discussion of *The Bruce*, a long narrative poem written in the 1370s by John Barbour (*c.* 1330–95), and ended with deserved praise for the novels of Neil Gunn, who was still alive and of whom Wittig wrote: 'More clearly even that C. M. Grieve, he embodies the aims of the Scottish Renaissance'. The modern reader, however, will quickly perceive in the book a flaw which, in the laudatory reviews of 1958, seems to have gone largely unremarked. The problem lies not in Wittig's magisterial tone nor in his judgements, which are generally sound, but in the fact that his work is not comprehensive at all. Of the 254 authors mentioned by name in the index, only nine are women, and two of these, Emily Brontë (1818–48) and Augusta, Lady Gregory (1852–1932) were not Scots. Most of the others were minor to the point of obscurity, and few are accorded much more than a passing reference or a one-sentence dismissal. Even allowing for historic inequality of education and opportunities for women, which meant that they were always outnumbered, it is hard to see this imbalance, as recently as 1958, as other than an indication of continuing male blindness to the quality of women's work.

Happily, due to scholarly enthusiasm and the great force of the modern Women's Movement, that imbalance is now well on the way to being rectified. In 1997, forty years after the publication of *The Scottish Tradition in Literature*, another book appeared which restored to women's writing its proper place in the literary canon. Edited by Douglas Gifford and Dorothy McMillan, and published by Edinburgh University Press, *A History of Scottish Women's Writing* consists of 43 scholarly essays, including two on Gaelic literature and several by men, covering the period from the 1560s, when Mary, Queen of Scots was writing poetry in French and feuding with her English cousin Queen Elizabeth, to the 1980s, when the poet and dramatist Liz Lochhead (b. 1947) turned the subject upside down in an energetic and ultra-modern play in Scots, *Mary, Queen Of Scots Got Her Head Chopped Off*. Eighteen of the essays deal at length with the work of nineteenth-century writers ignored by Kurt Wittig, who, in a different climate, are having their work republished and appreciated today.

And given the speed with which new works by Scottish women writers born after 1960 – among them Jackie Kay (b. 1961), Ali Smith (b. 1962), Kathleen Jamie

(b. 1962), A. L. Kennedy (b. 1965), Denise Mina (b. 1966), Gail Honeyman (b. 1972) Jenni Fagan (b. 1977) and Catherine Grosvenor (b. 1978) – are appearing, and the critical attention they now attract, the magnificent *History of Scottish Women's Writing* may need to be updated, but it is unlikely ever to be surpassed.

BIBLIOGRAPHY

Works

BAILLIE, LADY GRISELL: *The Household Book of Lady Grisell Baillie*, ed. R. Scott-Moncrieff (Edinburgh, 1911).

BAILLIE, JOANNA: *Poems: Wherein It Is Attempted to Describe Certain Views of Nature and Rustic Life* (London, 1790); *Arnold* [1790 unpublished]; *Plays of the Passions*, 3 vols (London, 1798–1812); *Miscellaneous Plays* (London, 1804); *The Family Legend* (London, 1810); *Metrical Legends of Exalted Characters* (London 1821); *A Collection of Poems, Chiefly Manuscript, and from Living Authors* (ed.) (London, 1823); *Recollections written at the Request of Miss Berry*, MS from the Hunter-Baillie Papers in the Royal College of Surgeons, (London, 1831); *Witchcraft* (London, 1836); *Fugitive Verses* (London, 1840); *Recollections written to please my nephew, William Baillie*, MS from the Hunterian Society Deposit in the Wellcome Institute for the History of Medicine Library (date unknown); *Ahalya Baee* (Printed for Private Circulation, 1849; London, 1904); *The Collected Letters of Joanna Baillie*, ed. J. Slagle (Newark DE, 1999).

BAILLIE, JOANNA and THOMSON, GEORGE (ed.) *Thomson's Collection of the Songs of Burns, Sir Walter Scott, Bart. and other Eminent Lyric Poets, ancient & modern, united to the select melodies of Scotland and of Ireland and Wales* (London & Edinburgh, 1822–25).

BERNSTEIN, MARION: *Mirren's Musings* (Glasgow, 1876); *A Song of Glasgow Town: The Collected Poems of Marion Bernstein* (Glasgow, 2013).

BIRD, ISABELLA (MRS BISHOP): *The Englishwoman in America* (London, 1856); *Six Months in the Sandwich Islands* (London, 1875); *A Lady's Life in the Rocky Mountains* (London, 1879); *Unbeaten Tracks in Japan* (London, 1880): *The Golden Chersonese and the Way Thither* (London, 1883): *The Yangtze Valley and Beyond* (London, 1899); *Chinese Pictures: China through the eyes of Isabella Bird* (New York, 1900).

BROWN née GORDON, ANNA. 'Mrs Brown of Falkland' letter to the jurist Alexander Fraser Tytler. MSS Collections, University of Edinburgh; MSS Collections, Harvard University.

BRUNTON, MARY: *Self-Control* (Edinburgh, 1811): *Discipline* (Edinburgh, 1814)
*Emmeline, with a Memoir by Alexander Brunton and extracts from her Travel
Diaries* (Edinburgh & London, 1819).

CARLYLE, JANE WELSH: *The Collected Letters of Thomas and Jane Welsh
Carlyle*, 49 vols to date, ed. Ian Campbell, Aileen Christianson et al.
(Edinburgh & Durham NC, 1970–2021).

CHILD, FRANCIS JAMES: *The English and Scottish Popular Ballads* (New York,
1882–98).

DIXIE, LADY FLORENCE: *Abel Avenged: A Dramatic Tragedy* (London, 1877);
Riding Across Patagonia (Edinburgh, 1880); *A Defence of Zululand and its
King* (London, 1882); *In the Land of Misfortune* (London, 1882); *The Horrors
of Sport* (Humanitarian League publication no. 4, 1891); *Gloriana, or the
Revolution of 1900* (London, 1892).

FERRIER, SUSAN: *Marriage* (Edinburgh, 1818); *The Inheritance* (Edinburgh,
1821); *Destiny* (Edinburgh, 1831); *Memoir and Correspondence of Susan
Ferrier 1782–1854, Based on her Private Correspondence*, ed. John A. Doyle
(London, 1898); 'Recollections of Visits to Ashiestiel and Abbotsford', *Temple
Bar*, 1874.

FLETCHER, ELIZA: 'Memoir of Grace Fletcher by her Mother', 1817, appended
to *Autobiography* (1874). *Elidure* and *Edward* (Privately printed, 1825); *The
Autobiography of Mrs Fletcher, with Letters and Other Family Memorials*, ed.
Mary Richardson (Edinburgh, 1874).

GERARD, EMILY: 'Transylvanian Superstitions', *The Nineteenth Century*, vol. 18,
July–September (London, 1885); *The Land Beyond the Forest* (London,
1888); *The Voice of a Flower* (London, 1893).

GORDON CUMMING, CONSTANCE FREDERICA: *From the Hebrides to the
Himalayas* (London, 1876); 'Across the Yellow Sea', *Blackwood's Magazine*
(1880); *At Home in Fiji* (Edinburgh & London, 1881); *Fire Fountains: The
Kingdom of Hawaii* (Edinburgh & London, 1883); 'The Offerings of the
Dead', *British Quarterly Review* (1885); *Wanderings in China* (Edinburgh &
London, 1886); *Memories* (Edinburgh, 1904).

GRANT, ANNE (OF LAGGAN): *Poems on Various Subjects* (Edinburgh &
London, 1803); *Letters from the Mountains* (London, 1806); *Memoirs of an
American Lady* (London, 1808); *Essays on the Superstitions of the Highlanders
of Scotland, with Translations from the Gaelic* (London, 1811); *Eighteen
Hundred and Thirteen: A Poem* (London, 1814); *Memoir and Correspondence
of Mrs Grant of Laggan*, ed. J. P. Grant (London, 1844).

GRANT, ELIZABETH (OF ROTHIEMURCHUS): *Memoirs of a Highland Lady
1797–1827*, ed. Jane Maria, Lady Strachey (London, 1898) and by Andrew
Tod (Edinburgh, 1992); *The Highland Lady in Ireland*, ed. Patricia Pelly and
Andrew Tod (Edinburgh, 1991); *A Highland Lady in France*, ed. Patricia

Patricia Pelly and Andrew Tod (Edinburgh, (2005).

HAMILTON, ELIZABETH: *Translations of the Letters of a Hindoo Rajah* (London, 1796); *Memoirs of Modern Philosophers* (London, 1800); *Letters on the Elementary Principles of Education* (London, 1801); *The Memoirs of the Life of Agrippina, the Wife of Germanicus* (London, 1804); *The Cottagers of Glenburnie* (Edinburgh, 1808; Glasgow, 2010); *Memoir of the Late Mrs Elizabeth Hamilton with a Selection from her Correspondence and Other Unpublished Writings* by Elizabeth Benger (London, 1818).

HAMILTON, JANET: *Poems and Essays of a Miscellaneous Character* (Glasgow, 1863); *Poems of Purpose and Sketches in Prose: Scottish Peasant Life and Character in Auld Langsyne, Sketches of Local Scenes and Characters, With a Glossary* (Glasgow, Edinburgh & London, 1865); *Poems, Essays and Sketches* (Glasgow, 1880).

JACOB, VIOLET: *The Bailie MacPhee*, as Violet Kennedy-Erskine, with Walter Douglas Campbell (Edinburgh, 1888); *The Sheep-Stealers* (London & New York, 1902); *The Interloper* (London & New York, 1904); *Verses* (1905); *The History of Aythan Waring* (London & New York, 1908); T*he Fortune Hunters and Other Stories* (1910); *Flemington* (London, 1911): *Songs of Angus* (London, 1915): *More Songs of Angus* (London, 1918); *Bonnie Joann and Other Poems* (1921); *Tales of My Own Country* (1922); *Northern Lights and Other Poems* (1927); *The Scottish Poems of Violet Jacob* (London & New York, 1944); *The Lum Hat and Other Stories: The Last Tales of Violet Jacob*, ed. R. Garden (Aberdeen, 1982); *Diaries and Letters from India 1895–1900*, ed. C. Anderson (Edinburgh, 1990): *Flemington and Tales from Angus*, ed. C. Anderson (Edinburgh, 1994).

JOHNSTON, ELLEN: *Autobiography, Poems and Songs of Ellen Johnston, The Factory Girl* (Glasgow, 1867, 1869).

JOHNSTONE, CHRISTIAN ISOBEL: *Clan-Albin, a National Tale*, 4 vols (London & Edinburgh, 1815; Glasgow 2003); *Elizabeth de Bruce*, 3 vols (Edinburgh, 1827); *The Cook and Housewife's Manual, Containing the Most Approved Modern Recipes, etc.* (Edinburgh, 1826); 'Marriages are Made in Heaven', *Tait's Edinburgh Magazine* (November 1832).

KEITH, CHRISTINA: *The Russet Coat* (London, 1956); *The Author of Waverley* (London, 1964); *War Classics: The Remarkable Memoir of Christina Keith on the Western Front*, ed. Flora Johnston (Stroud, 2014).

MILLER, LYDIA: *Little Amy's Birthday, and other tales* by Harriet Myrtle (London, 1846); *Home and its Pleasures: Simple Stories For Young People* by Harriet Myrtle (London, 1852); Aunt *Maddy's Diamonds: A Tale for Little Girls* by Harriet Myrtle (London, 1864) *Passages in the Life of an English Heiress; or Recollections of Disruption Times in Scotland* (London, 1847); (ed. L. M. Mackay) 'Mrs Hugh Miller's Journal', *Chambers's Journal* (6) **5**, 305–8, 369–72, 461–64, 513–16 (1902).

MURRAY, SARAH: *The School*, 3 vols; *A Companion and Useful Guide to the Beauties of Scotland* (London, 1799); *A Companion and Useful Guide to the Beauties in the Western Highlands of Scotland and in the Hebrides* (London, 1803, 1810).

NAIRNE, LADY CAROLINA: *Lays from Strathearn* (Edinburgh, Glasgow, Perth & Ayr, 1846).

OLIPHANT, MARGARET: *Passages in the Life of Mrs Margaret Maitland* (London, 1849); *Caleb Field: A Tale of the Puritans* (London, 1851); *The Life of Edward Irving* (London, 1862); *Salem Chapel* (Edinburgh & London, 1863); *The Perpetual Curate* (Edinburgh and London, 1864); *Miss Marjoribanks* (Edinburgh & London, 1866); *Hester: A Story of Contemporary Life* (London, 1883); *Tales of the Seen and Unseen* (Edinburgh, 1885); *Kirsteen: The Story of a Scotch Family Seventy Years Ago* (London 1890); *A Beleaguered City* (London, 1892); *Annals of a Publishing House: William Blackwood and his Sons, their Magazine and Friends* (Edinburgh, 1897); *The Autobiography of Margaret Oliphant*, ed. Mrs Harry Coghill (Edinburgh, 1899) and by Elisabeth Jay (Oxford 1990); *A Beleaguered City And Other Tales Of The Seen And The Unseen*, ed. Jenni Calder (Edinburgh, 2000).

RAMSAY, ALLAN: *The Tea Table Miscellany* (Edinburgh, 1723).

SCOTT, SIR WALTER (ed.): 'Auld Maitland', attrib. Margaret Maitland in *The Minstrelsy of the Scottish Border* (Kelso & Edinburgh, 1802–03).

SMITH, ROBERT ARCHIBALD: *The Scottish Minstrel: A Selection from the Vocal melodies of Scotland, ancient and modern, arranged for the Voice and Piano Forte* (Edinburgh, 1821–24).

SOMERVILLE, MARY: *The Mechanism of the Heavens* (London, 1831) with *Preliminary Dissertation to The Mechanism of the Heavens* published separately (London, 1831); *On the Connexion of the Physical Sciences* (London, 1834); *Physical Geography* (London, 1848); *Molecular and Microscopic Science* (London, 1869); *Personal Recollections from Early Life to Old Age*, ed. Martha Somerville (London, 1873) and as *Queen of Science: The Personal Recollections of Mary Somerville*, ed. Dorothy McMillan (Edinburgh, 2001).

SPENCE, ELIZABETH ISABELLA: *Summer Excursions* (London, 1809); *Letters from the North Highlands* (London, 1817).

STEEL, FLORA ANNIE: *The Complete Indian Housekeeper and Cook* [with Grace Gardiner] (London, 1888); *From the Five Rivers* (London, 1893); *Tales of the Punjab* (London, 1894); *On the Face of the Waters* (London, 1896); *India* (London, 1905); *The Garden of Fidelity* (London, 1929).

THOMSON, WILLIAM: *Orpheus Caledonius, or, a Collection of the Best Scotch Songs* (London, 1725).

WALDIE, CHARLOTTE: *Narrative of a Residence in Belgium during the Campaign of 1815 & a Visit to the Field of Waterloo: by an Englishwoman* (London, 1817); *Rome in the Nineteenth Century* (Edinburgh, 1820).

Criticism and Biography

ANON. 'Obituary of Margaret Oliphant', *Blackwood's Magazine* (1899).

ASHTON, ROSEMARY. *Thomas and Jane Carlyle: Portrait of a Marriage* (London, 2003).

BARR, PAT. *A Curious Life for a Lady: The Story of Isabella Bird* (London, 1970).

BARRETT, ELIZABETH and HORNE, RICHARD H. unsigned essay, 'A New Spirit of the Age' (New York, 1844).

BENGER, ELIZABETH. *Memoirs of the late Mrs Hamilton* (London, 1818).

BREWSTER, SIR DAVID. Review of *On the Connexion of the Physical Sciences* in *The Edinburgh Review* (April 1834).

BURY, LADY CHARLOTTE. *Diary Illustrative of the Times of George the Fourth* (London, 1838).

CULLINAN, MARY. *Susan Ferrier* (Boston MA, 1984).

CARHART, MARGARET. *The Life and Works of Joanna Baillie* (New Haven CT, 1923).

CARLYLE, THOMAS: *Collected Letters of Thomas and Jane Welsh Carlyle*, vol. 10 (1838), Duke-Edinburgh Edition, ed. Ian Campbell, Aileen Christianson, et. al. (Edinburgh & Durham NC, 1970). Also available at https://carlyleletters.dukeupress.edu/; *Sartor Resartus* (London, 1831); *The History of Friedrich II of Prussia, Called Frederick the Great* (London, 1858–65); *Reminiscences* (London, 1881).

ELTON, OLIVER. *A Survey of English Literature 1780–1830*, vol. 1 (London, 1912).

FOSS, PETER J. *The History of Market Bosworth* (Wymondham, 1983).

GIFFORD, DOUGLAS (ed.). *The History of Scottish Literature*, vol 3: *The Nineteenth Century* (Aberdeen, 1988).

GIFFORD, DOUGLAS and McMILLAN, DOROTHY (eds). *A History of Scottish Women's Writing* (Edinburgh, 1997).

HANSEN, LAWRENCE and ELIZABETH. *The Life of Jane Welsh Carlyle* (London, 1952).

HARDY, THOMAS. *Collected Letters of Thomas Hardy*, vol. 2 1893–1901, eds Richard L. Purdy and Michael Millgate (Oxford, 1980).

HUMBOLDT, BARON (ALEXANDRE). Letter (in French) to Mary Somerville, 12 July 1849.

JAY, ELISABETH. *Mrs Oliphant: A Fiction to Herself: A Literary Life* (Oxford, 1995).

KAMM, ANTONY. *Collins Biographical Dictionary of English Literature* (Glasgow, 1993).

McKINLAY, J. *Mary Somerville 1780–1872* (Edinburgh, 1987).

MAUDSLAY, ALFRED P. *Life in the Pacific Fifty Years Ago* (London, 1930).

McMILLAN, DOROTHY (ed.). *The Scotswoman at Home and Abroad: Non-Fiction Writing 1700–1900* (Glasgow, 1999).

MILLER, HUGH. Letter to Sir Thomas Dick Lauder 1837, MSS Letters, Notebooks and Manuscripts of and Concerning Hugh Miller, Geologist, National Library of Scotland.

NORQUAY, GLENDA (ed.). *The Edinburgh Companion to Scottish Women's Writing* (Edinburgh 2012).

OSEN, LYNN M. *Women in Mathematics* (Cambridge MA, 1974).

The Oxford Dictionary of National Biography, 60 vols (Oxford 2004). Also available at: www.oxforddnb.com.

PATWARDHAN, DAYA. *A Star of India: Flora Annie Steel, her Life and Times* (Poona, 1963).

ROSE, JONATHAN. *The Intellectual Life of the British Working Classes* (New Haven CT & London, 2001).

STURGIS, HOWARD. 'Obituary of Margaret Oliphant', *Temple Bar* (1899).

SUTHERLAND, ELIZABETH. *Lydia: Wife of Hugh Miller of Cromarty* (East Linton, 2002).

SWINDELLS, JULIA. *Victorian Writing and Working Women: The Other Side of Silence* (Minneapolis MN, 1985).

WELDON, FAY. 'Introduction' in Mary Brunton: *Discipline* and *Self-Control* (London, 1986).

WITTIG, KURT. *The Scottish Tradition in Literature* (Edinburgh, 1958).

WOOLF, VIRGINIA. *Three Guineas* (London, 1938).

YOUNG, JOHN. *Pictures in Prose and Verse, or Personal Recollections of the Late Janet Hamilton* (Glasgow, 1879).

Further Sources

BARRIE, J. M. *Auld Licht Idylls* (London, 1888).

BROWN, GEORGE DOUGLAS. *The House with the Green Shutters* (London, 1901).

BUCHAN, JOHN. *Witch Wood* (London, 1927).

COCKBURN, HENRY. *Memorials of His Time* (Edinburgh, 1856).

COLERIDGE, SAMUEL TAYLOR. 'The Rime of the Ancient Mariner' *Lyrical Ballads, with a Few Other Poems* (London, 1798).

COWPER WILLIAM. *Poems by William Cowper, of the Inner Temple, Esq.* (London, 1782).

CROFTON, EILEEN. *The Women of Royaumont* (East Linton, 1997).

DE QUINCEY, THOMAS. *Recollections of the Lakes and the Lake Poets*. A collection of biographical essays originally published in *Tait's Edinburgh Magazine* between 1834 and 1840.

FIELDING, HENRY: *The History of the Adventures of Joseph Andrews and of his Friend Mr. Abraham Adams* (London, 1742); *The History of Tom Jones, a Foundling* (London, 1749).

FINDLATER, MARY and JANE. *Crossriggs* (London, 1908): *Penny Moneypenny* (London, 1911).

FOOTE, SAMUEL. *Taste* (1752).

GALT, JOHN. *Ringan Gilhaize* (Edinburgh, 1823).

GIBBON, LEWIS GRASSIC. *A Scots Hairst* (London, 1967).

GOLDSMITH, OLIVER. *The Vicar of Wakefield* (Salisbury, 1766).

HAMILTON, CICELY. 'The Song of the Women' (WSPU anthem, music by Ethel Smyth, 1911).

HAMILTON, SIR WILLIAM. *Lectures on Quaternions* (Dublin, London & Cambridge, 1853).

HENRY THE MINSTREL (BLIND HARRY). *The Actes and Deidis of the Illustre and Vallyeant Campioun Schir William Wallace (The Wallace)* (c.1477).

HOGG, JAMES: *The Brownie of Bodsbeck* (Edinburgh & London, 1818); *The Private Memoirs of a Justified Sinner* (London & Edinburgh, 1824); *Familiar Anecdotes of Sir Walter Scott* (New York, 1834); *The Domestic Manners & Private Life of Sir Walter Scott* (London & Edinburgh, 1834).

INGIS, ELSIE. 'The Story of a Modern Woman' (unpublished, written c.1904).

JENKINS, ROBIN. *The Awakening of George Darroch* (Edinburgh, 1985).

JOHNSON, SAMUEL. *Rasselas* (London, 1759).

LE FANU, SHERIDAN. *Carmilla* published in *In A Glass Darkly* (London, 1872).

LEWIS, MATTHEW GREGORY. *Ambrosio, or, the Monk* (Waterford & London, 1796).

LINDSAY, SIR DAVID. *Ane Satyre of the Thrie Estaitis* (Edinburgh, 1602).

LINDSAY, MAURICE (ed.). *Modern Scottish Poetry: An Anthology of the Scottish Renaissance 1920–1945* (London, 1957). First published by Faber & Faber in 1946.

LOCHHEAD, LIZ. 'Mary Queen of Scots Got Her Head Chopped Off' (1987).

MACDIARMID, HUGH: *Northern Numbers* (Montrose, 1921–23); 'Contemporary Scottish Studies', *The Scottish Educational Journal*, 1925–27.

MACPHERSON, JAMES ['OSSIAN']. *Fragments of Translation from the Gaelic or Erse Language* (Edinburgh, 1760).

MELVILLE, ELIZABETH. *Ane Godlie Dreme* (Edinburgh, 1603).

MILNE, MARY LEE. Acc.6318: Journals, 1916–1917, of Mary Lee Milne, describing service with a unit of the Scottish Women's Hospitals in Russia and Romania, and her article 'The Dobruja Retreat', 1918. National Library of Scotland.

MILTON, JOHN. *The Minor Poems of John Milton* (London, 1866).

OSSOLI, MARGARET FULLER. *At Home and Abroad*, ed. Albert Fuller (New York, 1856).

The Oxford Companion to the Theatre (London, 1972).

POLIDORI, JOHN. *The Vampyre* (London, 1819).

Post Office Directory for 1874–1875.

RADCLIFFE, ANN. *The Mysteries of Udolpho* (London, 1794).

RAMSAY, ALLAN. *The Gentle Shepherd* (1725).

RICHARDSON, SAMUEL. *Pamela: or, Virtue Rewarded* (London, 1740).

ROBERTSON, JAMES. *The Fanatic and The Testament of Gideon Mack* (London, 2006).

SCOTT, SIR WALTER: 'A Postscript', *Waverley* (Edinburgh & London, 1814); *Old Mortality* (Edinburgh, 1816); *Paul's Letters to His Kinsfolk* (Edinburgh & London, 1816); *The Heart of Midlothian* (Edinburgh, 1818); *The Bride of Lammermoor* (Edinburgh, 1818); *A Legend of Montrose* (Edinburgh & London, 1819); *Redgauntlet* (Edinburgh & London, 1824); *Letters on Demonology and Witchcraft* (London, 1830).

Shorter Catechism of the Church of Scotland.

SMOLLETT, TOBIAS. *The Adventures of Roderick Random* (London, 1748).

SOMERVILLE, THOMAS. *My Life and Times, 1741–1814* (Edinburgh, 1861).

STEVENSON, ROBERT LOUIS: *The Strange Case of Dr Jekyll and Mr Hyde* (London, 1886); *Catriona* (London, 1893); *The Master of Ballantrae* (London, 1889).

STOKER, BRAM. *Dracula* (London, 1897).

STRACHEY, LYTTON. *Eminent Victorians* (London, 1918).

THACKERAY, WILLIAM M. *Vanity Fair* (London, 1848) (serialised in *Punch* 1847–48).

TROLLOPE, ANTHONY: *The Warden* (London, 1855); *Barchester Towers* (London, 1857).

Journals and Periodicals

Bell's British Theatre
Blackwood's Magazine
British Quarterly Review
Chambers's Edinburgh Journal
Daily News
Edinburgh Review
Edinburgh Weekly Magazine
Fraser's Magazine for Town and Country
Glasgow Examiner
[Glasgow] *Penny Post*
Glasgow Weekly Herald
Glasgow Weekly Mail
Inspector
Inverness Courier
Johnstone's Edinburgh Magazine

The Literature of Working Men
[London] *Morning Post*
Mathematical Repository
The Schoolmaster
The Scotsman
The Scottish Educational Journal
The Spectator
The Suffragette
Tait's Edinburgh Magazine
Temple Bar – A London Magazine for Town and Country Readers
Time and Tide
The Times
Westminster Review
The Witness
Working Man's Friend and Family Instructor

Online Resources
The National Library of Scotland
        www.nls.uk
The Scottish Poetry Library
        www.scottishpoetrylibrary.org.uk
Project Gutenberg (eBooks of classic texts)
        www.gutenberg.org/ebooks/author
The Victorian Web
        www.victorianweb.org
Electric Scotland
        www.electricscotland.com/history
Spartacus Educational
        www.spartacus-educational/women

INDEX